To Ted
with affection &
best wi[...]
Don

MORAL EXPERTISE

READINGS IN APPLIED ETHICS

Edited by Harold Bassford

Associate Professor of Philosophy, York University, Toronto, Ontario

MORAL EXPERTISE

Studies in practical and professional ethics

Edited by
DON MACNIVEN

ROUTLEDGE
London and New York

First published 1990
by Routledge
11 New Fetter Lane, London EC4P 4EE
29 West 35th Street, New York, NY 10001

Typeset in 10/12 Baskerville by Columns of Reading
Printed in Great Britain by TJ Press (Padstow) Ltd
Padstow, Cornwall

British Library Cataloguing in Publication Data

Moral expertise: studies in practical
and professional ethics.
1. Professional conduct. Ethical aspects
I. MacNiven, Don
174

ISBN 0–415–03576–7

Library of Congress Cataloging in Publication Data

Moral expertise / edited by Don MacNiven.
p. cm. — (Studies in practical and professional ethics)
Bibliography: p.
Includes index.
ISBN 0–415–03576–7
1. Ethics. 2. Professional ethics. I. MacNiven, Don.
II. Series.
BJ37.M818 1990
174—dc19   88–26814

CONTENTS

CONTENTS

LIST OF CONTRIBUTORS

Harry Arthurs, Professor of Law and the President of York University, Toronto, Canada.

H. A. Bassford, Associate Professor of Philosophy, Atkinson College, York University, Toronto, Canada.

James V. P. Check, Assistant Professor and Canada Research Fellow in the Department of Psychology at York University, Toronto, Canada, and the Chair of the Canadian Psychological Association – Section on Criminal Justice Systems.

Michael Creal, Professor of Humanities, York University, Toronto, Canada.

Leslie Green, Associate Professor of Philosophy and Law, York University, Toronto, Canada.

Robert H. Haynes, Distinguished Research Professor of Biology and Science at York University, Toronto, Canada.

Sue Hendler, Assistant Professor in the School of Urban and Regional Planning, Queens University, Kingston, Ontario, Canada.

Reg Lang, Professor of Environmental Studies, York University, Toronto, Canada.

Thelma McCormack, Professor of Sociology, York University, Toronto, Canada.

LIST OF CONTRIBUTORS

Christopher P. McKay, Solar System Exploration Branch, NASA Ames Research Center, Moffat Field, California.

Don MacNiven, Professor of Philosophy, York University, Toronto, Canada.

Neil M. Malamuth, Chair of Communication Studies at the University of California, Los Angeles.

Peter Penz, Associate Professor of Environmental Studies and Social Work, York University, Toronto, Canada.

David P. Shugarman, Associate Professor of Political Science, York University, Toronto, Canada.

Sol Tanenzapf, Associate Professor of Humanities, York University, Toronto, Canada.

David L. Wiesenthal, Associate Professor of Psychology, York University, Toronto, Canada.

H. T. Wilson, Professor of Administrative Studies and Law, York University, Toronto, Canada.

PREFACE

The articles in this book were originally presented as part of the Graduate Dean's Seminar series on Practical and Professional Ethics held at York University in the spring of 1987.

The academic community has not always responded very well to the moral challenges which the modern world presents to us. It tends to neglect practical ethics and moral education. Values are always someone else's problem. The idea that academic work should be morally neutral often means simply that it should be amoral. The seminars in practical and professional ethics, and the articles which developed from them, were designed to address these problems from the perspective of different academic disciplines, to place the insights derived from specialized expertise into an inter-disciplinary context, and to throw some light on the notions of moral expertise, professional ethics and moral education.

I would like to thank Dean David Bell for developing and supporting the York University Graduate Seminars. I would also like to thank Professor H.A. Bassford who helped organize these seminars with me, Dave Stamos who helped coordinate the series, Debbie McCrae who helped edit this volume, and Verna Mitchell and the staff of Secretarial Services, who did such an admirable job in helping to prepare the typescript.

Don MacNiven
York University
January 1989

INTRODUCTION
DON MACNIVEN

Many people believe that the western world is entering a period of moral decline, a period where greed, lust, mendacity, and false pride are the norm rather than the abnormal. Scandals have occurred in increasing numbers in every area of our social lives: in politics, in business, in medicine, in social and other scientific research, and even in the religious communities. The accuracy of this perception is less important than its existence, because it is accompanied by the sense not only that there is more evil now than at other times but that we as a civilization no longer think that evil matters. The western world is not becoming just more immoral; it is becoming amoral. We no longer believe that our professional lives have a moral dimension. If morality exists anywhere it might be found in the home, but certainly it has no place in our public lives. The law of the jungle pervades our offices, and survival, not duty, is the fundamental practical precept of social life. One reason for turning away from morality is that our intellectual community has embraced moral skepticism, a view which denies the reality of moral knowledge. Moral skepticism leads directly to the neglect of practical moral problems, a luxury we cannot afford in our complex and changing modern world. The articles in this volume all presuppose that moral knowledge is possible and that we must use what intellectual resources we currently have to deal with the moral challenges of our contemporary world. They also assume that our moral knowledge is imperfect and hence recognize that humility is the most important virtue of the wise.

In the introductory article "The idea of a moral expert," I

ask whether there can be experts in morality as there are in science, and the professions. The idea of moral expertise strikes us as paradoxical because we believe that individuals must decide for themselves what is right and wrong. Moral decisions are matters for autonomous moral agents, not moral experts. I argue that the idea of a moral expert is acceptable providing we see that moral reasoning is an organic creative process rather than the mechanical deductive one it is currently thought to be. Mechanical models of moral reasoning assume that we can develop an airtight hierarchical system of moral principles, secondary moral rules, and inference rules, which, when mechanically applied, will allow us to arrive at the correct solution to every particular moral problem. However, the complexity of lived moral experience will always defeat this kind of casuistry because it cannot capture the uniqueness of a developing society or a growing individual. The complexity of experience is not an insurmountable problem for organic casuistry because it involves searching for new ways to restructure experience into more highly integrated patterns, rather than applying rules to experience by logical fiat. The idea of the moral expert which emerges from the organic model is not that of the moral busybody who threatens moral autonomy but rather the moral educator who works in an interdisciplinary fashion with other professionals to search for creative solutions to professional and personal moral problems. All the articles in this volume can be seen as contributions to this interdisciplinary creative dialogue with moral philosophy.

David Wiesenthal, in his article "Recent developments in social psychology in response to ethical concerns," is concerned about the crisis which ethics has produced in social psychology. Once it became clear to social science experimenters that the use of deception in their work was inconsistent with the rights of their experimental subjects to informed consent and privacy, they were faced with a moral dilemma which appeared to threaten their science as a whole. The social scientists could have avoided the problem by claiming that their science was morally neutral and that morality had no place in the laboratory. Some did take this route but many opted for moral responsibility and tried to solve the moral dilemmas their research raised. But as Wiesenthal's research has shown they did not meet with much success as deception appeared to be integral to their work, and its use has actually increased rather than decreased. One result of the crisis was that young researchers left social psychology and began moving to other areas of research which do not involve such intractable moral problems. Wiesenthal's empirical research raises an important moral issue for ethicists who are concerned about the morality of scientific research. Should they be concerned about the negative consequences which might arise when ethics enters the domain of science? Do we need to think more about the ethics of ethicists? James Check and Neil Malamuth, in their article "Ethical considerations in sex and aggression research," continue the debate about ethics and research in social psychology, by presenting a research program which tries to cope with the ethical problems deception raises by emphasizing the need for the experimenter to care for the well-being and the dignity of his experimental subjects. It might be objected that this solution to the researcher's moral dilemma invites an unacceptable kind of paternalism on the part of the experimenter, but stressing the importance of an ethic of care in the laboratory context demonstrates that social science cannot avoid ethics, and must be concerned with the rights of the experimental subject.

In his article "Social ethics: two biblical perspectives," Michael Creal raises the question of the applicability of religious ethics to social issues. Most moral philosophers find little objection to anyone who wants to use religious ethics as a basis for developing a personal morality. Although many would not think this the most fruitful approach to ethics, most would agree that it is up to the individual to choose what sort of ethics to adopt. This is consistent with the principle of individual autonomy in ethics. However, most moral philosophers would be suspicious of using religious ethics as the basis for a social ethic. To impose a set of moral values on all members of a society appears to conflict with the principles of religious freedom, freedom of thought, and freedom of conscience. This objection to a religious social ethics is even more compelling in multi-cultural and democratic societies which accept the principle of the separation of church and state. Creal's paper raises important doubts about this general position. Surely religious ethics must have some valid public as well as private role to play in the life of a religious person. Creal argues that it has such a role and he provides a critical examination of two biblical perspectives which attempt to develop a social ethic. Is it possible for example for a Christian to live in an oppressive totalitarian state and to ignore the problems in social ethics this raises? It's not then so much a matter of whether a religious person should have a social ethics or not but rather what sort of ethics this should be. Sol Tanenzapf raises the same questions in his paper "Social ethics and religion." He agrees with Creal that a religious social ethic is possible in spite of its difficulties, but points out that such an ethic must be tempered with realism, and scrupulously ethical in its implementation. This is especially so with systems like Liberation Theology which advocate the use of violence in the name of justice.

At a recent meeting of the Ontario Professional Planners Institute, the membership called for a review of their Professional Code of Conduct because they recognized the need to provide professional urban planners with guidelines which would help them cope with the increasing complexity of the ethical issues which they encounter. Reg Lang and Sue Hendler in their article "Ethics and professional planners" develop a code of ethics for their profession. Some ethicists argue that moral codes do not provide an adequate solution to problems in professional ethics because they are artificial and out of touch with moral realities. Lang and Hendler argue that this objection does not hold if we recognize that a code of ethics is only part of a developing system of professional ethics which includes constant reflection and revisions of the code in the light of experience and the inclusion of moral education as part of the training of professional planners. On this view ethics becomes an integral part of the planners' activity rather than a postscript to professional decisions.

Affirmative action programs which are designed to redress the effects of historic and systemic discrimination in the workplace are commonplace features of modern industrial societies. There is widespread agreement among the western democracies that racist and sexist societies are undesirable and that one of the great moral challenges of the modern era is to create societies which are free from racial and sexual discrimination. The question now is not whether we should do this, but how we should do it. In capitalist economies one of the most invidious forms of discrimination is to pay minority groups less for doing the same or similar work. In his article "Industrial strategy: its challenge to social policy." Tom Wilson argues that the attempt to institute fair wage practices in capitalist economic systems is more difficult than was originally thought. It is important, he points out, to distinguish clearly between the principle of "Equal pay for equal work" and the principle of "Equal pay for work of equal value." The former is easily implemented and poses little danger to the health of the economy. The latter, however, is not that easy to implement because rating the value of different kinds of work becomes a subjective matter which puts inordinate power into the hands of those assigned to rate and compare jobs. Because of this it poses a danger to the economy, especially to the small business sector. Wilson does not recommend that we abandon either of these principles or affirmative action programs, only that if we do employ them we must develop industrial strategies that will neutralize any deleterious effects they might have on our economic systems.

Harry Arthurs in his article "Ideology, interest and implementation of a professional ethical code" questions the value of ethical codes in general. He was involved in developing and administering the current Code of Professional Conduct of the Canadian Bar Association, and his experience there undermined his confidence in this approach to professional ethics. He points out that the code had no significant effect on the ethical behavior of lawyers in Canada. It was a dead system of imprecise rules which was remote from the living morality which informed the practice of law in Canada. At best it focused attention on some new moral issues, like legal advertising, but for the most part it served as window-dressing for the Canadian legal profession. It presented a moral face to the public. Arthurs's experience suggests that if any professional moral code is to have value, it must be relevant and applicable to the concrete complex experience of the individual professional. If codes of ethics are to remain a vital part of professional ethics they must become living not dead parts of developing ethical systems. Leslie Green in his "Commentary:

legal ethics–sociology and morality" suggests that if we shift our perspective from codes of ethics to the ethical behavior of lawyers to develop our legal ethics we may simply be encouraging lawyers to avoid the ethical side of their profession, something which they are already inclined to do because they tend to resolve ethical problems by appealing to legal standards. The basic moral rule for lawyers becomes "If it is not illegal then it's not immoral." Acting on this rule does not require lawyers to enter into the moral arena. Green's analysis suggests that an adequate legal ethics requires more than observing lawyers' actual behavior. We need to evaluate as well as describe the principles of legal ethics.

One of the major moral problems of the modern world is the unequal distribution of wealth among its peoples. Some countries are very rich while others are very poor. Do those of us who are rich have any obligation to help the poor? The answer we give to this question depends, it appears, on the general ideology we adopt. If we are socialists who think that basic needs are more important than freedom and self-reliance, we are more likely to think that we have such an obligation. On the other hand if we are capitalists who hold just the reverse, we will think the opposite and deny that we have the obligation. In his article "Equality of opportunity: common ground for opposing ideologies" Peter Penz argues that a closer analysis of key concepts in these opposing ideologies suggests that consistent development of either will lead to the same conclusion, i.e. we have an obligation to help the poor but in ways that will not undermine their autonomy. In order to function optimally capitalistic societies need to adopt the principle of fair competition. For everyone to compete equally they also need to adopt the principle of equal opportunity. To meet the requirements of equal opportunity we have to see that people's basic needs for food, shelter, and so on, are met. Fair competition is possible only if everyone's basic needs are satisfied. Hence a capitalist requires the concept of need as much as a socialist does. Similarly socialism requires the idea of freedom to complete its ideology. If correct, Penz's analysis demonstrates that these opposing ideologies have sufficient common ground to solve the dilemma of societal obligations to the poor.

The idea of professional ethics is often thought to be redundant because it only involves the application of ordinary ethical norms to a specific professional context. In his article "The basis of medical ethics" H.A. Bassford argues that to establish a basis for any professional ethic we need to draw a distinction between "role-specific" and "general" moral norms. Role-specific norms are ones which arise from the nature of the profession and define its special obligations. In medicine, for example, the central norm is the obligation to promote the health of the patient. Anyone who sets out to undermine the health of patients cannot be considered to be a good doctor. General norms are the ordinary ones we appeal to in our everyday moral experience, like our obligation to respect people's rights to autonomy and privacy. An adequate professional ethics requires both an understanding of the values that are intrinsic to a profession and of how to resolve conflicts between professional and general norms. Should a doctor override a patient's rights in the name of patient care? Generally Bassford argues they should not. In cases of conflict human rights should normally take precedence over care.

One of the most significant recent developments in moral philosophy is the appearance of a feminist perspective in ethics. Feminist ethics suggests that current moral philosophy is dominated by a gender bias that prevents us from dealing adequately with many modern ethical questions. The status quo in morality, according to this view, is male dominated and tends to disregard women's quite different approach to moral problems. Masculine morality tends to be abstract, rationalistic and concerned with the rules of fair play. Feminist morality tends to be concrete, emotive, contextual and concerned with interpersonal relationships. The former is a morality of contract and justice, the latter one of care and personal responsibility. In her article "The bias of bioethics" Thelma McCormack applies a feminist approach to problems related to modern reproductive technologies, i.e. contraception, abortion, artificial insemination, and surrogate mothering. She argues that these problems are especially suitable for feminist ethics because they are essentially women's problems. If we shift from the justice to the care perspective we will likely be less concerned with the rights of fetuses and more with the need of women to establish their own personal perspectives with respect to their reproductivity. We will also begin to look on activities like surrogate mothering in human rather than economic terms. It becomes a matter of loving and giving rather than commercial contract.

One of the facts of modern life is that our scientific technologies develop faster than our morality. We only discuss the moral and social implications of these technologies after their creation. Usually it takes a disaster to turn our attention to the moral side of science. There are many reasons for this. Our blind faith in scientific progress as the cure of all our woes is perhaps one. But equally important is the assumption that science is a morally neutral project. Science deals with fact not value. Morality is extrinsic to science. Technologies are neither good nor evil, it is politics which make them what they are. It could even be argued that the principle of moral neutrality is essential for science because values undermine the objectivity of judgment which is at its core. Unfortunately we can no longer hold this simplistic view of the relationship between science and morality. Our experience of nuclear and other technologies has taught us differently. We are in the process of redefining this relationship and frequently it is the scientists themselves who are leading the way. In his article "Ecce ecopoiesis: playing God on Mars" Bob Haynes raises the question of whether we ought to create new biospheres and ecosystems on planets like Mars. His answer is a tentative yes. He argues that the answer must be tentative because the ethical theories currently available cannot adequately deal with the moral problems which ecopoiesis poses. Christopher McKay in his companion article "Does Mars have rights?" correctly shows that current ethical systems are essentially earthbound. This holds whether the ethical system is homocentric (human-centered) or biocentric (centered on the earth's ecosystem). These systems are both geocentric (earth-centered) rather than cosmocentric (centered on the universe). Only a cosmocentric ethics can provide us with adequate answers to the moral problems which the exploration of space raises. As Haynes points out this makes the question of ecopoiesis a novel moral question which could have a significant impact on ethical theory. Just as the recognition of the environmental crisis raised important questions about the limitation of homocentric ethics, so the new technology of planetary engineering will raise questions about the limitations of the geocentric systems of ethics we currently employ to solve our moral problems. One important implication of this shift in perspective is, as McKay points out, that we might have to assign intrinsic value to lifeless planets and so assign them rights of some sort to protect them from exploitation and wanton destruction.

As David Shugarman points out in his article "The use and abuse of politics" political corruption has been with us as long as we can remember. Currently in democracies like Canada false promising has become a way of life. We often think that morality and politics, like oil and water, cannot mix. Politicians, like the nations they govern, pursue their own self-interest and serve the public interest only when it is convenient for them to do so. Are ethics and politics naturally antagonistic? Is a moral politician a contradiction in terms? Shugarman argues that the opposite is true, that political systems presuppose specific sets of values without which they cannot function optimally. He points out that modern political theory, from Machiavelli and Hobbes onward, is based on the assumption that ethics has nothing to do with politics. But Shugarman argues that to adopt this so-called realistic theory of politics is simply to provide a theoretical warrant for corrupt political behavior. He recommends that we return to the classical view of politics found in Plato and Aristotle, in which ethics and politics are seen as integral to each other. The classical message suggests that democracies must necessarily be moral if they are to function properly. In a democracy we should expect the highest moral standards from our politicians rather than accept corruption as natural to political life.

1

PRACTICAL ETHICS
The idea of a moral expert

DON MACNIVEN

The idea that there can be experts in morals, as there are in medicine, law and engineering, strikes us at first sight as absurd. Moral questions are different from technical or scientific ones. With the latter we can legitimately appeal to an expert in the appropriate field for the best answer. With the former this is not the case. With moral questions surely we should each make up our own minds for ourselves about what we ought to do. Neither the philosopher nor anyone else can do this for us. Of course we can ask for advice from those we believe to be wise and experienced, but in the end we must each be our own moral expert. This commonsense opinion is consistent with the way most philosophers now see the relations between ethical theory and ethical practice.

Part of the charm of the current orthodoxy, which holds that the three traditional branches of moral philosophy – practical, descriptive, and theoretical ethics – are autonomous disciplines which are logically independent of each other, is that it reflects common sense. We can call this view the autonomous or specialist view. It has been dominant among English-speaking philosophers since 1903, the year in which G.E. Moore published *Principia Ethica*, until recently when it has been challenged by the revival of interest in practical ethics. The autonomous view involves the rejection of the idea of a moral expert.

Practical ethics, on this view, is the study of moral values which focuses solely on the normative aspects of morality. It is concerned with our attempts to think through and answer specific moral problems at both the personal and the social levels. Ought a doctor to tell the truth to a patient who has cancer? Ought students to cheat on examinations? Should we allow scientists to conduct experiments on human embryos? Is it ever right for an employee to blow the whistle on the boss? It is not concerned with problems in descriptive or theoretical ethics. It does not, for example, bother itself with scientific investigations into morality. Do Canadian doctors tell the truth to their cancer patients? Is academic dishonesty a widespread practice in Canadian universities? What sort of experiments, if any, do scientists perform with human embryos? These are interesting questions but not ones which normally concern the moral agent who is trying to solve a particular moral problem. Nor does it deal with logical or epistemological inquiries into morality. Is it a logical mistake to try and derive moral conclusions from scientific or metaphysical premises? How in general do we justify our moral judgments? Can moral judgments ever be rationally defended? Again these are interesting questions but not ones which are directly relevant to a moral agent, immersed in the world of practice.

Practical moral thinking involves making direct commitments to action. It makes a difference not only in the way we think about things but in the way we act and respond to the world we live in. If a doctor believes that it is morally irresponsible to tell the truth to cancer patients, he will likely lie to them. If a student believes that academic dishonesty is morally wrong he will not likely plagiarize an essay. If a scientist believes there is nothing morally wrong with using human embryos to advance knowledge he will likely use them in experiments. If an employee believes that he has an overriding obligation to be loyal to his employer, he will not blow the whistle on him. On the other hand descriptive and theoretical ethics appear to involve no direct commitment to action. Suppose a social scientist discovers that whistle blowing is considered an unforgivable moral offence in the business world. Would this imply that the social scientist should morally condemn whistle blowing by employees? Clearly not. Because whistle blowing is not an accepted practice doesn't mean that it is morally wrong. Social facts of this sort may have an effect on the way we act, but they cannot justify our conduct morally.

In *Principia Ethica*, G.E. Moore argued that all the great

moral systems of the western world rested on this simple logical fallacy – the attempt to deduce moral conclusions from non-moral premises. Moore called this mistake the naturalistic fallacy, but the error is now generally referred to as a breach of Hume's Law or the "no ought from is" rule: a moral conclusion cannot be derived from any set of non-moral premises. Consider the following argument. Lying to cancer patients is a widespread practise among doctors, therefore it is morally acceptable for doctors to lie to their cancer patients. The argument clearly contains, like the whistle-blowing case, an illicit move from fact to value. They both assume that what people generally do is directly relevant for deciding what we ought to do. Of course it doesn't follow from the fact that everyone does something that anyone ought to do the same thing. Just because everyone's doing it does not make it right. If we accept Hume's Law we must accept that fact and value are logically independent of each other, and that we cannot move directly from fact to value. Since science deals with fact, not value, we must also accept that science is morally neutral. It does not presuppose, nor can it alone establish moral values.[1] Social science is a morally neutral enterprise which does not commit its practitioners morally to anything.

The same is true for the moral philosopher. Suppose an ethical theorist were to establish that the rightness or wrongness of an action depends on its actual consequences. Nothing of moral substance would follow from the discovery. First, to make a moral decision we would have to establish what consequences would actually follow from performing a particular action. This is clearly an empirical rather than a philosophical task. Second, we need also to know whether these consequences are morally desirable or not. This is clearly a substantive moral question rather than a philosophical one. It is a problem in practical, not theoretical, ethics. If you cannot derive morality from factual truth, neither can you derive it from logical truth. There is no easy escape from Hume's law.

The ethical theorist, like the social scientist, appears not to be committed to substantive moral positions by his work. The analysis and understanding of the logic of moral language and moral reasoning are distinct from actually using the language or thinking morally. On the orthodox view theoretical and descriptive ethics are morally neutral, while practical ethics is autonomous and logically independent of both. It follows that practical ethics cannot be a professional discipline and there can be no professional moral experts. The specialist expertise of the philosopher or the social scientist does not give them a privileged position with respect to practical ethics. This is also supported by the commonsense view that being good at science or philosophy does not automatically make someone a better person or a better judge of right and wrong. Intellectual virtue is not a sufficient condition for moral virtue.

Practical ethicists, according to the orthodox view, fail to understand the autonomy of morality and hence ignore the logical canyon which separates ethical theory from ethical practice. They assume, because of their expertise in ethical theory and moral epistemology, that they can become experts in the same way as doctors and lawyers. They believe that others can turn to them for direct answers to their moral problems, the way they can to other experts. The moral philosopher is in a position to tell other people, including doctors and lawyers, what they ought to do. As a result they become involved in a kind of false paternalism which springs from moral conceit and denies the autonomy of the people they would have as clients. The mistake has bad consequences both for ethical theory and ethical practice.

It is true, as practical ethicists claim, that moral reasoning is controlled by the ethical theory implicit in it. If someone is a utilitarian who appeals to the principle of utility (a morally right act is one which brings about the greatest happiness of the greatest number), he will likely arrive at different moral conclusions from a Kantian who appeals to the principle of respect for persons (always treat persons as ends-in-themselves and never merely as a means). A utilitarian doctor is more likely to lie to a cancer patient than a Kantian doctor because he might believe that the truth would cause more harm than good. A Kantian doctor is more likely to tell the truth because lying fails to respect the personhood of the patient. Doesn't the patient have a right to know he is terminally ill?

To make this relation between ethical theory and ethical decision-making clear let's look at a moral dilemma. A middle-aged man went to his family physician for a check-up before

4

going on a holiday with his wife. This was a vacation he had been putting off for some time. The patient was diagnosed as having terminal cancer and was not expected to live for more than six months. Chemotherapy could perhaps prolong the patient's life but not without considerable undesirable side-effects. When the patient returned to inquire about his health the doctor told him that it was all right for him to take his wife on vacation. He did not inform his patient about the cancer, the chemotherapy or his impending death. He did inform the patient's wife about both her husband's condition and not telling him of his condition. Did the doctor do the morally right thing? The answer we give to the dilemma will depend upon the ethical theory we appeal to. If we appeal to utilitarian considerations we would likely conclude that the doctor did the right thing. If we appeal to Kantian considerations we would likely conclude that he did the wrong thing. Let's approach the doctor's dilemma first from a utilitarian, then from a Kantian perspective.

The utilitarian would argue that the doctor did the right thing because not informing the patient will bring about the greatest amount of happiness for everyone in the long run. Telling a patient he is terminally ill, especially when he is about to embark on a much-needed and long-awaited holiday with his wife, is unnecessary cruelty. Besides, telling the truth would be dangerous. The patient would likely become depressed and try to harm or even kill himself. The situation is bad enough for his wife and family but this would make it worse. The family, knowing the truth, will be able to provide the psychological and physical support the patient will need in the future. Not telling him is the only humane way to act.

The utilitarians also believe that we have a general duty to tell the truth and be honest with one another. Since telling the truth promotes the general welfare, because it helps facilitate human interaction while lying undermines it, then honesty is a useful social practice which should be promoted and protected. Doesn't this suggest that the doctor did the wrong thing? No, because in this case the doctor's dishonesty does more good than harm and presents no threat to the useful social practice. For the utilitarian there are no absolute moral rules which cannot be rightfully broken in specific sets of circumstances.

A benevolent deception is surely morally acceptable in this case.

The Kantian, on the other hand, would argue that the doctor did the wrong thing because lying to others shows no respect for them as persons. Kantians believe we have an unconditional duty to tell the truth and not to lie. They argue that truthfulness is a necessary condition of human relationships. Without a commitment to honesty we could not relate to each other as human beings because we could not develop the trust which a human relationship presupposes. No meaningful human relationships can be built on deceit. Nor could we communicate with each other. Using a language presupposes that normally we intend to tell the truth when we speak. If we always lied when we spoke, we would eventually fail to communicate because lying is parasitic on truth telling. It is only because others expect us to tell the truth that we can deceive them.

The Kantians also argue that honesty is a necessary condition of all contractual obligations. A lying promise is immoral not simply because it might harm others but because it denies a rule that is constituent for a practice. Lying promises literally make the practice impossible. Finally the Kantians would argue that in order to respect others as persons you have to respect both their legal and moral rights. The doctor–patient relationship is basically a human relationship which presupposes the principle of respect for persons, hence it involves respect for truth and human rights from both participants. The patient must be truthful with the doctor so he will be able to make a correct diagnosis. The doctor must respect the rights of his patients. Patients do have a moral, if not a legal, right to know the truth about their medical diagnosis and prognosis, and it is not up to the doctor to decide whether this right should be respected. He should then not have lied to the cancer patient. He should have told him the truth as it was his duty to do.

Certainly ethical theorists can analyze moral problems from different theoretical perspectives but what they cannot do is to say which theory is best. The decision to adopt an ethical theory appears to be purely arbitrary because philosophers have not developed a unified theory of ethics. The idea of a moral expert analogous to the scientific expert is then a chimera. It is also dangerous. If not checked it will become a threat to freedom of thought and conscience, values which are essential for a democratic society. Ethical theorists might soon become false philosopher kings, trying to impose their values on others on an ill-founded notion of moral expertise.

The orthodox view, however, has its difficulties. For if we accept this autonomous position then moral education in all its forms will disappear from the school system at all levels. This is in fact what did happen recently in our culture and universities. Descriptive ethics remained as the special province of the social scientist and theoretical (analytical) ethics remained the special province of the moral philosopher. Practical ethics got left out in the intellectual cold and became the province of anyone who had an axe to grind. The neglect of practical ethics has dire consequences for civilization. It may in part explain the widening gap which has developed between our technologies and our morality. The fact that the orthodox view leads to the neglect of practical ethics and moral education is a good reason why we should divest ourselves of it, in spite of its obvious merits. But if we abandon the orthodox view what do we put in its place? I would suggest an interdisciplinary or holistic view as an alternative. On the holistic view the three traditional branches of ethics are seen as logically interdependent. Although practical, descriptive, and theoretical ethics can be distinguished from each other for purposes of division of labor, they form part of a unified comprehensive system of understanding. At this highest level of thought descriptive and philosophical ethics cannot be morally neutral. Moral neutrality is a working hypothesis only, not an ultimate intellectual division. If we accept the holistic view then we are committed both to moral education and moral experts. Are these unacceptable implications which should make us abandon holism and scamper for the security of the autonomous view? I think not.

Let's take moral education first. To begin with, there are no morally neutral systems of education. Morality is always taught implicitly, if not explicitly, in any school system. The fact that universities, and I would hope all schools, consider academic dishonesty to be morally unacceptable and develop educational policies to outlaw it is a case in point. It is also clear that our

Canadian public schools teach the historic values of liberal democracy, i.e. respect for freedom of thought and religion, moral tolerance and respect for human rights. Again a case in point. Examples can be multiplied *ad infinitum*. Moral neutrality in the school system is simply a myth. Nor is moral education inconsistent with democratic values (see MacNiven 1984: 16ff). If we clearly distinguish between moral indoctrination and moral education, as we should, then moral education presents no problem for democracies. Since indoctrination denies that the learner is an autonomous moral agent, it defeats the primary purpose of any system of moral education which is to produce mature rational moral agents. It may be difficult to achieve this goal but there is no reason why moral education cannot be made consistent with respect for individual conscience and freedom of thought. Because holism commits us to moral education is no reason for rejecting it. But what of moral expertise which it is also committed to? Again I would argue that it does not constitute good grounds for rejecting holism.

The idea of the moral expert is unacceptable only if we see moral reasoning as a mechanical rather than an organic process. If we assume we can resolve moral dilemmas by using mechanical models of reasoning the criticism will be valid. The idea of moral expertise assumes that we can develop a hierarchical system of moral principles, secondary moral rules and inference rules which, when mechanically applied to any particular case, will allow us to arrive at correct moral conclusions. But in practice this is rarely the situation. What is correct in one set of circumstances seems inappropriate in others. The infinite complexity of concrete moral experience will always defeat a mechanical casuistry because it is too abstract to capture the uniqueness of individual moral experience. However, this criticism doesn't hold if we adopt organic as opposed to mechanical models of moral reasoning. According to organic casuistry, when obligations conflict to create moral dilemmas this indicates that the moral systems controlling our thought and conduct have become incoherent. We will be in intellectual and moral disequilibrium until it has been resolved. If we try to rid ourselves of this unease by mechanical methods of reasoning we are bound to fail, because the theory is applied to experience and experience is never applied to theory. Moral dilemmas are the death knells of mechanical casuistry but not of organic casuistry.

In order to solve a moral dilemma we need to grow morally either at the personal or social level. Moral dilemmas represent critical moments in the moral development of persons or institutions. They represent periods of personal or social discord. We need to rid ourselves of discord in order to restore meaning to our lives, for things to make sense once again. Dilemmas impel us to reach richer and more highly integrated states of affairs both personally and socially. When a moral dilemma has been successfully resolved the person or the institution will have developed morally. Moral problems signal not the death of living moral systems but present opportunities for moral growth. To grow we have to learn how to express the competing values in more complex personal and social structures. Should a doctor tell the truth to his cancer patient? Concern for the patient's well-being suggests that lying would do more good than harm. Respect for persons suggests that the truth must be told. The patient has a right to know. If we apply the utilitarian theory we express the value of care but not that of respect. If we apply the Kantian theory we express the value of respect but not care. So both solutions are wrong because they fail to give full expression to important values. What is needed is a way of relating to the patient which will express both values simultaneously. To do this we cannot simply apply a theory mechanically to a particular case. We need to engage in creative moral thought. We need to look at situations from different perspectives to see how we might restructure them in richer ways. Perhaps it is not a matter of whether the doctor should tell the truth or not but when or how he should do this. Are there not ways of being honest with the patient which also express concern for his welfare? Do you need to say straight out: "You're a dead man"? The idea that the way you tell the truth might be the solution to the dilemma came from a doctor, not an ethicist, which shows that the dialogue between the ethicist and other professionals is a two-way street, like the relation between ethical theory and practice.

The idea of the moral expert which emerges from an organic casuistry is not that of the moral busybody who goes around telling other people what to do (even if they want to be told). It is that of the moral educator working in an interdisciplinary fashion, both theoretically and practically, with other professionals to try to reach creative solutions to the moral problems of autonomous moral agents. The moralist becomes a humanist who respects the moral automony of those he is advising. The identification of the moral educator and the moral expert should not surprise us because moral indoctrination, which is foreign to both, is a mechanical rather than a creative method of teaching. Surely this conception of the moral expert which emerges from a holistic approach to ethics should be acceptable in both theory and practice.

REFERENCES

MacNiven, D. (1982) *The Moral Question, Ethical Theory*, Ontario.
—— (1984) "Moral Education," *Canadian Forum* (May 1984).
—— (1987) *Bradley's Moral Psychology*, Ontario.
Moore, G. E. (1903) *Principia Ethica*, Cambridge.

2

ETHICS AND SOCIAL SCIENCE

1 Recent developments in social psychology in response to ethical concerns

DAVID L. WIESENTHAL

ACKNOWLEDGMENTS

The author wishes to thank Dr Romeo Vitelli for providing his report and Ms Gloria Emerson for her bibliographic assistance.

In previous publications (Wiesenthal 1974, 1981), I described many of the problems and paradoxes that social psychology was faced with once researchers decided to conduct field research utilizing unobtrusive measures. These measures consisted of techniques to assess behavior without invoking the defensive reactions inherent in the use of questionnaires, surveys or experiments. My major point was that by eliminating many of the methodological and ethical problems inherent in deceptive laboratory experiments by switching to unobtrusive measurement, we were merely trading one set of problems for another one. The folk saying "Better the devil you know than the devil you don't know" may be an apt summary of some of these issues. This article will review recent developments in social psychological research in light of ethical concerns. I will highlight what changes the discipline has experienced and explain the influence of contemporary society on the culture of social psychology.

THE "CRISIS" PERIOD IN SOCIAL PSYCHOLOGY

A number of papers have been published documenting important changes in social psychological research with respect to the "crisis" that social psychology faced in the late 1960s and early 1970s (Argyris 1968; Baumrind 1964; Friedman 1967; Gergen 1973; Kelman 1967; McGuire 1967, 1973; Ring 1967, 1972; Rosenthal 1966; Rosenthal and Rosnow 1969). This crisis was characterized by the frustration over theory construction and methodological issues (i.e. experimenter effects, subject role related behaviors, statistical models, exclusive reliance on laboratory experimentation, etc.) as well as the fact that deception in the laboratory was the accepted norm. Deception in social psychology experimentation consisted of deception over: (a) the purpose of the experiment, (b) the implementation of the test procedure, (c) feedback provided to subjects regarding their performance, and (d) occasionally even the very debriefing designed to eliminate the deception and restore the subject to his or her original level of self-esteem prior to participation.

The arguments against deception are that: (a) deception violates the right to choose to participate since informed consent is not possible to obtain, (b) deception abuses the basic interpersonal relationship between experimenter and subject, (c) laboratory-based deception contributes to deception as a societal value and practice, (d) deception represents a questionable base for the development of social psychology, (e) deception represents a contradiction to our professional roles of teacher/scientist, (f) deception has led to the loss of trust in both psychology and psychologists, (g) society may retaliate against organized psychology by loss of funding, legal controls, and general noncooperation (modified from Adair, Dushenko and Lindsay 1985).

Baumrind (1985) has described the costs of deception research as consisting of: (a) the harm done to the subject in terms of threats to his or her identity and self-esteem, (b) the harm done to psychology by exhausting the pool of naïve subjects and by jeopardizing community support for the research enterprise, (c) the harm done to society by "snoopology" (Jung 1975) consisting of increased self-consciousness in public places, broadening the aura of mistrust and suspicion that pervades daily life, inconveniencing and irritating people by staging contrived situations, and desensitizing individuals to the needs of others ("boy-who-cried-wolf" effects) (Jung 1975;

MacCoun and Kerr 1987; Warwick 1975; Weinrach and Ivey 1975; Wiesenthal 1974, 1981). Graduate training in the 1960s consisted of indoctrination that deception was the correct way to perform research. Aronson and Carlsmith (1968), in their influential *Handbook of Social Psychology* chapter on research methods, described deception as an integral element of experimentation. This emphasis has been retained in their revision of this chapter for the third edition of the *Handbook*. These authors (Aronson *et al.* 1985: 456) state that "it might be said that part of being a good experimental social psychologist involves learning to say 'whoops' convincingly." Researchers who employed deception were the heroes and role models (e.g. Stanley Milgram and Philip Zimbardo) of a generation of graduate students who were socialized into accepting deception as the norm of the field.

DECEPTION AND METHODOLOGY

Adair *et al* (1985) have presented an analysis of published studies in one of the most influential journals (the *Journal of Abnormal and Social Psychology* and its successor, the *Journal of Personality and Social Psychology*) in social psychology over a thirty-one-year period. As can be seen in Figure 1, the percentage of published reports employing deception rose from 14.3% in 1948 to 58.5% in 1979. Adair *et al.* (1985) also analyzed seven social psychology journal volumes published in 1979 to examine the proportion of deception studies and the type of research methodologies represented in the articles. Figure 1 indicates that deception was very closely linked to laboratory experimentation. The journal (*Journal of Experimental Social Psychology*) with the highest percentage of deception papers (59%) also had the highest proportion of laboratory usage (88%). The *Journal of Social Psychology* had the lowest level of deception (32%) appearing in its reports and had the lowest level of laboratory experimentation, relying more than any other surveyed journal on survey methodology. Across all seven journals, 50% of their published reports utilized deception in the reported research, 67% of the reports were based on laboratory procedures, with only 19% and 14% respectively for survey and field-based methodologies, as can be seen in Figure 2.

Figure 1 Percentage of empirical studies employing deception in *Journal of Abnormal and Social Psychology/Journal of Personality and Social Psychology*

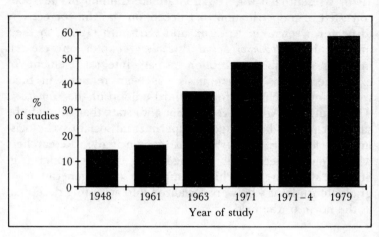

Figure 2 Summary of deception and research methodology from seven social psychology journals in 1979

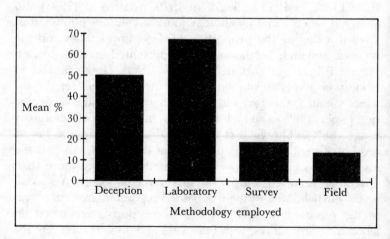

Figure 3 Use of deception over time

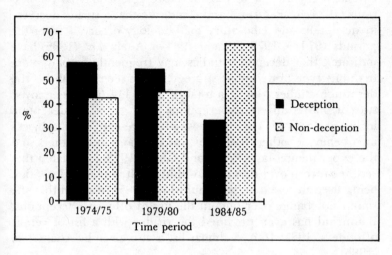

Figure 4 Research paradigms over time

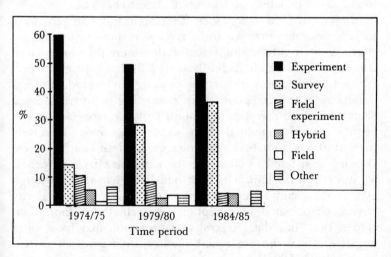

Vitelli (in press) performed a similar content analysis, but extended the review to include more recent journal publications (1984–5). Figures 3 and 4 indicate that a steady decrease in deception and laboratory methodology occurred from the periods 1974–5, 1979–80, and 1984–5. Adair *et al.* (1985) have indicated that deception studies may frequently employ more than one type of deceptive strategy. It was seen that of the 166 deception studies (out of a total of 284), 114 (69%) employed two or more different deceptions. The types of deception included deceit over the purpose of the research, the subject's own behavior, others' behavior, information about others and the experimental tasks. West and Gunn (1978) speculated that recent concern over deception would result in milder deception being used in research, but Baumrind (1985) reported that she found no change over time in the use of offensive deceptions. Baumrind has even provided the reader with a list of recent offenders (1985: 166). A similar list is also given by Adair *et al.* (1985).

The issue of the after-effects of laboratory deception experiences was addressed by Silverman, Shulman and Wiesenthal (1970). They reported that subjects who had taken part in deception experiments and were then debriefed, behaved differently from nondeceived subjects when they subsequently took part in later psychological research. The deceived-debriefed subjects were seen to respond defensively in a socially desirable manner and were less responsive to demand characteristics in following research than were the nondeceived controls. Smith and Richardson (1983) have recently performed a questionnaire survey probing undergraduates' experiences with deception and debriefing in psychological research. These investigators found that participants who had been deceived evaluated their experiences more positively than students who had not engaged in deception research. Debriefing seemed to eliminate the negative effects perceived by students who indicated they had been harmed. Although 20% of their sample reported experiencing harm, the majority having participated in deception research, the authors concluded that "our data suggest that deception may have more negative effects on researchers than on their research participants" (1983: 1081)!

In Adair *et al.*'s (1985) previously reported analysis of seven major social psychology journals published in 1979, deception was used in 50% of published research, ranging from 32% of articles published in the *Journal of Social Psychology* to 59% of articles appearing in the *Journal of Experimental Social Psychology*. Informed consent was mentioned in only 6% of the 1979 articles, with withdrawal rights mentioned in 4% of the papers.

Adair *et al.* (1985) report the results of a content analysis of empirical papers published in the *Journal of Personality and Social Psychology* for the year 1979. Informed consent was reported in only 8% of the 284 empirical studies, while informing subjects of their right to leave the experiment was reported in only 5% of the papers. To follow up their initial survey, other social psychology journals published in 1983 were coded (*Journal of Personality and Social Psychology, Journal of Experimental Social Psychology* and the *Personality and Social Psychology Bulletin*). Overall, this analysis found no appreciable changes in ethical practice. Reports of informed consent and publicizing the ability to withdraw were infrequent. Reported debriefing was seen to drop by three percentage points.

Perry and Abramson (1980) examined two key journals, *Journal of Personality and Social Psychology* and *Journal of Consulting and Clinical Psychology* from 1975 to 1978 and reported that over two-thirds of the studies failed to mention that debriefing had occurred. Adair *et al.* (1985) stated that reported debriefing occurred in 33% of the articles published in the seven major social psychology journals published in 1979. In an extension of this research, Ullman and Jackson (1982) examined every article published in the *Journal of Abnormal and Social Psychology* and its successor, *Journal of Personality and Social Psychology* from 1960 to 1980, searching only on alternate years. Ullman and Jackson reported a steady increase in studies describing debriefing, compared to 47% of studies reporting debriefing in 1980. The average increase between the examined years was 4.38%. Researchers tended to report debriefing university students more than any other group (e.g. convicts, mental patients, juvenile delinquents and pre-school children). The irony of deceiving our own students has been previously described (Wiesenthal 1981), but it is made even more problematic when one considers the overreliance of social psychology upon university student subjects. Higbee and Wells (1972) and Higbee *et al.* (1982) analyzed published research in major social psychology journals and found that earlier trends for experimental methodology and the use of university students as subjects predominated over correlational research and non-university samples. Vitelli's previously described data (in press) may suggest only a very recent downturn in this trend.

SENSITIVITY TO ETHICAL ISSUES

Despite the actual ethical practices in research, or perhaps because of them, social psychology textbooks seem to show concern for ethical issues in their coverage of the field. This concern for text coverage was significantly greater than industrial and clinical psychology texts, although clinical psychology journal articles contained more citations to ethics than did social psychology (Giacalone *et al.* 1982). Adair *et al.* (1983) analyzed experimental psychology textbooks' coverage of research ethics from the early 1970s to 1981. More recently published texts tended to have increased attention devoted to research ethics. Adair *et al.* (1983) report that only 11% of the recent texts failed to provide coverage of ethics and more than three-quarters gave substantial coverage to this topic. Many of the texts reprinted the American Psychological Association's ethical code.

Latané (1986) has reported the results of a survey of experimental social psychologists where he was informed by respondents that deception research would not be funded by the National Institutes for Mental Health (NIMH) and internal ethical review committees were reluctant to approve even "innocuous research" in social psychology.

To examine this issue of increased sensitivity to ethical concerns from another perspective, we searched citations to the American Psychological Association's ethical principles in the *Social Science Citation Index*. The search covered the years from 1966 to August 1986, examining every other year. Only 39 citations to the ethics code were seen in the five years examined for the 1970s, while a total of 122 citations were counted for the 1980s. If we view the citing of the ethical principles as reflecting a concern with ethical practice, then this tripling of citations means that psychologists are probably cautiously referring their procedures to the ethical code for propriety and/or may be writing more about ethical principles in general.

Vitelli's data indicate that deception and laboratory methodology may have since passed its peak and now be on the downturn. In addition to the rise of non-laboratory techniques, there are other indications that the behavior of social psychologists may have been changed in response to the concern over research ethics. Since the 1960s, whole new sub-fields have arisen with a strong applied orientation that opposes deceptive laboratory techniques. These would be the fields of environmental psychology, applied social psychology, program evaluation research, and parts of health psychology. If the concern in the 1960s over deception in social psychology experimentation was linked to the disgust over the conduct of the Vietnam war, with its history of presidential deception felt by American social psychologists (Kelman 1968), then the contemporary research of social psychologists may reflect the current conservative resurgence in North American society.

SOCIETY AND SOCIAL PSYCHOLOGY

Psychology and its practitioners are influenced by the surrounding society. Some historical examples may be germane here. Kurt Lewin is generally credited as being the father of modern social psychology (Morrow 1969). Lewin, a German Jew, served with the German army during the First World War, being decorated with the Iron Cross for his performance. After the war, Lewin researched in the areas of memory, learning, and perception. Forced to flee Germany during the Hitler era, he set up laboratories in the United States where his research shifted to the study of prejudice, democratic leadership styles, and exploring the usefulness of group discussion to change behavior in a positive manner. During World War II, Konrad Lorenz was functioning as a Nazi propagandist in perverting ethological principles to appear as supporting the Nuremburg laws (Eisenberg 1972; Kalikow 1983). When Lorenz received the Nobel Prize in 1973, his interests centered on explaining human aggression. The point here is that we are all sensitive to the cultural matrix that surrounds us and this matrix influences what we choose to research and what methodology we will employ. Sears has recently described (1986) a shift in the content of social psychological research. Sears states that the change is away from "hot" domains to "cool" research topics. By "hot" Sears is referring to the study of topics like obedience, conformity, aggression, and altruism, while "cool" refers to cognitive processes. Another way of describing this trend would be to state that problem areas in society are not being investigated. Rather than study the issues involved with what is outside the body, social psychology is studying what is inside the head.

Social psychology has abandoned many of Lewin's real world concerns to environmental and health psychology. Perhaps the fear of stirring up ethical controversies has had a deterrent effect on many investigators, who now prefer to avoid these "hot" topics. Gross and Fleming (1982) point out in their content analysis that the following proportions of research in these areas of social psychology used deception: compliance/conformity (96.7%), altruism (96.6%), aggression (90%), equity (84.6%). A similar analysis by Stricker (1967) surveying four key social-personality journals (*Journal of Abnormal and Social Psychology, Journal of Personality, Journal of Social Psychology*, and *Sociometry*) published in 1964 found comparable results. Research that challenges how we perceive the fundamental nature of human behavior may be more likely to arouse ethical concerns than research that does not disturb our conceptualizations (Milgram 1964; Wiesenthal 1974). Schlenker and Forsyth (1977) had high school and university students judge the propriety of two obedience paradigms: Milgram's original laboratory study (1963) and West *et al.*'s (1975) field study where undergraduates were persuaded to perform burglaries. Subjects judged experiments that investigated obedience to an authority as generally less moral and more threatening to the participant's dignity and welfare when the proportion of total obedience was high rather than low. The proportion of those described as being upset by the manipulations did not affect the subject's judgment of morality. West and Gunn (1978: 31) point out that "this bias if it is shared by ethics committees and journal editors, is particularly troublesome. It will tend to discourage research in potentially important areas that involve negative aspects of the human character." West and Gunn argue that psychologists will be pressured to study only positive behaviors. In addition to concentrating on pleasant events, non-motivational models will be proposed and tested because of the avoidance of deception manipulations necessary to study motivation (p. 381). Recent articles by researchers in the areas of sexuality and aggression have signalled their scrupulous concern over ethical matters (Abramson 1977; Check and Malamuth 1983, 1984; Malamuth and Check 1984). Perhaps researchers in "hot" areas feel compelled to justify their actions in an effort to prevent or forestall objections from others.

Another change that has arisen relates to the establishment of tightened ethical codes. The American Psychological Association has recently revised its *Ethical Principles in the Conduct of Research with Human Participants* (1982) to reflect more of the finer points than its predecessor did in 1972. There has also been interest in developing a distinctly Canadian set of ethical principles in psychology (Brandt 1978; Sinclair *et al.* 1987). I am quite concerned about the variety of differing national codes that are arising. A wiser course would be the establishment of a truly international ethical code for social science. The history of the Nuremburg trials, culminating in the World Health Organization's statement of informed consent (Bower and de Gasparis 1978), should be seen as forever questioning the notion that each nation can be relied upon to follow the highest level of ethics. Lifton (1986), Kogon (1975) and Shirer (1960) have described the practices of Nazi scientists and physicians engaged in research that they saw as vital to national interests. Warwick (1980) highlights the issues of researchers working in cross-cultural settings where issues may raise strong ethical and moral concerns that would not arise in their home country. Social science needs a fairly strict ethical code that should have as its goal equal applicability across nations.

In describing the State University of New York at Albany's violation of both state and federal laws aimed at protecting research subjects, Smith (1977) mentioned that the psychology department requirement that introductory psychology students participate in experiments or write an essay (as an alternative requirement) was declared to constitute coercion under both

New York State and federal law by the state health department. (For more on the Albany incident, see Tedeschi and Rosenfeld's report (1981).) Subject pool requirements are common at many Canadian universities and, in fact, there was a suggestion last year from a new faculty member that we implement such a requirement in our department. The only merit to a Canadian ethical code may be its "made in Canada" label. Since the Canadian legal system seems less sensitive to civil liberties than what exists south of the border (Friedenberg 1980), we may find less practical concern with coercion, privacy, and informed consent, than adherence to American models would afford.

REFERENCES

Abramson, P. R. (1977) "Ethical Requirements for Research on Human Sexual Behaviour: From the Perspective of Participating Subjects," *Journal of Social Issues* 33: 184–92.

Adair, J. G., Dushenko, T. W. and Lindsay, R. C. L. (1985) "Ethical Regulations and Their Impact on Research Practice," *American Psychologist* 40: 59–72.

Adair, J. G., Lindsay, R. C. L. and Carlopio, J. (1983) "Social Artifact Research and Ethical Regulations: Their Impact on the Teaching of Experimental Methods," *Teaching of Psychology* 10: 159–60.

American Psychological Association (1982) *Ethical Principles in Conduct of Research with Human Participants*, Washington, DC: American Psychological Association.

Argyris, C. (1968) "Some Unintended Consequences of Rigorous Research," *Psychological Bulletin* 70: 185–97.

Aronson, E. and Carlsmith, J. M. (1968) "Experimentation in Social Psychology," in G. Lindzey and E. Aronson (eds) *The Handbook of Social Psychology, Vol. 2*, Reading, Mass.: Addison-Wesley.

Aronson, E., Brewer, M. and Carlsmith, J. M. (1985) "Experimentation in Social Psychology," in G. Lindzey and E. Aronson (eds) *The Handbook of Social Psychology, Vol. 1*, 3rd edn, New York: Random House.

Baumrind, D. (1964) "Some Thoughts on the Ethics of Research: After Reading Milgram's 'Behavioral Study of Obedience'," *American Psychologist* 19: 421–3.

—— (1985) "Research Using Intentional Deception," *American Psychologist* 40: 165–74.

Bower, R. T. and de Gasparis, P. (1978) *Ethics in Social Research: Protecting the Interests of Human Subjects*, New York: Praeger.

Brandt, L. W. (1978) "Don't Sweep the Ethical Problems under the Rug! Totalitarian versus Equalitarian Ethics," *Canadian Psychological Review* 19: 63–6.

Check, J. V. P. and Malamuth, N. M. (1983) "Ethical Considerations in Sex and Aggression Research." (Unpublished manuscript.)
—— and —— (1984) "Can There Be Positive Effects of Participation in Pornography Experiments?" *Journal of Sex Research* 20: 14–31.
Eisenberg, L. (1972) "The *Human* Nature of Human Nature," *Science* 176: 123–8.
Friedenberg, E. Z. (1980) *Deference to Authority: The Case of Canada*, White Plains, NY: M. E. Sharpe.
Friedman, N. (1967) *The Social Nature of Psychological Research*, New York: Basic Books.
Gergen, K. (1973) "Social Psychology as History," *Journal of Personality and Social Psychology* 26: 309–20.
Giacalone, R. A., Robinson, B., Gracin, L., Greenfeld, N. and Rosenfeld, N. (1982) "Concern for Ethics in Social, Industrial, and Clinical Psychology as Reflected in Textbooks and Journal Articles," *Bulletin of the Psychonomic Society* 20: 1–2.
Gross, A. E. and Fleming, I. (1982) "Twenty Years of Deception in Social Psychology," *Personality and Social Psychology Bulletin* 8: 402–8.
Higbee, K. L. and Wells, M. G. (1972) "Some Research Trends in Social Psychology During the 1960's," *American Psychologist* 27: 963–6.
Higbee, K. L., Millard, R. J. and Folkman, J. R. (1982) "Social Psychology Research During the 1970's: Predominance of Experimentation and College Students," *Personality and Social Psychology Bulletin* 8: 180–3.
Jung, J. (1975) "Snoopology," *Human Behaviour* 4: 56–9.
Kalikow, T. J. (1983) "Konrad Lorenz's Ethological Theory: Explanation and Ideology, 1938–1943," *Journal of the History of Biology* 16: 39–73.
Kelman, H. (1968) *A Time to Speak: On Human Value and Social Research*, San Francisco: Jossey-Bass.
Kelman, H. C. (1967) "Human Use of Human Subjects: The Problem of Deception in Social Psychology Experiments," *Psychological Bulletin* 67: 1–11.
Kogon, E. (1975) *Theory and Practice of Hell: The German Concentration Camps and the System Behind Them*, trans. Heinz Norden, New York: Berkley Windhover.
Latané, B. (1986) "The State of Social Psychology." Invited address presented at the annual meeting of the Society for Personality and Social Psychology, Division 8 of the American Psychological Association, Washington, DC, August 23, 1986.
Lifton, R. J. (1986) *The Nazi Doctors: Medical Killing and the Psychology of Genocide*, Toronto: Fitzhenry & Whiteside.
MacCoun, R. J. and Kerr, N. L. (1987) "Suspicion in the Laboratory: Kelman's Prophecy Revisited," *American Psychologist* 42: 199.
McGuire, W. J. (1967) "Some Impending Reorientations in Social Psychology," *Journal of Experimental Social Psychology* 3: 124–39.
—— (1973) "The Yin and Yang of Progress in Social Psychology," *Journal of Personality and Social Psychology* 26: 446–56.

Malamuth, N. M. and Check, J. V. P. (1984) "Debriefing Effectiveness Following Exposure to Pornographic Rape Depictions," *Journal of Sex Research* 20: 1–13.

Milgram, S. (1963) "Behavioral Study of Obedience," *Journal of Abnormal and Social Psychology* 67: 371–8.

—— (1964) "Issues in the Study of Obedience: A Reply to Baumrind," *American Psychologist* 19: 848–52.

Morrow, A. J. (1969) *The Practical Theorist: The Life and Work of Kurt Lewin*, New York: Teacher's College Press.

Perry, E. B. and Abramson, P. R. (1980) "Debriefing: A Gratuitous Procedure?", *American Psychologist* 35: 298–9.

Ring, K. (1967) "Experimental Social Psychology: Some Sober Questions about Some Frivolous Values," *Journal of Experimental Social Psychology* 3: 113–23.

—— (1972) "Let's Get Started: An Appeal to What's Left in Psychology," mimeograph, University of Connecticut.

Rosenthal, R. (1966) *Experimenter Effects in Behavioral Research*, New York: Appleton-Century-Crofts.

Rosenthal, R. and Rosnow, R. L. (1969) "The Volunteer Subject," in R. Rosenthal and R. L. Rosnow (eds) *Artifact in Behavioural Research*, New York: Academic Press.

Schlenker, B. R. and Forsyth, D. R. (1977) "On the Ethics of Psychological Research," *Journal of Experimental Social Psychology* 13: 369–96.

Sears, D. O. (1986) "College Sophomores in the Laboratory: Influences of a Narrow Data Base on Social Psychology's View of Human Nature," *Journal of Personality and Social Psychology* 51: 515–30.

Shirer, W. L. (1960) *The Rise and Fall of the Third Reich: A History of Nazi Germany*, New York: Simon & Schuster.

Silverman, I., Shulman, A. D. and Wiesenthal, D. L. (1970) "Effects of Deceiving and Debriefing Subjects on Performance in Later Experiments," *Journal of Personality and Social Psychology* 14: 203–12.

Sinclair, C., Poizner, S., Gilmour-Barrett, K., and Randall, D. (1987) "The Development of a Code of Ethics for Canadian Psychologists," *Canadian Psychology* 28: 1–8.

Smith, R. J. (1977) "Electroshock Experiment at Albany Violates Ethics Guidelines," *Science* 198: 383–6, 708.

Smith, S. S. and Richardson, D. (1983) "Amelioration of Deception and Harm in Psychological Research: The Important Role of Debriefing," *Journal of Personality and Social Psychology* 44: 1075–82.

Social Science Citation Index, Philadelphia: Institute for Scientific Information.

Stricker, L. (1967) "The True Deceiver," *Psychological Bulletin* 68: 13–20.

Tedeschi, J. J. and Rosenfeld, P. (1981) "The Experimental Research Controversy at SUNYA: A Case Study," in A. J. Kimmel (ed.) *Ethics of Human Subject Research*, San Francisco: Jossey-Bass.

24

Ullman, D. and Jackson, T. T. (1982) "Researchers' Ethical Conscience: Debriefing 1960 to 1980," *American Psychologist* 37: 972–3.

Vitelli, R. (in press) "The Crisis Issue Assessed: An Empirical Analysis," *Basic and Applied Social Psychology*.

Warwick, D. P. (1975) "Social Scientists Ought to Stop Lying," *Psychology Today*, February 1975: 38–106.

—— (1980) "The Politics and Ethics of Cross-Cultural Research," in H. C. Triandis and W. W. Lambert (eds) *Handbook of Cross-Cultural Psychology: Perspectives, Vol. 1*, Toronto: Allyn & Bacon.

Weinrach, S. G. and Ivey, A. E. (1975) "Science, Psychology and Deception," *British Psychological Society Bulletin* 28: 263–7.

West, S. G. and Gunn, S. P. (1978) "Some Issues of Ethics and Social Psychology," *American Psychologist* 33: 30–8.

West, S. G., Gunn, S. P. and Chernicky, P. (1975) "Ubiquitous Watergate: An Attributional Analysis," *Journal of Personality and Social Psychology* 32: 55–65.

Wiesenthal, D. L. (1974) "Reweaving Deception's Tangled Web," *Canadian Psychologist* 15: 326–36.

—— (1981) "Sweating at Night: Some Ethical Paradoxes Confronting Social Psychological Research," *Social Science and Medicine* 157: 33–37.

2

ETHICS AND SOCIAL SCIENCE
2 Ethical considerations in sex and aggression research

JAMES V. P. CHECK and NEIL M. MALAMUTH

INTRODUCTION

Over the past several years of conducting sex and aggression research, it has become apparent to us that there are a fairly large number of special ethical issues to be addressed in such research, and that these issues should be communicated to other researchers. This paper presents a discussion of these concerns, and describes the ethical precautions we have developed for use in our own research. These procedures concern the materials used, voluntary participation, deception and debriefing, and monitoring. It is hoped that by communicating what we have learned from our own experiences, we can help other researchers to avoid ethical pitfalls in their own research programs.

ETHICAL CONSIDERATIONS IN SEX AND AGGRESSION RESEARCH

The purpose of this paper is to: (a) outline general ethical principles and concerns with sex and aggression research, as well as some specific concerns, (b) outline the precautions we have developed in our own sex and aggression research, and (c) indicate our past experience with ethics at the University of Manitoba. We will make reference to both the sex and the aggression areas of study for each of the three topics referred to above. We should like to note at the outset that our research is fully consistent with the Ethical Standards of the Canadian and American Psychological Associations, and, as will be apparent from the following detailed discussion, our general policy is to be overly cautious.

ETHICAL PRINCIPLES AND CONCERNS

As Malamuth (1983) has detailed elsewhere, there are a number of ethical principles that are applicable to aggression research but especially to sex research, because "society has often treated sexuality as a taboo topic and many people understandably wish to keep their sexual lives private. It is clear that research in this area needs to be particularly sensitive to ethical safeguards" (p. 231). Malamuth has indicated five basic ethical safeguards, all of which we typically employ in our research at the University of Manitoba:

1. Only volunteers who are fully aware of the procedures to be used in the research should serve as subjects.
2. Pressures should not be exerted on people to volunteer.
3. Subjects should not participate in any new activities as part of the research that they have not previously chosen to engage in.
4. Subjects must be free to leave at any time, for any reason, without any penalty whatsoever.
5. A thorough debriefing must be held to explain any procedures that may involve deception.

With respect to sex research in general, Paul Abramson (1977) has found that subjects in sex studies which employ these ethical safeguards almost uniformly report that they found their experience with the research to be positive and devoid of any negative after-effects. With respect to our own sex research at the University of Manitoba, however, there was an additional ethical concern regarding the effects of exposing research subjects to depictions of forced sexual encounters which, for example, portray the victim as enjoying the assault. Since our research has demonstrated that such exposure can, for example, lead to attitude change regarding the acceptability of force in sexual encounters (Malamuth and Check 1981), it is for ethical reasons necessary to debrief subjects (in order to counteract these attitudes), and to follow up these debriefings with an assessment of their effectiveness. With respect to

27

aggression research, Smith and Richardson (1983) have found that subjects who participate in a variety of deception studies (including aggression studies) experience no ill effects if a proper debriefing procedure is used.

ETHICAL PRECAUTIONS

The precautions we have developed at the University of Manitoba over the past several years concern (a) materials to be used, (b) voluntary participation (points 1 to 4 above), (c) deception and debriefing (point 5 above), and (d) monitoring.

Materials

Since there may be some general concern about the nature of the sexual materials we use, it should be noted that we use sexual depictions (both rape depictions and consenting sex depictions) which are adapted from those currently available to subjects in varied mass media outlets (e.g. *Playboy* and *Penthouse* magazines).

Voluntary Participation

In general, introductory psychology students at the University of Manitoba are given the option of writing a paper or participating in seven hours of experiments. The regulations regarding recruitment of subjects stipulate that each experiment is advertised in class, where a sign-up booklet is usually circulated.

Sex Research

In our sex research studies, we typically state on the sign-up booklet that the research involves the use of detailed questionnaires about a variety of sexual and other personal matters, that the research involves exposure to "sexually explicit pornography" (where applicable), and involves the physiological assessment of sexual arousal (again, where applicable, such as in studies which employ penile tumescence measures of sexual arousal). Thus, subjects are free to sign up or not sign up as they choose. When subjects arrive at the research room (in groups), their experiment credit cards are immediately signed, and it is explicitly stated that they are free to leave at any time, without any penalty whatsoever, if there is anything which they find objectionable about the study. For some studies the sexual depictions are typewritten and included at the end of the questionnaire, so that subjects can just leave if they do not wish to read the sexual depiction. For other studies we are interested in the physiological assessment of males' sexual arousal (*vis-à-vis* penile tumescence), and we usually use tape-recorded depictions. The usual procedure in this latter type of study is to have subjects participate (in groups) in an "orientation session," where they first fill out a large questionnaire and receive one experimental credit. They are then given a detailed description of the procedures which are used to assess penile tumescence. Subjects are told to (1) read over the description, (2) decide if they wish to participate in this "second experiment," and (3) if they wish, sign up for one of the sessions (where they participate individually in private rooms), or (4) simply leave if they do not wish to participate further. Thus, subjects sign up for the physiological assessment phase in an active manner, with no coercion whatsoever, and they receive experimental credit for the questionnaire phase regardless of whether they also sign up for the physiological assessment phase. All those who participate in the physiological assessment phase are, of course, given another experimental credit as soon as they arrive at the laboratory. They are then left in complete privacy, to (1) read the instructions on how to connect the equipment, (2) sign the following informed consent form:

Participation in this study involves placing a small band around one's penis, reading written stories, and listening to audiotapes with explicit sexual content. These procedures have been fully explained to me. I AM AWARE THAT I MAY LEAVE NOW OR AT ANY TIME DURING THE EXPERIMENT, IF I SO WISH, WITHOUT HAVING TO GIVE ANY EXPLANATION AND WITH NO PENALTY WHATSOEVER. I am also aware that the data gathered in this research are confidential and anonymous with respect to any individual's identity. (Signed or initialed.)

29

and (3) either close the research room door and proceed with the experiment or (4) simply leave without having to speak to the experimenter (the experimenter is in a separate room and communicates via intercom). Once again, subjects give informed consent, are not coerced in any way, and are made to feel that they are free to leave at any time without penalty.

Aggression Research

In our aggression studies (which employ ostensible delivery of aversive noise as the measure of aggression), we use an "ESP" task as the cover story. Briefly, in a rigged lottery, the subject is assigned to the role of "transmitter," and is instructed to attempt to send numbers via ESP to another subject (actually a confederate of the experimenter) whose ostensible task is to guess the numbers. The subject is instructed to "punish" the confederate for incorrect guesses, ostensibly using aversive noise (no noise is actually sent). A sample of noise is given ahead of time (a 70 db tone). Subjects are then given an informed consent form to sign, which explicitly states that they will not be penalized if they withdraw (as with the sexuality studies, subjects' experiment credit cards are signed as soon as they arrive at the research setting).

Deception and Debriefing

In general, we place a great emphasis on debriefing, with respect to both our sex research studies and our aggression studies.

Sex Research

The major ethical concern relevant to debriefing following exposure to explicit sexual depictions concerns the use of rape depictions. The reason for this is that much of our research is directed toward examining the antisocial effects of exposure to rape depictions in which, for example, the rape victim is portrayed as enjoying the assault, or in which the victim is likely to be seen as responsible for her own rape. These types of depictions are hypothesized to increase subjects' rape myth acceptance attitudes (e.g. beliefs that rape victims enjoy rape or beliefs that victims are to be blamed for their own rapes). This being the case, our overall policy is to (a) give subjects a debriefing at the end of the experiment which is designed to counteract or reverse the effects of such exposure, and (b) assess the effectiveness of the debriefing. For example, the debriefing we typically use in our research on victim blaming is as follows:

> While the following is probably obvious to all subjects, we would like to emphasize that the story you read [or heard] was COMPLETE FANTASY. Some of you read a story which depicted a rape. In reality, as you are hopefully aware, rape is a serious crime, punishable by many years in prison. As well, rape victims suffer severe psychological damage as well as the more obvious physical effects of the assault. Unfortunately, many people still believe a number of *falsehoods* or *myths* about rape. For example, one totally unfounded myth is that if a woman does not immediately report a rape, or hesitates to report it, then the act is somehow not considered a real rape. A second falsehood that many people mistakenly believe is that if a woman does anything which puts her at greater risk or makes her more vulnerable to being victimized (e.g., going to a man's apartment, or kissing with a man when alone with him), then it is her own fault if she is subsequently raped, i.e., she somehow brings the rape upon herself. Clearly, a woman should not feel guilty about being raped just because she let a man kiss her but decided not to go any farther with him. A third totally false myth is that women want to be raped or are turned on by rape. All of these are in fact just myths and are in fact totally unfounded. Hopefully, if you realize that these myths are totally false, you will leave this experiment with a more realistic and accurate view of rape.

With respect to the effectiveness of these debriefings, we have found that the overall impact of exposure to the rape depiction followed by an appropriate debriefing is actually to reduce subjects' rape myth acceptance below the level of subjects who were not exposed to rape (Check 1982, 1984; Check and Malamuth 1984; Malamuth and Check 1984).

Aggression Research

There are two deceptions in our aggression research which necessitate debriefing: the fact that the subject is insulted (given a false negative evaluation) by the confederate, and the fact that the ESP cover story is false. Therefore, the following debriefing is given at the end of the experiment:

> Now that your active participation in the study has come to an end, we would like to offer you a more extensive, and accurate description of the experiment. If you have any questions, or concerns about any aspect of the study, please feel free to discuss them with the experimenter. It was never the intent of this study to focus on your ability to transmit ESP. The actual purpose of the experiment, was to demonstrate how an unpleasant personal evaluation would affect a subject's selection of an unpleasant stimulus.
>
> You were initially informed that you would be involved in an ESP experiment, so that you would not feel unnecessarily self-conscious about the delivery of an unpleasant stimulus. This deception was unavoidable, because it has been shown that when subjects are aware that a particular behavior is being studied, they have a tendency to change that behavior.
>
> The receiver in this experiment was not an actual subject, but a "confederate." This means he (she) was a part of the experiment, and he (she) plays this role for each of the sessions we run. Furthermore, the negative evaluation you received was prepared well before the experiment began, and each subject who participates receives the same evaluation. The confederate never actually used your answers, nor did he (she) write the evaluation you received. The evaluation was intended to give you a negative impression of the confederate. It is extremely important that we assure you that in no way does the evaluation reflect any meaningful statements or valid opinions concerning yourself.
>
> At no point during the study, did the confederate hear the "aversive noise" or attempt to receive the numbers you were transmitting. The numbers the computer gave you to transmit, and the correct or incorrect responses to these numbers were all programmed before the study began.
>
> Finally, we would like to apologize for the deception that

was involved in the experiment. Unfortunately, we are not aware of any alternative methods that are available for performing a study of this nature. We would also like to assure you that we are not suggesting that the delivery of an unpleasant stimulus, such as the aversive noise used in this study, is any indication of undesirable behavior on the part of the subject. The subject is expected to deliver the stimulus, and the experiment is arranged in such a manner, so as to increase the likelihood that he will do so.

Again we thank you for participating and we hope that you found the experiment at least mildly interesting.

We have just recently completed a study of the effectiveness of this debriefing, and the preliminary findings suggest that it was very effective in alleviating subjects' concerns about the negative evaluation. As well, it seems that the vast majority of the subjects found the study to be the most interesting and worthwhile research experience that they had had all year. In fact, several subjects spontaneously indicated that their biggest complaint about participating in psychological experiments was that they found them to be boring!

Monitoring

In addition to requiring the evaluation of the Human Subjects Ethical Review Committee at the University of Manitoba, we have established an independent Advisory Committee composed of members of the general community (including a lawyer), who review and monitor all the procedures used, and to whom an Ombudsman reports. The name and phone number of the Ombudsman is given to each and every subject who participates in our research, and subjects are asked to report their concerns to this person if they have any which we do not satisfactorily deal with. The Ombudsman is not otherwise affiliated with the project or department. While we have not had a single complaint from over 2,000 subjects so far, we none the less feel that the position of Ombudsman serves an important function, if for no other reason than that it allows subjects to feel that they have an independent agent to whom they can voice any concerns.

PAST EXPERIENCE WITH ETHICS

All of the procedures outlined above have been reviewed by a number of reviewing bodies, including our Department of Psychology Human Ethical Review Committee, our Faculty of Arts Ethical Review Committee, and the Social Sciences and Humanities Research Council of Canada (Research Grants Division). As well, several smaller granting agencies have made final judgments with respect to small individual projects. Through a continual process of interaction with these bodies and with ethics researchers in this area, we have evolved the ethical safeguards outlined above. While we have occasionally been requested to revise minor aspects of our procedures, there has never to our knowledge been a single major question raised about the ethicality of our current research procedures. None the less, we realize that it would be imprudent for any researcher to assume that his/her ethical behavior is perfect, and therefore we would appreciate feedback about any aspects of our procedures which any reader feels may be improved.

REFERENCES

Abramson, P. R. (1977) "Ethical Requirements for Research on Human Sexual Behaviour: From the Perspective of Participating Subjects," *Journal of Social Issues* 33(2): 184–92.

Check, J. V. P. (1982) "Rape Attitudes Following Participation in Pornography Experiments Employing Debriefing Procedures." Paper presented at the meeting of the American Psychological Association, Washington, DC.

—— (1984) "Rape Myths and Sexual Violence in the Mass Media: Recent Canadian Findings." Paper presented at the meeting of the International Society for Research on Aggression, Turku, Finland.

Check, J. V. P. and Malamuth, N. M. (1984) "Can There Be Positive Effects of Participation in Pornography Experiments?" *Journal of Sex Research* 20: 14–31.

Malamuth, N. M. (1983) "Human Sexuality," in D. Perlman and P. C. Cozby (eds) *Social Psychology*, New York: Holt, Rinehart & Winston.

Malamuth, N. M. and Check, J. V. P. (1981) "The Effects of Mass Media Exposure on Acceptance of Violence against Women: A Field Experiment," *Journal of Research in Personality* 15: 436–46.

Malamuth, N. M. and Check, J. V. P. (1984) "Debriefing Effectiveness Following Exposure to Pornographic Rape Depictions," *Journal of Sex Research* 20: 1–13.

Smith, S. S. and Richardson, D. (1983). "Amelioration of Deception and Harm in Psychological Research: The Important Role of Debriefing," *Journal of Personality and Social Psychology* 44: 1075–82.

THEOLOGY AND PRACTICAL ETHICS

1 Social ethics: two biblical perspectives

MICHAEL CREAL

I need to acknowledge from the outset that there are certainly more than two biblical perspectives on social ethics but the two I have selected have prominence today and both are deeply concerned, in a total sense, with social justice. One is the perspective of Liberation Theology. The other is identified as Biblical Realism and is usually associated with the name of Reinhold Niebuhr, whose views seem to be enjoying something of a revival currently, for instance in the recent writing of Christopher Lasch.

What I want to attempt is a brief statement of these two perspectives, identifying some of the assumptions associated with each, as well as their practical meaning in the area of social/theological/ethics.

Let me begin with Liberation Theology. Liberation Theology originated in, but is by no means restricted to, Latin America. Its intellectual origins were in Germany but its origins as a major theological force were in Latin America. The Roman Catholic Archbishop of Durban, South Africa, speaking in Toronto on February 15, 1987, in response to the question: "Do you support Liberation Theology?" responded, "Certainly, with all my heart." Its relevance to Southern Africa could hardly be more obvious. And in North America, many feminist theologians locate their theological position within the framework of Liberation Theology and so do black theologians like the American, James Cone.

So while Liberation Theology had its origins in Latin America, it has established roots in many parts of the world. A common factor in these different settings is a perceived order of oppression which works injustice against some particular group: the poor in Latin America, women (perhaps everywhere), blacks in South Africa and native peoples (among others) in North America. It appears that Liberation Theology arises today wherever Christian writers or thinkers develop a social, political or economic analysis which identifies two classes: the oppressors and the oppressed. In his book *The Theology of Liberation* published first in Spanish in 1971 and later in English in 1973, Gustavo Gutiérrez, a Peruvian theologian whom most would see as the earliest prominent and powerful exponent of Liberation Theology, distinguishes two classical approaches in theology. The first understands theology as a form of wisdom. It was monastic in setting and was "geared towards spiritual growth where spiritual life was removed from worldly concerns" (Gutiérrez 1973: 4). The second classical approach regarded theology as a rational science, an intellectual discipline bringing faith and reason together. This was the theological approach of the thirteenth-century theologian Thomas Aquinas. In a later period, the period of the Reformation – and specifically at the Council of Trent in the mid-sixteenth century – scholastic theology which had grown out of the medieval tradition became the discipline of the "magisterium" of the church. Its function was to define and explain revealed truth, to denounce and condemn false doctrines and to teach revealed truths authoritatively. This is still theology seen as a "rational science." In recent times, however, as Gutiérrez sees it, theology has taken on a new character. In Latin America and elsewhere, theology has become "critical reflection on praxis." "Charity," he writes, "has been fruitfully rediscovered as the center of Christian life." In this light faith appears "not as the memorization of truths but [as] a commitment, an overall attitude, a particular posture toward life" (ibid.: 6). It could be said that theology has always been seen as "faith seeking understanding" and if faith is now seen as charity-in-action (or praxis), theology can properly be seen as reflection on praxis.

What does all this imply? An expression which turned up in some of the Vatican II deliberations (notably the Vatican II document, *Gaudium et Spes*), an expression, incidentally, which was prominent in Reinhold Niebuhr's writings, was "discerning the signs of the times." These words and the discipline implied in them became a key item on the agenda of Vatican II. And, as a matter of fact, because "discerning the signs of the times" was seen by Vatican II as the responsibility of every Christian, every Christian was implicitly called to be a theologian: to engage in reflection on the "signs of the times," to engage in reflection on the experience of faith at work in the world, to engage in reflection on praxis.

There isn't space to outline the history of the church in Latin America following Vatican II but there were two important – post Vatican II – conferences of the Latin American Catholic Bishops. The first was at Medellin in Colombia in 1968. It was at Medellin that Liberation Theology became recognized as a force. As Gutiér-rez (1973: 135) put it, a fundamental question came to the fore at that conference: What is the meaning of faith in a life committed to the struggle against injustice and alienation? To understand the sources and character of injustice and alienation, the methods of the social sciences were called upon, including – particularly including – Marxist analysis of class conflict. Now clearly, a theology which utilized a form of Marxist social/historical analysis was not everybody's cup of tea at the meeting of the Latin American Conference of Bishops but that form of analysis certainly met with an astonishing measure of acceptance. Whether accompanied by Marxist analysis or not, poverty and oppression were placed at the top of the church's agenda in Latin America. At the succeeding conference of Latin American Bishops, held at Puebla in Mexico in 1979, and attended by the present Pope, there was agreement on the part of the bishops to make "a preferential option for the poor." That this agreement was more than just theological rhetoric was reflected in a number of ways but in none more dramatic than Archbishop Romero's stand against the repression in El Salvador in the early 1980s which led to his assassination. Another indication was the victory of the Sandinistas in Nicaragua in the summer of 1979 among whom Catholics – clergy and laity – have been so prominent *as Catholics*. In fact, in his article in the *Atlantic Monthly* of August, 1986, Conor Cruise O'Brien argued that "Marxism – even of the home-made variety – is now recessive within Sandinismo and that the Christian revolutionary element is becoming dominant."

Acknowledging that recent movements for social transformation – or even revolution – in Latin America have been supported and often led by Catholics – bishops, clergy, laity (laity functioning notably through base communities where the relationship between biblical faith and social, political and economic life is the primary material for reflection and study), noting all that, let's go back to Gutiérrez and see how he understands these developments in terms of theology, theological ethics and biblical perspectives.

"What is at stake in the south as well as in the north," says Gutiérrez, "in the west as well as in the east, on the periphery and in the center is the possibility of a truly human existence, a free life, a dynamic life which is related to history as a conquest" (1973: 28). Liberation, says Gutiérrez, "expresses the aspirations of oppressed peoples and social classes" and in this context, the context of oppression, Gutiérrez does not back away from the inevitability of conflict. Like most Liberation Theologians, he is suspicious of the concept of "developing nations" as a way of understanding the countries in Latin America.

"Developing nations" seems to imply gradual, evolutionary change. But Gutiérrez is distrustful of this concept because he sees it as enfolding all the principles of capitalism and particularly American economic imperialism which in his view reinforces and undergirds structures of oppression in Latin America. This is his first level of understanding liberation: liberation from forms of North American capitalism which oppress the poor in Latin America. At a deeper level, Gutiérrez sees liberation as meaning that humans take responsibility for their own destiny. Horizons of social change begin to open up. Oppression is seen for what it is, not as a God-given inevitability. It is a particular group of humans oppressing another group of humans. Finally, according to Gutiérrez, the meaning of liberation is illuminated by the biblical story. The story of the exodus in the Hebrew Bible is the paradigm: the story of a people delivered from slavery. And in the New Testament, it is the story of Jesus. Both are stories of liberation from bondage of one kind or another. Both point, as Gutiérrez sees it, to the possibility of a community or society where justice becomes reality.

Let's scrutinize a bit more closely what is involved in these points so that we can better understand Gutiérrez' method and assumptions.

If theology is seen as a reflection on praxis, the setting for praxis or action must be understood. In this connection Gutiérrez adopts a concept developed by Paulo Freire in his book *The Pedagogy of the Oppressed* (1968), the concept of "conscientization." Conscientization means an awakening to the structures and forms of oppression, an awakening to the limits imposed on one's freedom by various social, religious, political, and economic forces. Once conscientization has begun to occur, the initial focus of liberation becomes clear: the structures of oppression must be broken. But it must be noted that for theologians like Gutiérrez, liberation involves more than just breaking forms of oppressive control. It includes a particular understanding of community; community characterized by a love which is not sentimental, which does not back away from conflict but which implies a mutuality, an interdependence and a rejection of the modern concept of individualism.

In what sense can this kind of thinking be described as a biblical perspective? I have already made reference to the exodus theme which is central in the Hebrew Bible. In the New Testament, it is the eschatological promises of freedom, peace, justice and reconciliation which are seen as marks of the Kingdom which Jesus proclaimed. And referring back to the Nicaraguan assessment of Conor Cruise O'Brien (1986: 55),

> among Sandinistas in Nicaragua those words "the Kingdom of God" crop up in speech and in print with a frequency disquieting to the secular visitor and to some religious visitors as well. What is most striking is the casual way in which the words are used. People refer to the coming of the Kingdom of God as if they were waiting for a bus.

Now it is clear from the vast amount of conflicting New Testament commentary on both the meaning of the Kingdom of God and the role of Jesus as "revolutionary" that one cannot assume that liberation theologians have had the final word on these matters. What is clear is that while there are many differences among the liberation theologians themselves on these hermeneutical questions, they all see a connection between the transformation of society in the direction of social justice and "the Kingdom of God." They all see a radical challenging of the status quo as consistent with the prophetic tradition and the role and teaching of Jesus. They all see a connection between liberation and what has been classically referred to as "salvation" which they understand as meaning nothing less than the ending of alienation and the achievement of community among humans. The essential point in all this is that Liberation Theology is a theology very much focused on present social realities seen within the horizon of hope and confidence in God and humans.

How far does this perspective make sense outside the Latin American setting? The answer seems to be that it is potentially illuminating and energizing wherever oppression is experienced and identified. It obviously has informed feminist theologians like Rosemary Radford Reuther, Isabel Carter Heyward, Elizabeth Schussler Fiorenza and others. Increasingly, it is related to the conditions of native peoples in Canada, to the critique of so-called "expertise" in a variety of professional and bureaucratic structures in western society. I won't elaborate further on this but simply offer the proposition that a liberation theology grounded in, and energized by, a central biblical perspective provides an important base for social critique and has the potential to become a significant social ethical force in many parts of the world including North America.

I will begin my comments on the second perspective which some refer to as Biblical Realism (or others as "Christian Realism" and certainly this perspective emerges out of a Christian ethos) by recalling a lecture which Christopher Lasch gave at York University in Toronto in January 1985 entitled "Modernity and its Critics." In that lecture, Lasch identified three critical stances toward modernity and the problems which modernity has brought: a Marxist, a romantic and a Biblical. The Marxist he rejected because among other things it already included many of the elements of modernity which were themselves part of the problem (for instance the confidence placed in technology, the assumptions about historical progress, etc.). The romantic perspective he rejected because in order to achieve a more harmonious relationship between humans and the world of nature, he felt that it sought "to turn the clock back," a strategy which Lasch felt was simply not achievable. The perspective he found most congenial was that of Biblical Realism because, in his view, it most adequately grasped what humans were up to. What do I mean by that phrase? Simply this: that humans are limited creatures with unlimited aspirations. In his book, *The Minimal Self*, Lasch argues that the Promethean self, nourished by modern western culture, the self which saw itself as a "conqueror" virtually without limits, has given way, in the face of enormous social ethical issues in the twentieth century, to the "minimal" self. This is a self which sees itself as minimal, as virtually powerless in the face of those issues: environmental devastations, threat of nuclear holocaust, poverty, starvation and near starvation of vast populations, refugees in the millions and so on.

As Lasch sees it, the biblical view acknowledges, on the one hand, human powers and potentialities and, on the other, recognizes human limits. It acknowledges the tension between these two realities as central in human history. It recognizes the devastation that can occur if human limits are not acknowledged, when individuals or groups, political movements or religious movements, or even whole nations presume that they have a monopoly on truth or that there are no legitimate boundaries to their exercise of will and power. On the other hand, it recognizes the abdication of moral responsibility, the passivity, the trivializing of human life that results where a sense of powerlessness or a sense of fatality prevails. In this connection, his chapter on "The Survival Mentality" is particularly illuminating. The "survivor" whom he describes is the person who sees sheer physical and emotional survival as a major achievement in itself and as the central goal for the individual in our society. Any larger ethical concerns simply do not exist for such a person. Personal survival is everything. To say "I am a survivor" is to say the best thing one can hope to say. Lasch (1984: 20) summarizes his argument in these terms:

A new culture – a post industrial culture if you like – has to be based on a recognition of those contradictions in human experience (the contradiction of human limits and unlimited aspirations), not on a technology that tries to restore the illusion of self-sufficiency, or, on the other hand, radical denial of selfhood that tries to restore the illusion of absolute unity with nature (Gregory Bateson). Neither Prometheus nor Narcissus will lead us out of our present predicament. Brothers under the skin they will only lead us further down the road on which we have travelled too far.

Lasch makes it clear that in opting for what he refers to as the perspective of Biblical Realism, he is indebted in a significant way to Reinhold Niebuhr. So let me now try to identify briefly some of the key elements in Niebuhr's theological ethic because, in its mature development, it is probably the clearest expression of "Biblical Realism." The most complete formulation of Niebuhr's mature thought is found in his Gifford Lectures, *The Nature and Destiny of Man*, delivered and published in the 1940s. One needs to recognize a certain trajectory in Niebuhr's life in order to identify the changes and continuities in his thinking. Let me put this in the briefest form. In the 1920s he had a pastoral charge in Detroit but he emerged as more than the pastor of a congregation. He became a leading figure in interracial issues in Detroit, and a fierce critic of Henry Ford's labor policies. He was an eloquent spokesman on social issues and wrote a regular column on such matters in the Detroit *Times*. Toward the end of the 1920s he assumed a teaching post at Union Theological Seminary in New York and the questions which he subsequently addressed were no longer local but national and international. At that point he was a pacifist and a socialist but the Great Depression, the rise of Hitler and the Soviet purges changed his views significantly. He abandoned pacifism and pushed for American intervention in the European crisis. (Incidentally, he was one of the very few American intellectuals who argued publicly that the US should open its doors to Jewish refugees.) He rejected the Liberal Protestant Social Gospel which was so confident about the possibility of social transformation because, as his recent biographer Richard Fox puts it (1985: 140), Niebuhr came to see society not "as a garden in need of regeneration" but as "a realm of power blocks to be adjusted." It was not a matter of expecting Utopia but a matter of preventing human disaster.

Following the war, Niebuhr advocated a policy of western strength in the face of Soviet power. He never saw communism as the incarnation of evil (as some current American leaders appear to) nor did he see the US as the incarnation of good. It was his view that power on the one side had to be confronted with power on the other. That certainly did not mean that he was neutral. Political democracy was something he believed in deeply. In a book published in the mid-1940s he made his point in words which were frequently quoted: "Man's capacity for justice makes democracy possible," he said, "but man's inclination to injustice makes democracy necessary" (Niebuhr 1944). This was a distinctive and, I think, original way of expressing the importance and meaning of democracy.

Let me now state what I see to be the key elements of Christian Realism which can be put in terms of a view of human nature and a view of human history. These were the two central themes of *The Nature and Destiny of Man*. Niebuhr derived his views of both human nature and human destiny from the Bible but he read the Bible in terms of myth and symbol. "It is important to take biblical symbols seriously" he said, "but not literally" (1943: 50). For Niebuhr, the myth or symbol of creation signified that humans were made in the image of God and marked the human quality of freedom and the human capacity for self-transcendence. This he saw as the glory and greatness of human life. It was from this that human creativity derived. But secondly there was the myth or symbol of the Fall. Because man is both "strong and weak, both free and bound, both blind and far seeing" he is constantly tempted

to obscure his blindness by over-stating the degree of his sight and to obscure his insecurity by stretching his power beyond its limits... He is tempted to deny the limited character of his knowledge and the finitude of his perceptions. He pretends to have a degree of knowledge which is beyond the limit of finite life. This is the ideological taint in which all human knowledge is involved.

(ibid.: 181, 183)

This is how Niebuhr understood man's rebellion against God: the attempt of man to deny his finitude.

The third myth or symbol – and let it be understood that I

44

am summarizing an enormous amount in all that I am saying – implies a distinctive view of human history. It sees human history as a territory of meaningful human activity and the measure of this meaning is expressed ultimately in the symbol of "the Kingdom," the symbol of fulfillment, both individual and social. Niebuhr read the New Testament to say that the Kingdom has both come and is still to come. This means that the best that can be achieved in this world is incomplete, imperfect, and distorted by human pretensions (which Niebuhr called sin). To the extent that the Kingdom has come, it means that humans have an idea of justice and can work for it, and an experience of reconciliation which makes the possibility of full reconciliation of all humans a meaningful aspiration. To the extent that the Kingdom has not come, idolatry and all the forms of oppression which go with idolatry constantly lurk as a threat. One of his friends at Columbia in those days characterized Niebuhr's position as "Realism with Vision." It is the vision which animates and energizes toward justice and human fulfillment. It is the realism which recognizes the potential for distortion, self-deception, and corruption.

Clearly an enormous number of questions have to be asked and answered before an adequate assessment can be made of the full meaning and implications of these two perspectives as well as their relative strengths and weaknesses. Both take the issue of social justice seriously. Both are grounded on a biblical foundation. Christian Realism carries the risk that it may become too complacent about given social, political and economic realities although if Niebuhr himself were taken as the test, complacency is hardly a word that comes to mind. Liberation Theology on the other hand may be too naïve in its confidence that the Kingdom is on its way and thus the proponents of Liberation Theology may be susceptible ultimately either to disillusionment or to that form of tyranny which frequently replaces the tyranny which the revolutionary seeks to overthrow. But what is clear is that proponents of both views have a contribution to make in contemporary discussions about social and political ethics.

REFERENCES

Fox, Richard (1985) *Reinhold Niebuhr*, New York: Pantheon Books.

Freire, Paulo (1968) *The Pedagogy of the Oppressed*, New York: Hender & Hender.

Gutiérrez, Gustavo (1973) *The Theology of Liberation*, Maryknoll: Orbin.

Lasch, Christopher (1987) *The Minimal Self*, New York: Norton.

Niebuhr, Reinhold (1943) *The Nature and Destiny of Man*, New York: Scribners.

—— (1944) *The Children of Light and the Children of Darkness*, New York: Scribners.

O'Brien, Conor Cruise (1986) "God and Man in Nicaragua," *Atlantic Monthly* August, 1986.

THEOLOGY AND PRACTICAL ETHICS
2 Commentary: social ethics and religion
SOL TANENZAPF

Professor Creal's paper examines two approaches to the questions of social ethics in the contemporary world: that of Liberation Theology and that of Biblical Realism. He analyzes the writings of Father Gustavo Gutiérrez as representative of the thinking of many Latin American bishops, and points out that Liberation Theology has influenced theological thinking outside of Latin America; in particular, that it has influenced the thinking of feminist and black theologians. Furthermore, Liberation Theology has influenced events, most conspicuously in Nicaragua, but also throughout Latin America where grassroots communities are being organized by exponents of Liberation Theology and where the church is the only institution powerful enough to resist despotic governments. Professor Creal goes on to examine the Biblical Realism of Reinhold Niebuhr and Christopher Lasch. He demonstrates that Biblical Realism, like Liberation Theology, is grounded in the ethical teachings of the Bible. He concludes that the biblical tradition is capable of generating a vital and relevant social ethic.

I accept Professor Creal's conclusion, but I would argue that what gives these formulations of social ethics their vitality and relevance is that they combine biblical ethics with a very sophisticated analysis of the contemporary political, economic, and international situations. From biblical ethics they derive some basic ideas: (1) No society or government is the final arbiter of what is right and wrong. All societies and government policies stand under God's judgment. (2) The basic norms of biblical ethics are justice and benevolence. These norms are supported by a metaphysic that includes God and that sees man as the object of God's concern. The dignity of the human person is grounded in his metaphysical status as the child of God his Father and as the very image of God in the world. That it is God's will that we act with justice and benevolence toward others is confirmed by the central revelatory events of both the Hebrew Bible and the New Testament. The Israelites experienced the exodus from Egypt as God's action in history. In leading the Israelites from Egypt "with a strong hand and an outstretched arm" God revealed His will to redress the injustices of Egyptian oppression and His benevolence toward the weakest and least important members of society. The prophets then took *Mishpat* (justice) and *Tsedakah* (benevolence toward the weak; usually translated as "righteousness") as criteria for judging their own societies. In the central revelatory event of the New Testament, the early Christians also experienced God's justice and benevolence: justice in Jesus' accepting death as the penalty for man's sins, and benevolence in God's so loving man that He emptied Himself of His divinity, took the form of man and accepted death as atonement for man's sins.

Norms, however, must be applied contextually. It is difficult to know precisely what justice demands in any particular situation, and it is even more difficult to act with benevolence, since benevolence toward one person or group might conflict with the just claims of other persons or groups. Good will is not enough. What is required is knowledge of the facts and intelligence in applying general norms to particular situations. No one can anticipate the consequences of any proposed course of action for redressing injustices or for increasing the opportunities for individuals to realize their potential, unless he has knowledge of causal connections and of probable trends from the social sciences and personal observation, and unless he is able to assess the situation that confronts him with intelligence. This is why the authors Professor Creal has chosen for examination present social critiques that are so powerful. The thinking of Father Gustavo Gutiérrez, of Reinhold Niebuhr, and of Christopher Lasch is indeed informed by the biblical ethic, by an awareness of divine judgment, of the preciousness of the human personality, and by the norms of justice and benevolence. More important, perhaps, is the fact that the application of the norms of biblical ethics is made possible in each case by a sound understanding of the contemporary global situation. This is also why the three authors examined by Professor Creal are so controversial. Their critics are found not only among persons who reject their religious worldview and ethics, but also among co-religionists who object to their descriptions and analyses of contemporary social, political, and economic situations. This is especially evident in the case of Liberation Theology. It is the Marxist analysis of the dynamics of social, political, and economic change that is objected to by their opponents within and outside of the Roman Catholic Church.

It is my own view that the social, political and economic theories of Liberation Theology are plausible, notwithstanding their Marxist derivation. I agree that justice requires the elimination of violence and oppression, and that violence against persons can take many forms. There is overt physical violence – direct physical assault by one person against another, and direct assault by the army or police against single persons or groups; there is also covert violence – non-physical assaults causing psychological damage to individuals and groups, and institutional or structural violence in which the very laws and institutions of society prevent people from realizing their full human potential by keeping them illiterate, unemployed or in low-paying jobs, living in slums and powerless to influence legislation or government administration (Brown 1973: 29–38).

Joseph Cardinal Ratzinger, speaking for The Congregation for the Doctrine of the Faith, objects to the Marxist theories that underlie Liberation Theology, and to the Liberation Theologian espousing armed violence as the necessary path to liberation. He contends that revolutionary violence is not likely to lead to the creation of a more humane society; it is more likely to lead to the setting up of totalitarian regimes. Reform within the political system, reform of education and of working conditions, and passive resistance are the proper means to social change. They conform to moral principles and have no less a prospect for success than armed resistance. Armed struggle should be a last resort only. Reprisals against the general population, torture, terrorism, deliberate provocations aimed at causing death during popular demonstrations, and smear campaigns are crimes, whether they are perpetrated by the established powers or by the insurgents (Ratzinger 1986).

It should be noted that Cardinal Ratzinger's critique of modern nationalist and communist movements is consistent with Reinhold Niebuhr's critique of these same movements. He writes that the quest for freedom is the principle characteristic of the modern era, beginning in the Renaissance. Yet, the modern era has produced totalitarian systems, acts of genocide and terror, and unscrupulous regimes and tyrannies in formerly colonial countries. The movements to liberation have not fulfilled their promises; instead, they have produced new and unprecedented forms of slavery. His analysis of the situation is that this outcome is due to the fact that these liberation movements are based on ideologies that alienate man from God and that misconceive human nature. Man stands in need of liberation from sin as well as from political and economic oppression. Change of social and political structures and of technical organization will not lead to liberation unless the changes are effected by people willing to act and capable of acting for the social good. "It is therefore necessary to work simultaneously for the conversion of hearts and for the improvement of structures" (ibid.: 45). Reinhold Niebuhr and Christopher Lasch, I think, would both agree with this part of Cardinal Ratzinger's argument.

All the difficult issues surrounding the relationship between ethics and religion are raised once more by Professor Creal's paper. There is a longstanding philosophical tradition from Plato's *Euthyphro* to George Edward Moore's *Principia Ethica* defending the autonomy of ethics. We are all of us familiar with great men whose dedication to the principles of justice and benevolence is not grounded in a theistic metaphysic nor motivated by a vision of the Kingdom of God; and whose moral concepts are not shaped by a religious upbringing. John Stuart Mill and Bertrand Russell are historical examples; Brand Blanshard, Professor of Philosophy at Yale University, a personal example. Moreover, we know that governments cloaking themselves in the garb of defenders of the faith have perpetrated atrocities, and that individuals continue to find religious justification for crimes against other human beings.

When that has been said and fully acknowledged, it still remains the case that for large numbers of human beings ethical concepts are transmitted by religious traditions and moral behavior is learned by members of particular religious communities. One of the most effective instruments of moral education is still the tradition of a religious community, where moral ideas are taught by means of powerful narratives, reinforced by ritual and liturgical practices, and crystallized in ethical codes. The moral views of large numbers of people are made more balanced and inclusive by the great religious traditions; and their conception of the goals of life and of the legitimate aspirations of society are elevated by religious teachings. For many, religious commitment provides the motivation to overcome selfish tendencies that resist doing what a larger, social good requires, and enable the individual to overcome a sense of futility and moral despair. We are often overcome with a sense of futility because of our ineffectiveness in changing things, so that we withdraw into our "minimal selves." We are overcome too by our guilt and despair over whether we ourselves or people in general will be able to control the darker sides of their personalities, our seemingly irrepressible tendencies to do what is cruel and destructive. Thousands of people have testified that their awareness of God and God's will for humanity has enabled them to overcome selfishness and to do what is right, and has enabled them to overcome a sense of futility and moral despair.

The authors Professor Creal has examined also provide evidence of another sort. They give evidence in support of the claim that the biblical tradition has nurtured men of large moral vision, who, when they add knowledge and intelligence to that vision, are capable of producing incisive social critiques and of providing the leadership needed to remedy society's failings.

REFERENCES

Brown, Robert MacAfee (1973) *Religion and Violence*, Philadelphia: The Westminster Press.

Moore, George Edward (1903) *Principia Ethica*, Cambridge: The University Press.

Ratzinger, Joseph Cardinal (1986) "Instruction on Christian Freedom and Liberation," *Origins* 15 (April 17, 1986).

4

ENVIRONMENTAL ETHICS
Ethics and professional planners[1]

REG LANG and SUE HENDLER

Urban and regional planning, as a professional activity, is ethically complex. The variety of contexts, subject matter and obligations confronting individual practitioners creates a broad spectrum of ethical issues ranging from quasi-legal matters such as conflict of interest to profound philosophical and political questions such as whose interests the planning profession ought to serve.

At the inaugural meeting of the Ontario Professional Planners Institute (OPPI) in March 1986, the membership passed a motion calling for a comprehensive review of the Professional Code of Conduct. It's not clear whether this reflected real concern about ethical behavior of planners or was simply an adjunct to a review of the bylaws. Whatever the motive, the endeavor is timely; there are compelling reasons for a fundamental re-examination of the ethics of planning. Clear signals are coming from a number of directions in society, indicating growing public concern about right- and wrong-doing by professionals, politicians, bureaucrats and others who are or should be serving the public interest. Although planners as a group have not yet been singled out for attention, individual planners do face difficult ethical and moral choices. OPPI's ethical code provides little aid or comfort on matters such as confidentiality, conflict of interest, bribery and whistle blowing. ("Whistleblowers" are persons who believe that others in the organization, or perhaps the organization as a whole, are engaged in unethical or even illegal activity, and who-usually-having failed to correct the situation through internal channels, "go public" with their charges.) Nor does it give any guidance on deeper issues, such as what planning is for and how practitioners are to choose among conflicting values.

This paper considers the potential contribution of the field of ethics to the field of planning, explores the boundaries of ethical/unethical behavior, and outlines directions toward making ethics an integral part of planning practice.

MORALITY IN TODAY'S WORLD

Matters of right and wrong seem to be gaining prominence on the public agenda. Consider this selection from recent media reports:

Canadians have witnessed a steady stream of politicians under investigation for and/or charged with conflict of interest. Typically, these individuals first try to stonewall, then claim there was no wrong in what they did. A recent study of MPs found agreement that such practices as bribery and misappropriation of funds are "dishonorable" but found no consensus on grey areas such as conflict of interest.

(Howard 1986)

A provincial government forester was fired after he went public with his concerns about poor forest management [a US study, cited by Sagel (1985), found that only one person in ten who blew the whistle was back on the job]. The Ontario Professional Foresters Association's code of ethics calls for its members to maintain the honor and integrity of their profession but many members remain silent, according to one veteran forester, because they are employees and "they like to eat."

Members of a city council complained that aggressive developers are stepping up efforts to influence politicians, most of whom rely on developers as their prime source of campaign contributions.

(York 1985)

Developers were said to be sending councillors unsolicited cheques, openly attempting to bribe them, courting citizen groups, offering public benefits such as day care centres in order to gain approvals, and putting heavy pressure on planners. Although none of this is new, somewhere a line appears to have been crossed.

During the Westchester Classic, professional golfer Raymond Floyd called a penalty shot on himself even though it was likely that no one else had witnessed the infraction. One astounded reporter headlined his article, "Floyd's honesty broke the rules of cheating." Pollster George Gallup, providing support for this cynical view, told the Empire Club in Toronto that "cheating is both epidemic and big business".

(Howard 1985)

These reports appear to suggest that apparently ethical behavior is somehow deviant. Certainly, a sense of right and wrong is changing in a society characterized by the waning of influence of such institutions as the church and the family. While morality may have become uncertain, however, expectations of ethical behavior appear to be alive and well, especially with regard to people in positions of power, influence, public trust, and public service. Yet there is little to guide such individuals, professional planners among them, toward the ethical behaviors expected of them.

ETHICAL ISSUES IN PLANNING

Wachs (1985) defines four categories of ethical issues in planning practice:

Everyday behavior

Conflicts of interest, leaking reports and distorting information fall into this group, routinely encountered in professional and social relationships.

Administrative discretion

Ethical dilemmas result from the fact that planners exercise judgment on behalf of the public but are not directly accountable to an electorate.

Planning techniques

Supposedly value-neutral tools such as cost-benefit analysis and impact assessment are suffused with values that predispose their users toward certain options or interests and against others.

Plans and policies

Ethical principles are embodied in plans and policies which reflect community values, deal with choices among ends and means, impinge directly on people's lives, and often involve redistribution of resources and impacts. The very purpose of planning is called into question: Why is it done? Whose interests does and should it serve?

Complex ethical issues arise in planning practice with its numerous actors, contending interests and conflicting responsibilities (e.g. to the public interest, employer or client, the community, the profession, an immediate peer group of colleagues, and our own consciences). What is a planner to do? No one likes to be caught in an ethical dilemma in which the only choices are to abandon one's principles or resign. Most of us try to avoid getting painted into that corner. The fluid, messy world of planning provides plenty of escape routes – for example, withdrawing behind the mantle of the employing organization and assuming an instrumental role, treating ethics as merely "situational," turning a blind eye to unethical behavior, or putting personal loyalties ahead of the public good.

A code of ethics and professional conduct is one means that a profession has to remind its members of their ethical obligations and to provide guidance in meeting them. Such a code establishes standards to which the profession aspires, expresses general agreement on what is best, and imposes obligations. In devising its code, a professional organization can let itself be guided by the general values of society, draw upon the collective experience of the organization's members, and exercise commonsense judgment. But can the field of planning also get help from the field of ethics? We think so.

CONNECTING PLANNING AND ETHICS

A branch of philosophy, ethics is the study of moral behavior and judgments. A key concept from the field of ethics is that it is possible to evaluate a given behavior and give coherent reasons why it is good or bad. Kaufman (1980) argues that planners need to cast aside the notion that moral choice is murky and best left to intuition. Rather, careful thought based on ethical analysis can aid the professional in determining right or wrong in specific situations.

What criteria can be used to decide whether a given action is ethical? In everyday life people rely on culturally received behavioral norms from such sources as family upbringing, formal and informal education, religion, and role models. Most of us try to Do Unto Others, Seek Truth and so on. Wise as these axioms may be, though, they are seldom sufficient, especially in complex situations. Consider the admonition to Do Good, or at least Do No Harm – prudent counsel for planners. As Bolan (1985) points out, planners often find themselves in situations where their proposals will produce some good and some harm (a new industry creates both jobs and pollution) or, worse still, where harm will result no matter what is or isn't done (siting a hazardous waste management facility here, there, or not at all). When the choice is to do more or less harm, the professional is in an ethical bind.

A philosopher would remind planners that, in deciding what is right and what is wrong, there is often a tendency to fall back on one of two fundamental and differing positions: ends-oriented (teleological) and means-oriented (deontological). In the former position, ends are what count and "good" ends can justify "bad" means; in the latter, an act in and of itself determines whether it is good or bad. And so, proponents of a project that will forcibly relocate people argue that its benefits to the many justify the disruption it will cause for a few; meanwhile, opponents argue just as strenuously that doing harm to people is wrong in itself and cannot be justified by good intentions. The clash between ends- and means-oriented positions and the need often to seek balance between them is a common feature of planning problems. It can also be found in planning principles and methods. Arguing "the greatest good for the greatest number" and seeking an excess of "benefits" over "costs" exemplify practices rooted in teleology while statements such as "land is a sacred trust that should never be abused" reflect deontology. Planners who add ethical analysis to their repertoire of knowledge and skills therefore can become more adept at systematically analyzing difficult situations, addressing the moral content of competing claims, and arriving at sounder and more defensible bases for informed ethical judgments.

The sub-field of applied ethics offers a specific form of ethical analysis that has been attracting attention: the development of what Bayles (1984) and others have called "bridging principles." These are guidelines for behavior that mediate between abstract ethical theory and actual practice situations. An example is telling the truth in professional relationships. This principle, derived from the field of ethics, responds to the planning field's practical need for trust between client and professional. But truth-telling is seldom a clear-cut imperative; conflicting responsibilities can create difficult choices. Bok's (1979) provocative book on lying illustrates how practitioners may be aided by bridging principles. She suggests that before practicing deception or some similarly questionable tactic, such as whistle blowing or leaking information, we (1) consider alternative ways to achieve the purpose underlying that tactic, (2) weigh the moral reasons for and against, and (3) ask ourselves how a jury of our peers would judge the contemplated action. Similarly, the use of bridging principles might help planners reconcile such ethically based conflicts as open access to information vs. confidentiality to client, full public participation vs. representative democracy, and the public interest vs. equity (as in the familiar Not-In-My-Backyard syndrome).

Although some disagreement between theory and practice is inevitable (and a potential stimulant to the field's growth), bridging principles could focus the controversy on difficult cases while usefully guiding the remainder. In this way, ethical analysis and the formulation and testing of bridging principles offer planners a rational and defensible means of promoting moral behavior.

BUT WHAT IS ETHICAL/UNETHICAL?

What specifically constitutes ethical and unethical behavior for planners? To probe the views of practicing planners on this question, we presented a self-survey (Appendix A) in the journal of the OPPI. It consisted of fifteen planning practices which respondents were invited to rate on a scale ranging from ethical to unethical.[2] "Ethical" was defined as good, right or correct behavior while "unethical" meant the opposite. A final question tried to get at planners' positions on the teleological vs. deontological dichotomy. The results, from the fifty responses received, are summarized here and detailed in Appendix B.

A strong consensus emerged (from over 70% of respondents) that the following practices are unethical:

- Distorting information to facilitate acceptance of a development proposal the planner feels meets a public need (3 in the survey in Appendix B)
- Not providing members of the public with the full range of information available to the planner working on a planning proposal (11)
- Accepting a loan from a developer with whom the planner's employer or client regularly does business (6)
- Threatening a developer with costly delays in order to secure concessions the planner believes to be in the public interest (2)
- Submitting a report on a bylaw that affects a property owned by a member of the planner's family, without declaring a possible conflict of interest (10)
- Downplaying the value judgments in a forecast or analysis to make it appear more objective than it really is (8)
- Presenting an opinion known to be one the planner's client/ employer will find acceptable, even though it is not the view held by the planner as a professional (13)
- Seeking to avoid responsibility for giving full consideration to environmental impacts of a planning proposal or project (12)
- Knowing that another planner is behaving unethically but not informing one's superiors or the professional organization (15).

Similarly, respondents felt strongly that the following practices are ethical:

- Within the planning department, openly taking a position on an issue which the planner knows to be contrary to the declared position of the employer or client (9)
- Planning for the needs of disadvantaged groups, and working to alter policies and decisions which oppose such needs, whether it is part of the planner's mandate or not (14).

Three other practices were considered unethical even though the consensus was somewhat weaker (i.e. smaller majority and a high proportion of "probably" responses):

- Leaking information to the media when the planner feels strongly about something but believes the employer/client is being unduly secretive (4)
- Writing a letter to the editor, signing only one's name and home address, criticizing the municipal council for approving a development against the recommendations of the department that employs the planner (7)
- Organizing support among community groups and lobbying for one's planning proposal without the planning director's approval (5).

A final practice – assisting, in one's own time, a citizens' group to prepare a position counter to that of one's employer (1) – split respondents evenly between those who think this is ethical and those who believe it is not.

Our last question attempted to probe planners' positions on teleological vs. deontological. A strong preference was shown for the latter. Over three-quarters of the planners responding believed that an act or behavior is right or wrong in itself, without regard to the consequences. Full members of the OPPI, two-thirds of the sample, especially favored this position while most students took the opposite view, namely, that "the rightness or wrongness of an act should be judged solely by its consequences." Although our respondents may have been turned off by the word "solely," many of the choices made in the survey did seem to be based not directly on consequences but more on underlying value positions: honesty is right, making threats and engaging in conflict of interest are wrong, helping the disadvantaged and protect-ing the environment are right, and so on. A consequentialist perspective would have focused on the results of these actions (e.g. deception in the public interest may be acceptable in some circumstances), which would have produced different answers to our questions. The responses we received suggest that the planners, often laboring in contexts beset by moral ambiguity, tend to fall back on basic values to guide them in deciding whether actions are right or wrong.

In general, our survey produced results comparable to other research in the field. Ontario planners' views on distorting information, threatening developers, leaking information, protecting the environment, and planning for disadvantaged groups are similar to those held elsewhere, as documented by Howe and Kaufman (1979). The responses to our question on deontological vs. teleological moral thought, however, were somewhat surprising. Many writers, including Kaufman (1985) and Hodge (1986), have "grounded" the planning profession in consequentialist, often utilitarian, principles such as "the greatest good for the greatest number." OPPI planners, by favoring deontological positions, appear to depart from this conventional view.

Overall, our results, have significance for the OPPI's proposed new Code of Professional Conduct. Planners in our sample believe strongly that concealing conflict of interest and turning a blind eye to unethical practices are wrong, and that dishonesty and deceit are to be avoided. These are obvious candidates for emphasis in a strengthened code but they are not specific to planners. However, some of the practices described in our question-naire – such as paying special attention to environmental quality and social equity, and to the value bases of planning analysis – are uniquely planners'. Respondents felt strongly about these also, which suggests that they could find a place in the code.

WHY AN ETHICAL CODE?[3]

A profession's ethical code serves a variety of purposes, two of which stand out: articulating minimum acceptable behavior, and establishing standards of conduct to which practitioners should aspire. The code expresses general agreement on the beliefs that members of the profession share, imposes constraints on individual choice, provides the basis for acting on charges of unethical conduct, and informs the public of the profession's collective commitment to excellence and the public interest.

Ethical codes are not without difficulties. They are open to a range of interpretations and can be difficult to enforce. They may be regarded as "window-dressing" – public-relations gimmicks that look good to outsiders but are not taken seriously by practitioners. An ethical code may even be counterproductive by helping to maintain the very status quo that it seeks to change (Marcuse 1976).

A code of professional conduct for planners is open to this potential and this risk. But the planning field exhibits at least five additional problems that affect ethical practice. First, planners face a confounding array of conflicting allegiances and obligations. Second, they often find it difficult to know who "the client" is; the majority of planners are employees, not autonomous problem-solvers in the classic professional tradition (Mandelbaum 1985). Third, the planning field presents great and growing diversity – process, content, context and role combine in many different ways. Fourth, the practice of planning seems to be experiencing some kind of fundamental change, as it moves beyond physical and land use planning to other forms and to the generic application of planning knowledge and skills. Finally, planners' roles are shifting, e.g. from technical/analytic to more interactive/political (Baum 1983).

All this naturally makes practitioners wary of imposing norms of professional conduct that, in advance, give some considerations supremacy over others and that may unduly constrain needed freedom of action. Perhaps as a result, the typical ethical code that planners are prepared to adopt tends to be quite limited in scope, weak in its provisions and vaguely stated. Such a code gives planners flexibility but at a price: it provides little guidance in coping with ethical issues, is therefore not taken seriously or enforced, and ultimately deserves the "window-dressing" label. These criticisms apply to the OPPI Code, essentially the same as the Code of the

Canadian Institute of Planners (CIP, OPPI's national counterpart), which has remained more or less unchanged since the 1950s and has resulted in few disciplinary actions.[4]

Our position is that an up-to-date professional code, meaningful to the work planners, is needed and is long overdue. We believe that, if carefully developed and maintained, fairly interpreted and properly enforced, a code can be of real value by providing ethical standards, and can be a way of exposing unethical practice, and a means of renewing the profession. However, as we will argue, the code must be part of a system and process of ethics if these potential advantages are to be captured.

WHAT MIGHT THE CODE CONTAIN?

Five categories of professional responsibility are commonly cited in codes of ethics for planners.

1. *Responsibility to the public.* This category, which automatically comes first for any profession, is particularly important for planning which makes a special claim to guarding and interpreting the public interest. The preamble to OPPI's Professional Code of Conduct acknowledges this "primacy of the public interest" but makes no specific provisions for it. By contrast, the code of the American Institute of Certified Planners and the draft ethics statement of the American Planning Association include references to: the comprehensive and interrelated nature of planning and the need to seek integrated balance of physical, social, economic, and environmental considerations in planning; provision of full, clear and accurate information, on an equal basis, to the public and decision-makers; giving citizens adequate opportunities to have meaningful inputs to planning processes; expanding choice and opportunity for all persons; and protecting, enhancing and conserving the natural and built environments.[5]

2. *Responsibility to client and employer.* Addressed here are such matters as confidentiality, public disclosure "where the public interest may be adversely affected," conflicts of interest, and so on. The OPPI Code covers these but not

fully. For example, it offers little guidance on exceptions to maintaining confidentiality.

3. *Responsibility to the profession.* Of concern in this category are professional autonomy, relations among professionals, advertising, compensation, etc. Missing from the OPPI Code are such matters as guidelines for "whistle blowing" on unethical colleagues.

4. *Responsibility to employees and colleagues.* Only two concerns are addressed in this part of the OPPI Code: discrimination and facilitating employee development. The OPPI Code leaves out a section that is included in the CIP Code: the planner's special obligation to the professional advancement of students and junior members.

5. *Responsibility to self.* This concerns the planner striving for high standards of integrity, proficiency, and knowledge; maintaining competence through such means as continuing education; and voluntarily assisting groups who lack adequate professional services (the CIP Code says something about this but OPPI dropped it). It is also the place where reference can be made to the incorporation of critical reflection and ethical analysis in planning practice.

Provisions of the code in each of the foregoing five categories ought to address the four types of ethical issues defined earlier: aspects of everyday behavior, administrative discretion, planning techniques, and plans and policies. The code should address itself to behaviors that are specific to planners (such as revealing and not knowingly concealing values in planning analyses, forecasts and proposals), not merely those that are part of ordinary moral behavior and expected of any professional, in fact of any person (e.g. avoiding conflict of interest, being loyal to employer/client, and treating peers fairly). In addition, the code needs a preamble that clearly establishes why it exists, what it is for, and how it is to be used.

ETHICS AS SYSTEM AND PROCESS

By itself, however, even the best ethical code can do only so much. As a framework of principles, it can express the planning profession's commitment on certain matters – a few initially and more as time goes on – but a code can seldom be precise enough to define what is appropriate in specific situations. This does not mean that ethics returns to being a matter solely for the individual's conscience. Rather, it suggests that professional ethics be considered a process in which guidance on what is right and wrong emerges out of experience, critical reflection and discussion amongst peers and publics, and where the results are fed back to the code which may then be amended to enhance its utility and maintain its relevance. Like the law, an ethical process ought to involve ongoing interplay between principles and cases. Like laws, ethical codes have to be dynamic instruments if they are to be justified.

We visualize professional ethics as a process functioning within a system that could include these components:

- The Code of Ethics and Professional Conduct.
- A capacity, on the part of individual practitioners, to engage in ethical analysis – taking a systematic approach to examining situations in order to arrive at bases for informed ethical judgment – and its regular application to planners' work.
- Mechanisms and channels for ethical reflection and discourse, in order to legitimize and facilitate the application of ethics to everyday planning (this might include "ethical advising" from the Institute, as now offered by the American Institute of Certified Planners).
- Inclusion of ethics in planning curricula, continuing education programs and Institute examinations (following the example of engineers and lawyers in Ontario).
- Enforcement and discipline, together with encouragement to and protection for whistle blowers, to enable exposure of unethical behavior and to make the profession more accountable.
- Continuing review and updating of the Code.

What about next steps? Typically, these would involve establishment of a committee to review the existing Code, circulation of draft proposals for comment, discussion at meetings, and formal proposals ratified (or not) at an Annual General Meeting. Such an approach has two important shortcomings.

First, its proposals might not be sufficiently grounded either in the realities planners face or in ethical analysis; proposed changes often lean far too heavily on what other jurisdictions have done and overly reflect the biases of their proponents. Second, creation of a new Code would not fully address the central issue: the appropriate role of ethics in the practice of planning. Confronting this issue necessitates a rigorous effort to think through the need for ethics in planning and alternative means by which this need could be met. We feel this should include:

- Identifying, through broad consultation, what planners and others concerned about the profession perceive to be the real ethical issues (our survey made a start in this regard) and going through several iterations to expose deeper concerns and problems in planning practice.
- Marshalling facts and other evidence (e.g. case studies) concerning the nature and extent of these ethical problems.[6] Defining them more clearly, paying attention to what Schon (1983) calls the "frames" within which they occur. Clarifying and attempting to narrow areas of disagreement.
- Establishing broad principles – e.g. related to the public interest, confidentiality, truthfulness, openness of information, etc. – and then linking these via "bridging principles" to issues in practice.
- Formulating a new Code including norms of conduct, principles and procedures. The intent would be to create an instrument, part of a system and backed by a process, that would actually help planners to work through specific ethical problems, resolve conflicting aims and desires that block action, and determine what is ethically appropriate.

Rather than rushing into revision of the Code, the planning profession would be well-advised to step back and initiate a longer-term and more fundamental inquiry of the kind just outlined, perhaps beginning with a series of workshops on ethics and planning. Such a process would yield the kinds of information needed to produce a Code in which professional planners could have pride and toward which they would show respect.

IN CLOSING...

Since planning is intended to lead to action, many planning decisions unavoidably become moral judgments, not just conclusions. Responsible behavior then becomes the central issue. Professionals naturally want to be competent and effective, to do things right. But the responsible professional also strives to do the right things, to be ethical. To assist its members in this regard, a profession can do several things. One is to guide practitioners toward appropriate planning behavior; that is the role of a code of ethics. Another is to enhance the planner's ability in ethical analysis – to think through what is right and wrong in specific circumstances. Paralleling these is a further need, to make the discussion of ethics and the "ethical impacts" of planning a legitimate and routine part of the professional planner's work – to transform ethics into a process, within a system of related components of which the code is one.

Interest in ethics on the part of planners appears to be high. Perhaps at a time when many individuals are questioning the meaning of their work, ethics offers a pathway to greater personal satisfaction. For planners collectively, the time is similarly opportune for giving ethics attention. As the profession continues down the road of inevitable change, an ethical process could be an attribute that distinguishes the planning field, anchors and unifies the profession, and enables it to show leadership to others.

APPENDIX A THE SURVEY: RIGHT OR WRONG? YOU BE THE JUDGE

Assign each of the following practices a score as follows: 1 ethical; 2 probably ethical; 3 probably unethical; 4 unethical; 5 undecided.

a. Assisting, in your own time, a citizens' group to prepare a position counter to one taken by your employer.
b. Threatening a developer with costly delay in order to secure concessions you believe to be in the public interest.
c. Distorting information to facilitate acceptance of a development proposal you feel meets a public need.

d. Leaking information to the media on a matter you feel strongly about and on which you believe your employer or client is being unduly secretive.

e. Organizing support among community groups and lobbying for your planning proposal without your planning director's approval.

f. Accepting a loan from a developer with whom your employer or client regularly does business.

g. Writing a letter to the editor, signing only your name and home address, criticizing the municipal council for approving a development against the recommendations of the planning department, of which you are an employee.

h. Downplaying the value judgments in a forecast or analysis, thereby making it appear more objective than it really is.

i. Openly taking a position on an issue, within the planning department, which you know to be contrary to the declared position of your employer or client.

j. Submitting a report on a bylaw that affects a property owned by a member of your family, without declaring a possible conflict of interest.

k. Not providing members of the public with the full range of information available to you as a planner working on a planning proposal.

l. Seeking to avoid responsibility for giving full consideration to the environmental impacts of a planning proposal or project.

m. Presenting an opinion that you know is the only one that your client/employer will find acceptable, even though it does not represent the view held by you as a professional.

n. Planning for the needs of disadvantaged groups, and working to alter policies and decisions which oppose such needs, whether this is part of your mandate or not.

o. Knowing that another planner is behaving unethically but not informing your superiors or the professional organization.

Which of the following statements comes closest to expressing your view of ethics?

— An act or behavior is right or wrong in itself, without regard to the consequences.

— The rightness or wrongness of an act should be judged solely by its consequences.

APPENDIX B SURVEY RESULTS: ETHICAL/UNETHICAL PLANNING PRACTICES

Practice	E %	PE %	U %	PU %	UN %	NR %
1. Assisting citizens	14	32	22	24	6	2
2. Threatening developers	8	16	40	34	2	0
3. Distorting information	0	4	74	20	2	0
4. Leaking information	10	30	36	20	2	2
5. Organizing support	4	18	36	32	8	2
6. Loan from developer	4	2	90	0	4	0
7. Letter to the editor	16	20	38	22	4	0
8. Downplaying values	2	8	46	40	2	2
9. Contrary position	84	12	4	0	0	0
10. Conflict of interest	0	2	4	90	2	2
11. Withholding information	0	18	44	34	4	0
12. Disregarding environmental impacts	0	0	56	36	6	2
13. Suppressing professional opinion	2	6	64	28	0	0
14. Planning for disadvantaged groups	62	28	4	4	2	0
15. Not whistle blowing	8	2	32	42	16	0

16. Deontological   76%   (act is right/wrong irrespective of consequences)

    Teleological   8%   (right/wrong depends on consequences)

    Undecided   16%

The Sample
- 22% consultant, 56% local government, 2% provincial government, 20% other
- 36% director level, 32% senior, 27% intermediate, 5% junior
- 73% full members, 16% provisional, 9% student, 2% other

E=ethical   PE=probably ethical
U=unethical   PU=probably unethical
UN=undecided   NR=no response and uncodable
Total responses=50   (Figures shown are % of respondents.)

NOTES

1. This paper is a revised consolidation (with expanded references) of four articles by Reg Lang and Sue Hendler in *Ontario Planning Journal*: "Ethics: Drawing the Boundaries for Professionals" (July-August, 1986); "Planning and Ethics: Making the Link" (September-October, 1986); "Right or Wrong? Planners Respond" (November-December, 1986); and "Towards a New Ethical Code" (January-February, 1987).
2. For other sets of such planning-practice scenarios, refer to American Institute of Certified Planners (1983) and Barrett (1984). The latter included a self-survey, the results of which can be found in *Planning*, May, 1985.
3. For the sake of simplicity, the terms "code of ethics" and "code of professional conduct" were used more or less synonymously in the four articles.
4. Reference here is to: General By-Law of the Ontario Professional Planners Institute, Appendix 1, Professional Code of Conduct, 1986; and Canadian Institute of Planners National Charter By-Laws, Procedures and Appendices, Schedule B, Code of Professional Conduct, 1986. According to the CIP national office, there have been no disciplinary actions since the early 1970s. The Ontario chapters of CIP, now the OPPI, have had several such actions.
5. Reference here is to: American Institute of Certified Planners, Code of Ethics and Professional Conduct, adopted September, 1981; and the American Planning Association's proposed Statement of Ethical Principles for Planning, presented in *Planning*, March, 1986.
6. An example of how this can be approached is provided by: Marvin L. Manheim, "Ethical Issues in Environmental Impact Assessment," *EIA Review* 2 (1981): 315–34.

REFERENCES

American Institute of Certified Planners (1983) *Ethical Awareness in Planning*, Washington: AICP.
Barrett, Carol (1984) "Ethics in Planning: You Be the Judge," *Planning*, November.

Baum, Howell (1983) *Planners and Public Expectations*, Cambridge, Mass.: Schenkman.

Bayles, M. (1984) "Moral Theory and Application," *Social Theory and Practice* 10: 97–120.

Bok, Sissela (1979) *Lying: Moral Choice in Public and Private Life*, New York: Vintage Books.

Bolan, Richard (1985) "The Structure of Ethical Choice in Planning Practice," in Martin Wachs (ed.) *Ethics in Planning*, New Brunswick, NJ: Rutgers University, Center for Urban Policy Research.

Hodge, Gerald (1986) *Planning Canadian Communities*, Toronto: Methuen.

Howard, Ross (1985) "Pollster Favors Forced National Service," *Globe and Mail*, March 8.

—— (1986) "Study of Honorable Members Finds Some Are a Little Less So," *Globe and Mail*, January 2.

Howe, Elizabeth and Kaufman, Jerome (1979) "The Ethics of Contemporary American Planners," *Journal of the American Planning Association* 45: 243–55.

Kaufman, Jerome (1985) "American and Israeli Planners: A Cross-Cultural Comparison," *Journal of the American Planning Association* 51: 352–64.

Kaufman, Jerome L. (1980) "Land Planning in an Ethical Perspective," *Journal of Soil and Water Conservation*, November-December: 255–8.

Mandelbaum, Seymour J. (1985) "The Institutional Focus of Planning Theory," *Journal of Planning Education and Research* 5: 3–9.

Marcuse, Peter (1976) "Professional Ethics and Beyond: Values in Planning," *Journal of the American Institute of Planners* 42: 264–74.

Sagel, J. Frederick (1985) "Whistleblowing – and What It Means for All of Us," *Engineering Dimensions*, January-February: 37–9.

Schon, Donald A. (1983) *The Reflective Practitioner: How Professionals Think in Action*, New York: Basic Books.

Wachs, Martin (1985) "Introduction," *Ethics and Planning*, New Brunswick, NJ: Rutgers University, Center for Urban Policy Research.

York, Geoffrey (1985) "City Councillors Back Away from Aggressive Developers," *Globe and Mail*, May 21.

5

ETHICS AND ECONOMIC POLICY

Industrial strategy: its challenge to social policy in Canada

H. T. WILSON

SECTION I

Lindblom concludes a chapter on "The Market-Oriented Private Enterprise System" in his *Politics and Markets: the World's Political-Economic Systems* (1977) by stating that:

> However poorly the market is harnessed to democratic purposes, only within market-oriented systems does political democracy arise. Not all market-oriented systems are democratic, but every democratic system is also a market-oriented system. Apparently, for reasons not wholly understood, political democracy has been unable to exist except when coupled with the market. An extraordinary proposition, it has so far held without exception.

Lindblom's argument is not restricted to the immediate present, or even the last fifty years, but addresses origins and the subsequent development of both market-oriented systems and democratic institutions. Thus he speaks of political democracy arising only in nation-states that were already market-oriented to some extent. The fact that democratic institutions do not always arise in nation-states which have market-oriented systems cannot gainsay the main point. Historically, when such institutions have arisen, they have done so in nation-states with economic systems that are market-oriented. Lindblom makes the point cited in summary form at the very beginning of the study, *en route* to suggesting how little we know about the relationship between capitalism and democracy (ibid.: 5).

71

The idea of a historic institutional linkage, coupled with the priority of market to democratic arrangements in the circumstances in which they have been found together, draws our attention to the need to look carefully at the mix of institutions and the types of combinations that have occurred among them. It is commonplace nowadays to note that "free enterprise" economies were rarely if ever "free" of the helping hand of government and the state in one form or another, even from the earliest times. But this is not to dispute Lindblom's point in any way, since governments have always been directly involved in commercial, financial, and economic activity to the extent that taxes were required for military and public purposes. My concern here is with democratic governments, by which I mean the institutional mechanisms and processes of liberal democracy, more recently overlaid by more socially focused allocation and distribution schemes aimed at extending political equality (suffrage and political participation) and equality under the law to new, more distinctly social, forms of equality, all inside putatively market-oriented systems (Macpherson 1973, 1977, 1984; Wilson 1985a).

Lindblom uses the term "market-oriented" rather than "market" on its own in order to comprehend in his analysis of market systems the new forms that I have cited as an overlay on traditional market economies. His point is that these more distinctly social forms are far more understandable as an overlay on the traditional conception (often incorrect) of the market system than they are on political democracy (Lindblom 1977: 93–116). Yet it is important to see them both in process and in form as an alteration of the liberal democratic scheme no less than the market system. What do people, organized or unorganized, use their political and legal rights for (if at all) in a democratic polity, and how have they used these rights in the past? To what extent must we see social policies of the sort I have alluded to as the result of this citizenly and/or interested activity, and to what extent must they be acknowledged to be a response to actual local, national and international events by established elites? Questions like these only underscore the new way we have come to view the purpose of wealth creation in advanced industrial societies, namely as a device to provide jobs, benefits, social services and social administration generally.

Even the Canadian Chamber of Commerce has justified its concern about productivity in this way (Smith 1976: 4–7)!

Thus numerous commentators have argued, within the auspices of the market-oriented system, that we cannot possibly expect to have a decent and progressive social welfare system if we do not maintain certain levels of productivity and innovation – domestically and in competition with other countries in the new international market. This leads quickly to the claim that capitalism must be nurtured and protected all the more if the social policy overlays that I have alluded to are to continue in their present form and maintain or improve in quality with increases in the cost of living, as well as both unemployment and inflation, coupled with decreasing dollar value. A very important undercurrent is being appealed to here, which I would like to isolate and thereafter address off and on in the remainder of this text. If we treat social administration and social services as a set of institutions in their own right, rather than merely an "overlay" on either market-oriented or democratic institutions, we can see that an attempt is being made to create a coalition of common interest based on mutual support for social policies and the market and against political democracy.

This coalition is implicit, when not explicit, in Offe's observation (1983: 225–46) that if the party system, interest groups and "representation" in and through government agents makes democracy safe for capitalism, it is social services and benefits and social administration generally that make capitalism safe for democracy. While this observation is certainly valid as far as it goes, it does not take adequate account of the way that political democracy, employing representative forms, has been either obviated, or criticized when this has not been possible, by those concerned about the need for continuous system steering through speedy decision-making by specialized, expert and interested elites. In effect, while this refrain has long been a feature of the political-economic landscape in discussions of domestic economic activity, it has acquired a more recent status in concerns about Canada's position in the world-trading system. Democratic institutions, particularly of the parliamentary and deliberative kind, are increasingly viewed as an impediment to effective steering, where by "effective" is understood the sort of international comparative advantage which is the only guarantee of quality social services, alongside economic growth and profitability.

I want to argue against this coalition, whether in principle or in practice, in the strongest possible terms. If democratic institutions can be successfully bypassed, to the point of being rendered virtually "obsolete" by reference to prevailing conceptions of progress biased toward techniques and technology, then the basis on which capitalism and democracy have sustained their precarious equipoise will be sundered, here and elsewhere (Wilson 1987). I am not addressing ideas and events that are just now beginning to occur and take shape, nor am I speaking of practices which lack the support of earlier developments in the same direction. The very emergence of party discipline, and its use over the past forty to fifty years to guarantee Cabinet and Prime-Ministerial control over Parliament, has left individual sitting members with little or no opportunity to represent their constituents in the face of a full-fledged government agenda for Parliament. The percentage of votes for which a disciplined response is demanded from back-benchers by the leader and members of the Cabinet (shadow cabinet or caucus) has gone from 35% in the 1930s to 98% today.

While this example is the most important one for me, involving as it does significant and operational changes in the most important of all the institutions of representative democracy – the legislature – numerous others could be cited. The fact that Parliament does not make law, and has only a peripheral role to play in the law-making process relative to Cabinet and the relevant ministries and consulted interests, must be of serious concern to anyone schooled in the basic tenets of representative democracy. From the standpoint of the theory and practice of representation, it should hardly be surprising to hear that social and political scientists, themselves so often unconcerned with the defense of democratic institutions, have explained much of this signal difficulty away by noting that non-elected personnel, either appointed or scheduled, "represent" the people better than they can be represented in and through elections anyway. The argument here

74

is that the most salient sociological characteristics of the population being governed are more accurately reproduced in microcosm in such structures than formal elections can ever hope to accomplish (Wilson 1985a: 69–122).

Without laboring the obvious, I think that we ought at least to be clear on what we are giving up when we acknowledge and accept such facts for whatever reasons. Neither am I unaware of the limitations and shortcomings of the established mechanisms and processes of liberal democracy. Indeed, it is precisely because I appreciate what has historically made democracy safe for capitalism that I am so concerned about these further developments, and the attempt to justify them by reference to society's need for quality social services and a governmental presence in the area of distinctly social policy. The point remains, however, that it is only the presence of representative democracy, with all its faults, that has guaranteed through the aegis of partisan politics that these services and benefits will be provided regardless of "affordability". While it is true that social policies have existed in the absence of political democracy (e.g. under Bismarck), there is no denying the fact that they have come about elsewhere as a consequence of the extension of the franchise and the further development of political democracy, and will not for long be tolerated in their present form without it.

None of this is to ignore recent attempts, so often successful, albeit in the short term, to contain the pace of development of social policy in market-oriented systems which are also liberal democratic. Even in the case of the United States since 1980, however, the argument has been that only the private sector can create jobs, and social service "payouts" in the form of "entitlements" must accommodate themselves to this fact of government policy-making accordingly. In the instances where this has translated into sustained employment for individuals formerly on social welfare, they too have been beneficiaries of a government-managed (re)allocation scheme of gigantic, and consequential, proportions. One wonders whether the absence of staggering defense and space program costs, even in the face of the employment it provides, would not make most of this (re)allocation noticeably less attractive, as well as unnecessary. In Canada, the "social compact" conception of society has made such a policy shift all but impossible for the present government, however much it might wish to make it. Yet here, far more than in the United States, can it be said that we acknowledge and accept a politics of deference to established elites (Presthus 1973, 1974).

Developments recently afoot to democratize party structures so that citizen members can have a greater impact on the parliamentary wing of the party, while highly significant, are no substitute for bringing Parliament once again into the law-making process and cutting back the amount of disciplined voting so that individual Members of Parliament can endeavor to represent their constituents and speak their mind.[1] It is the institutionalization of the practice of crisis government, maintained after the Second World War and defended for various reasons connected with the "Cold War" and fiscal management of the economy, that first suggested the necessity for, and the likely viability of, the coalition between capitalism and social policy, with government the mediator when not the director of operations. Even if it was a combination of elite fears and citizenly concerns expressed through the party process (if not more directly) that led to initial government concern with fiscal as well as monetary management, the result since that time, in spite of all the efforts to roll it back, has been an alliance between capitalism and social policy which has gradually been undermining the institutions of political democracy.

To be sure, it is difficult to take issue with those who argue that liberal democracy and capitalism have been institutionally compatible for a very long time in the absence of massive and continuous government intervention in the economy through fiscal and monetary management and in society as a whole through social policy. My point in *Political Management* (Wilson 1985a) was that these institutions, archaic and compromised by the past (and present) as they may legitimately appear to be, cannot be transcended until they have been fully utilized, and in any case are absolutely indispensable in their present or a modified form if constructive social policies are to continue to have their proper impact on both the economic and the political system. The idea that an alliance or coalition of capitalism and social policy will constitute no problem because of the requirement that it operate in and through governmental structures ignores the fact of governmental centralization and concentration, and the declining role of elected officials in making political decisions, in favor of cabinets under strict party discipline, combined with bureaucrats, technocrats, regulators, and – especially since patriation of the Constitution and entrenchment of a Charter of Rights – judges and magistrates.

Confusing politics with the established governmental system is problematic precisely because so much in representative politics has been effectively pre-empted by rigid structures on the one side and the total lack of any alternative for translating needs and goals into policy on the other. In the absence of a willingness to fully utilize already established institutions of representative democracy, it will be impossible to sustain continuous support for present social policies and to provide for further developments toward egalitarianism and fundamental democratization. This becomes clear from more recent concerns about the viability of the market that only echo earlier tales of woe and damnation. I am speaking here of affirmative action, but particularly equal pay for work of equal value, and the apparent fear for the system's viability that has been expressed by all manner of persons and groups, as if system failure (unlikely in any case) would return us to a veritable state of nature, very much as it was supposed to do fifty years ago when novel market-threatening solutions were proposed during the Depression. I want to look first at the major characteristics of these two proposals, then contrast them with the new mode of "industrial strategy" thinking that is becoming so influential.

SECTION II

Two excellent and timely examples of social policies proposed and, in some cases, being implemented by government are affirmative action and equal pay for work of equal value. Both might seem to constitute more extensive intrusions into the market, as well as the "merit" principle, than have ever before taken place. But reflection makes it clear that while this may perhaps appear to be the case now, it is only from the present vantage point that those sincerely concerned are making such a comparison. To those who were similarly worried in the 1930s, the very development of the so-called "welfare" (or service) state, accompanied by increasing government intervention in the economy focused on monetary and fiscal controls, must have seemed the end of capitalism. Later, many of those who were most staunchly opposed to these developments would admit that their effect may well have been to save capitalism more than anything else, but this is not my concern here.

Indeed, I am not so sure that capitalism can absorb affirmative action and equal pay fully and still remain capitalism. Systematic wage discrimination is so deeply embedded in capitalism that we understand it, alongside the kind of surplus value extraction that is not gender and visible-minority specific, to be absolutely essential to innovation in the entrepreneurial and small business sector. This does not even begin to address the "free labor" performed by vast numbers of women, and children and the aged as well, in the form of housework, food preparation, shopping and work in the voluntary sector (Illich 1982; Wilson 1988a). My point here is that these goals are now part of the political process, and must be dealt with in one way or another. If they do not become compulsory (as opposed to voluntary), at least in firms in the private sector with over 100 employees, their effective operation in civil and public service employment alone may generate job ghettos of a new kind. The private sector has already begun to curtail the hiring of women and visible minorities, and the small businesses where 40 to 45% of Ontario women presently work may be effectively exempt from the requirements of these two policies.

Here too we can see a parallel which those presently worried about government interventions in the labor market and employment relationship often ignore. Successive government demands beginning at the turn of the century focused on hours of work, working conditions, child labor and later on benefit schemes, all supported by majorities, had the same effect in humanizing capitalism in and through work and labor activities and mutual obligations that affirmative action and pay equity now seek in the new circumstances. To be sure, the circumstances in which such reforms occurred were either apocalyptic, as in the case of the Depression, or the result of governmental initiatives and good sense in the wake of severe

78

and continuing economic abuses. No matter how ineffective democratic practice may have appeared at the time, and there is increasing evidence that it was much more effective than we have been led to think, it was the backdrop of democratic institutions that made it possible, in the absence of such practice, for change in the direction of the humanization of capitalism to occur.

More recently, we can point to the doctrines of corporate social responsibility and good corporate citizenship as central vehicles getting us to rethink the nature of the employment relationship. While initial concerns in the 1960s were very much concerned with environmental despoliation and pollution, as well as the misuse of renewable and non-renewable natural resources, efforts were also made to address the need for fair hiring, advancement and compensation policies as well. In effect, what was beginning to take shape was a new view of the social functions of firms and corporations which stressed the central role of their non-economic obligations and responsibilities to society as a whole. Thus did certain notions of social responsibility come to be accepted as a minimum condition for the right to do (and keep doing) business. Employment, while certainly not an absolute right, is increasingly seen to constitute more a right and less a privilege, though this is of course more clearly the case in public sector employment than anywhere else (Wilson 1988b).

The upshot of all these changes, even in the face of concerted, and in many cases successful, resistance to affirmative action and equal pay, is that either the market is much more flexible than anyone thought, and is capable of absorbing structural modifications without long-term negative consequences, or that we no longer have a market and therefore live under a vastly different form of capitalism (if any form) than we are aware of. I am almost certain that the first understanding is the correct one, which is to say, with Lindblom (1977: 93–116), that the permutations and combinations of political and economic systems go far beyond any simplistic rendering of the market concept. What remains of central importance is the practice of democratically elected governments, however much they are supposed to be based on party structures and systems which make democracy safe for capitalism. What this suggests to me is that sometimes it is democracy, and governments elected through and accountable to the democratic mechanism, which make capitalism safe for capitalism!

Looking at affirmative action in this light, we can see it as an attempt to take "merit" seriously in practice by making sure that it is applied in a way which gives women and visible minorities who are as meritorious as others the first chance at initial placement and advancement. If it turns out that merit is no more objective a basis for allocating functions and positions than the market, understood to operate autonomously from government and politics, then it can be argued that recourse to either one as the basis of an effort to forestall affirmative action (or equal pay), especially by those who have never invoked them before, amounts to little more than special pleading. The market, and merit in practice (as opposed to principle), come to seem more like rhetoric and ideology than they do a description of some past or present state of affairs. The truth is that they have all too often been used in the past to favor the occupancy of work and labor positions and functions by groups and individuals other than the ones for whom affirmative action is intended.

Looked at from this standpoint, affirmative action does constitute something of a quota system in given organizations and occupations, but then there is nothing necessarily wrong with quotas if market and merit criteria have been used in the past to favor some individuals and groups over others (Winn 1985). On the other hand, if such criteria are alleged to be objective, in their application as well as their conceptualization, then it is possible to meet the requirements of both while still achieving the implementation of affirmative action legislation. In the case of merit, this would happen whenever any one of those considered to be most (equally) meritorious was picked, including a member of the underrepresented group. In the case of the market, it would occur whenever a choice was made about intake or advancement at a specified time and following a specified interval on the basis of who of those available was most meritorious for a given position or function. Here merit would be conditioned (as above), but not compromised, by the demands of affirmative action in the event that there were members of an underrepresented group whose quota in the particular organization (position or function) had not been met.

The point here is that merit only favors the member of the underrepresented group if he or she is as (or more) meritorious than anyone else, no matter what indicators are used. As far as the market is concerned, it depends on availability during a particular period of time. Anyone may apply, but the choice must be made on the basis of merit, conditioned only by the requirement that the member of an underrepresented group be chosen where he or she is as (or more) meritorious. None of what I have said so far is intended to constitute a defense of either the market or merit as objective concepts for which clear criteria exist and can be applied equitably. In addition, there is the fact that merit in practice, in contrast to merit in principle, at best allows for an initial judgment of competence. Ironically enough it is precisely tenure, and related forms of job security, whether *de jure* or *de facto* in nature, which have the effect of taking employees who have survived probation out of the market, no less in the private than in the public sector, thereby precluding subsequent judgments of performance that might lead to displacement by those in a subsequent intake group.

Equal pay for work of equal value, in contrast to equal pay for equal work, is perceived to be no less radical in its intent and effects than affirmative action. But here the focus is on compensation rather than representation, and on the function or position rather than on specific underrepresented groups. Note that in neither case is the emphasis explicitly on the individual, but then individual performance has all too rarely mattered when it came to displacing already protected persons with newcomers offering superior qualifications. Equal pay for work of equal value is far more radical than equal pay for equal work, which has been law in Ontario since 1952, and reflects a determination to overcome the problem of job ghettos for women and visible minorities. Not surprisingly, equal pay for equal work has failed to deal with the problem of job ghettos, and it may well turn out that equal pay for work of equal value will be no more successful in this endeavor. Still, it does constitute an attempt to bring merit evaluations to bear, while opening up job opportunities to people who have been channelled into stereotyped employment in the past. The core of such legislation is a rating scheme which can be used to compare jobs in ways that the market apparently fails to take adequate account of.

An important point about these rating and comparison schemes is that they are at present confined to the function of upgrading traditionally female jobs by comparison with traditionally male jobs. A second point is that application of these schemes is at present restricted to jobs with a great amount of task predefinition and little discretion, though it is possible, if not likely, that male/female jobs in the higher echelons will also be compared and rated. At present, these latter positions are mainly covered by affirmative action legislation, which favors women over all other underrepresented groups for the obvious reason that women are the one underrepresented group which is not a minority in society. The limits of the present scheme, or any scheme contemplated for the immediate future, are clearly evident in the fact that it is highly unlikely that elite and non-elite jobs will be compared and rated, which is to say that such schemes do not presently threaten the class and stratification order in any way. The result might otherwise be that male jobs would be upgraded, and male/male and female/female jobs compared and rated. Note finally that equal pay for work of equal value is inflationary, at least in the short term, because no job will take (or has taken) a cut in pay, but is only adjusted upward (Government of Ontario 1985: 4).

Let me provide some examples of what has already become a light industry of sorts in provincial governments in Canada and in some state governments in the United States. It has been argued, for example, that a carpenter and a secretary should be paid the same amount because their jobs accumulate the same number of points when assessed by a standard rating scheme. This scheme is used to break down given jobs into their component parts based on the skills and demands that each requires. The example is apt because it compares a traditionally male with a traditionally female job and comes to a conclusion at substantial variance with the "market" (and union), which pays the secretary two-thirds of what the carpenter makes. Similar male/female comparisons with the same conclusions have been carried out rating clerk typists and truck drivers, laundry workers and laborers, retail clerks and offset duplicator operators, library technicians and gardeners, licensed practical nurses and campus policemen, and administrative assistants and electricians.

The criteria usually isolated in such comparison and rating schemes include the following: (1) *knowledge and skills* (a) job knowledge; (b) interpersonal skills; (2) *mental demands* (a) independent judgment; (b) problem-solving; (3) *accountability* (a) freedom to take action; (b) impact on results; (4) *working conditions* (a) physical effort; (b) hazards; (c) discomfort. Each of the subsets has four or five boxes which can be checked off. For example (1)(a) offers five levels of experience, ranging from no previous experience to technical expertise in a specialized area. Interpersonal skills (1)(b) is more subjective, and gives a clear advantage to people (e.g. women) who must respond to the requests of superiors and be tactful with customers or clients. It also favors organizational and interactional activities over relatively solitary and technical ones. Under independent judgment (2)(a), and problem-solving (2)(b), the carpenter and the secretary received the same number of points. Under accountability the secretary gets a substantially higher rating than the carpenter, in contrast to working conditions, where an opposite result obtains.[2]

I have attempted to examine briefly two legislative programs which are regularly accused of jeopardizing or threatening both the market system and the merit principle in Canada and the United States. My point has been to argue that the transmogrifications of the market, from its inception at the dawn of capitalism in its most primitive forms to today, make it virtually impossible to argue that any and all "interventions" in some fictional dyadic trading relation lie uniformly outside it. Fears of the demise of the market are all too similar to Mark Twain's purported death. Yet even if this fear turns out to be warranted in the instances cited, it would constitute a significant triumph of democratic and egalitarian political values over market values based on classical liberal individualism. On the other hand, when merit is examined, in particular the substantial gap between meritocracy in principle and meritocracy in practice, we see it as something less than the objective indicator it is alleged to be. Reliance on it in the contemporary context can hardly be criticized in light of its past uses, especially when the impact of tenure and job security provisions exempting those who have survived a probationary period are taken into account.

SECTION III

I would now like to turn from scrutiny of the two social policies cited to consider what is fast becoming the operative mode for conceptualizing the desired interface between political and economic systems in advanced industrial societies. "Industrial strategy" and "industrial policy" are the names most often used to describe this emerging phenomenon, one whose significance lies, to a considerable extent, in its view of the nation-state, or discrete sectors therein, as a "firm" for purposes of international competition and market share. In effect, this new form of capitalism appears more and more to constitute a new *mercantilism*, particularly when some of the more monopoly-designating and initiative-taking approaches of central governments are considered. At the same time that industrial strategy can be said to have arisen in response to international market conditions, it would be senseless to deny that such programs impact directly, often in unexpected and contradictory ways, on structures and processes already in place to "manage" the domestic economies of the countries in question.

My point here is to underscore how much pressure is being put on representative democratic, allocative and distributive, and structural and legal mechanisms by the strategy-making approach to the "management" of government. The very idea of managing a governmental system already presumes the validity of distinctly technocratic approaches whose consequences are almost certain to include what I have elsewhere called political regression (Wilson 1985a). Thus the installation of crisis-style government as a permanent feature of central and executive politics in most advanced industrial societies can be seen as a natural upshot of the system of cabinet government already alluded to, with its tight party discipline and continuous management and control of parliamentary members of parties. Centralization and concentration favor not

84

only central governments over provincial, state or local and municipal forms, but the executive and administrative, however comprised, over legislatures. Concepts of efficiency and effectiveness allegedly characteristic of the private corporate sector have been brought to bear on these governments over the past twenty-five years in ways which imperil not only legislatures and federalism as forms and practices, but citizenship and citizenly activities as well.

I mentioned at the outset that a useful way of conceptualizing the problem which I see emerging on the horizon would be to see it in terms of a three-cornered hat of sorts. That is, we can distinguish the technocratic structures of planning, management and organization, along with Cabinet, institutionalized bureaucracies and plebiscitary politics and government as one subsystem, the linkages between citizens, voting constituencies, interests, parties, "local" concerns and legislatures as a second subsystem, and the client-centered organization and operation of social administration, service and welfare apparatuses in both legal jurisdictions as a third subsystem. My point was to emphasize that those in influential positions in the first subsystem are beginning to argue that citizens in the second who need the services and programs provided by the third should seriously consider (or reconsider) some of the loyalties they may have to other elements in the second subsystem which evidence a commitment to representative democracy, the partisan and electoral process, and the deliberative and investigative role of legislatures.

What makes this argument (or admonition) all the more amazing is the fact that it is precisely the institutional mechanisms and processes of representative democracy operating in and through political parties that have been responsible for the rise of programs and services in both jurisdictions, programs and services that no party, regardless of its mandate, can seek to undo in any fundamental way without serious repercussions. Offe's argument (1983), while sound in a number of respects, thus appears a bit too pat on the matter of what makes democracy safe for capitalism to apply to Canada with unfettered confidence. Political parties of all types, partly as a result of Canadian tendencies to "risk-averse" cross-voting between jurisdictions, but also because of the way the "social

85

compact" has been institutionalized in ongoing political and administrative practices, are even more clearly devices to make capitalism safe for democracy rather than the reverse. Add to this the relatively undeveloped practice of interest group politics and organized pressure in all jurisdictions, and the tie between citizenship, partisanship and the emergence and development of social programs and services is beyond dispute.

Structures which aggregate as well as articulate the needs, desires and interests of Canadian men and women constitute *intermediaries* between individual citizens and their families on the one hand, and formal bodies and groups exercising tremendous powers of initiative, intervention, allocation, distribution, regulation, enforcement, and privilege on the other. Only the presence of the democratic franchise organized around existing and proposed ways of articulating between citizens and such bodies can guarantee the continued viability of these programs and services. The same thing can be said about the two forms of legislation to which I alluded in Section II. Both affirmative action and equal pay for work of equal value will only be guaranteed if the existing structures of the second subsystem continue in their present form and, ideally, are improved in their effectiveness so that they become more viable than they already are. Like the politics of display as a substitute for, rather than a supplement to, established processes and mechanisms of representative democracy, heightened interest in close linkages between the first and third subsystems will lead to political regression rather than political development (Wilson 1985a: 69–122).

Yet it is all too easy to understand how we are (and have been) persuaded that social services and programs, to be good, must be underwritten by a strong, productive, and profitable economy. Otherwise, we are convinced that we shall not be able to "afford" such social services (Smith 1976). This is hardly a new argument on its own. What is new about it is the way it has been tied into emergent thinking on industrial strategy and industrial policy not only in the advanced countries, but in the so-called "Third World" as well. This has occurred at precisely the time when we have become legitimately concerned about international competition, and the felt need to treat the nation-state for certain purposes as a firm if we are to secure our fair share of the export market. On the other side of this justification for industrial strategy approaches to conceptualizing the problem and its solution is the apparent demand that the domestic economy be brought increasingly into line in order to serve these new concerns and objectives.

We should never forget who our competitors in this emerging international market system are, and what some of their most important and salient country characteristics are. First, they are either dictatorships or countries with a history of non-democratic forms of government which have only recently been (to varying extents) democratized through representation and electoral processes and mechanisms, with the assistance of elements of the rule of law. Second, they are almost never federal or confederative, because federalism and variations on the idea and practice of a division of powers premised on coordinated jurisdictions with certain spheres of exclusivity (not levels) present a clear structural obstacle to industrial strategy-making.[3] A third characteristic is the absence in these countries of wide-ranging social services and programs, which, I submit, goes hand in hand with the absence of representative democracy. A fourth characteristic, which is the only one of the four that Canadians increasingly share with these countries, is a low to non-existent level of mass (as opposed to organized) participation in political matters in the absence of an electoral campaign.

Instead of saying that the technical and related "complexities" of contemporary issues demand (even) less citizenly activity and participation, I would argue that they require more of it than ever before. Concentration and centralization have led to the effective bypassing of legislatures and provincial and state governments in favor of executive (Cabinet) centralization and central government concentration, undergirded by the technocratic thinking of "central agents" and other key appointees and civil servants. Constitutions and Charters of Rights allow more and more *political* questions and issues to be settled by non-elected judges, magistrates and human rights officers, often with little regard to past practice, present needs, or proper procedures based on the presumption of innocence. Economies have become progressively subject to the allocation decisions (or lack of same) of regulators and other interveners, all too often with no appreciation whatsoever of the mutual interdependence between political/legal and economic/social rights so central to our present system. This shrinking or stagnating sphere of political and citizenly activity, when compared to the vast increase in decisional matters whose complexity allegedly makes debate and discussion a luxury we can no longer afford, and parliamentary and federal institutions obsolete, augurs poorly for real human progress and political development.

What has made this all too apparent for me is the way that concentrated and centralized technocratic thinking in the first subsystem is increasingly determined to follow an economizing rather than an egalitarian agenda, based on the presumption, implicit in some forms of industrial strategy thinking, that affirmative action and equal pay policies are a new element of the third subsystem – social services and programs. I am not concerned about the ethical or moral issues that arise from permitting "the market" and "merit" to rule, when we all too often know the outcome. What concerns me is that those who head democratically elected governments at the center now take a position toward the nation-state as a firm that is virtually indistinguishable from the way business and industrial leaders, and their henchmen in the discipline of economics, dealt with the urgent need for social services and programs at an earlier date. Again, it may not be out of order to suggest that the real issue, even in the face of the probable consequences of properly functioning affirmative action and equal pay programs, is what needs to be done to make capitalism safe for capitalism in a democracy!

The view of affirmative action and equal pay legislation as problematic in the absence of a substantial surplus (which we never seem to have "available" at the time) is part and parcel of the idea that they are to be understood as forms of social administration, and those who make use of them as objects of such services and programs. Economistic accounting mechanisms (GNP), notorious for taking no account of the "free labor" performed mainly by young and middle-aged women, but by children and the aged as well, in homes and in the "voluntary" sector, as well as society at large, also fail to see the public sector as a creator, rather than only a disposer and spender, of value. Thus, when it is stated that such legislation will have its initial impact on employees in the public sector, the response is all too predictable. My point is that fair employment, advancement and compensation practices are *sensible* as well as moral and ethical when looked at in terms of the long-range goals and objectives of productivity and profitability in our form of collective life. Only where the means had become their own justification could the sense and value of such practices, in the face of present disparities, inequities, and misallocations and misuses of talent, experience and interest, be lost sight of.

The fact that affirmative action and equal pay programs ought not be construed as part of the social administration sector, in the form of a "handout" to individuals who will consume but not create wealth, is not put forward as a criticism of this particular subsystem. The object is to respect the fact that since virtually every adult is now required to work for money, employment itself needs to be reconceptualized in the same way that social assistance and related programs had to be in the past. People should be compensated on the assumption that they are unfortunate enough not to be able to find secure employment like everyone else. In the same vein, employment, whenever possible, ought ideally to be available to anyone who can meet the requirements, particularly those in underrepresented groups, and compensated accordingly. It is important that we realize greater consistency in our attitudes toward both social programs and employment schemes, not in the way that we presently do – by treating them as a "frill" of the system that only our productivity makes possible – but rather by realizing that we must take a "total system" approach which focuses on how society gets *all* its work done, and on how those who cannot or do not participate in this endeavor feel!

The tie between these social programs and services and the larger system of benefits, and industrial strategy thinking, has taken a new twist since Canada decided to conclude a "free trade" deal with the United States. Instead of the refrain already alluded to which argues for technocratic steering and industrial strategy thinking in domestic and international affairs as a prerequisite to good social services and programs, US negotiators are arguing that our more intensive and comprehensive social administration sector is precisely what is giving *Canadians as a whole* an unfair competitive advantage. If there ever was a time for a heightened political activity and process reaffirming the link between representation, elections and the franchise and the need to preserve and enhance these programs and services, it is now.

It is in this regard that Canadian uniqueness with respect to capital preference, financial capital dominance, risk aversion, preoccupation with capital "scarcity" and our "fall back" attitude to renewable and non-renewable natural resources now appears far more consistent with the "social compact" view of politics as "peace, order and good government" than we may have thought. This suggests that the preservation and development of our political and social values and institutions requires not so much a continental free trade zone which could very well presage the end of Canada, but rather selective strategies of a sectoral or case-by-case type which would aid rather than inhibit our already well-developed sense of internationalism. Canada has been an ongoing experiment in adaptation to external economic realities since (if not before) its inception, which is to say that Canada has always had one or another form of industrial strategy, and that it may be time to change it. I have suggested elsewhere (Wilson 1985b) the range of policy options in this regard, to the end of arguing that free trade could all too readily generate continental isolation as the price of a formalized Canadian-American economic integration.

Above all, it is important that we not so completely take for granted our representative, electoral, political-party and citizenly institutions, processes, mechanisms, values and practices that we forget their central role in securing and maintaining social services and programs, thereby falling prey to the "pay as you go" fetishization of productivity as something which can only be realized in the new circumstances where established political and governmental institutions are sidestepped in favor of models of governmental practice originating in creditable, but manifestly non-democratic, activities and circumstances in the private sector. If we refuse to be hoodwinked by this sort of thinking, which has become a staple of yellow journalism as well as racism and what is nowadays incorrectly (but often effectively) called sexism, we can begin to see more clearly the parallel between such programs and the right to fair employment in hiring, advancement and compensation. This, in its turn, will allow us to remember our collective sense of priorities when it comes to the role that we assign to industrial strategy *vis-à-vis* the preservation and enhancement of democratic institutions.

While it might be argued that I have placed too much confidence in what are, after all, liberal and individualistic political forms and institutions, I would respond that present concerns with social equality may require certain modifications of the operative sense of individualism in Canadian society, but not its displacement. Indeed, our ongoing commitment to the social compact conception of government already cited may suggest that far fewer modifications have been needed here than will be required in the United States at some future date. In any case, my point has been to underscore the fact that economic activity is a means to realize non-economic values; as Macpherson (1973, 1984) has shown, this always has been and still is central to the liberal–democratic vision. Social equality is hardly at variance with this vision for reasons that he has pointed out forcefully. The fact that the two "belong together" argues, as feminists in particular are now increasingly aware, for a stronger, not a weaker, commitment to representative and electoral politics, combined with sensitivity to the importance of a person's being employed or being denied this opportunity and right.

NOTES

1. See James Gillies and Jean Pigott (1982) "Participation in the Legislative Process," *Canadian Public Administration* 25 (2): 254–64. The entire issue is devoted to analysis of the role of interest groups and legislatures in Canada.
2. See *Toronto Star*, February 3, 1985, F1, for discussion of this scheme for comparing and rating jobs.
3. The tendency throughout federal systems to redefine this arrangement in organizational and hierarchical terms as a relation of levels rather than coordinated jurisdictions is clearly directed to the objective of centralized management and planning in the industrial strategy mode.

REFERENCES

Government of Ontario (1985) *Pay Equity*, Green Paper, Toronto.

Illich, Ivan (1982) *Gender*, New York: Pantheon.

Lindblom, Charles (1977) *Politics and Markets: the World's Political-Economic Systems*, New York: Basic Books.

Macpherson, C. B. (1973) *Democratic Theory: Essays in Retrieval*, London: Oxford University Press.

—— (1977) *The Life and Times of Liberal Democracy*, London: Oxford University Press.

—— (1984) *The Rise and Decline of Economic Justice*, London: Oxford University Press.

Offe, Claus (1983) "Competitive Party Democracy and the Keynesian Welfare State: Factors of Stability and Disorganization," *Policy Sciences* 15 (3): 225–46.

Presthus, Robert (1973) *Elite Accommodation in Canadian Politics*, London: Cambridge University Press.

—— (1974) *Elites and the Policy Process*, London: Cambridge University Press.

Smith, A. J. R. (1976) "Equality and Efficiency: the Big Trade Off," *The Canadian Business Review*, Autumn: 4–7.

Wilson, H. T. (1985a) *Political Management: Redefining the Public Sphere*, Berlin and New York: Walter de Gruyter.

—— (1985b) "Once Again: the Industrial Strategy Debate," *Atkinson Review of Political Studies* 2 (2): 33–40.

—— (1987) "Industrial Democracy Reconsidered," in Wolfgang Dorow (ed.) *The Business Corporation in the Democratic Society*, Berlin and New York: Walter de Gruyter.

—— (1988a) *Sex and Gender*, Leiden: E. J. Brill.

—— (1988b) "Anti-Discrimination Legislation and its Impact on the Employment Relationship: The Case of Affirmative Action and Equal Pay," in Klaus Weiermair and Günter Dlugos (eds) *Managerial Discretion in the Labour Market and Employment Relationship*, Berlin and New York: Walter du Gruyter.

Winn, Conrad (1985) "Affirmative Action for Women: More than a Case of Simple Justice," *Canadian Public Administration* 28 (1): 24–46.

6

LEGAL ETHICS

1 Ideology, interest, and implementation of a professional ethical code

HARRY ARTHURS

BACKGROUND

I am going to begin by describing my methodology and thus by confessing my own bias.

My perspective is that of a participant observer in the process of forming and administering professional ethics as a member, first, of the Committee of the Canadian Bar Association (CBA) which drafted its 1974 Code of Professional Conduct and, second, from 1980 to 1984 as a bencher of the Law Society of Upper Canada and a member of its discipline committee.

In addition, as the first Canadian law professor with an interest in legal professionalism, I have had twenty years to ponder the significance of legal ethics as a device of internal ordering and of external accountability.

Neither of these perspectives has left me with any confidence that codes of professional ethics do have, should have, or can have, a significance which compels us to deal with them on their own terms, as if they meant what they said. On the other hand, perhaps my limited perspectives seriously qualify my conclusions; perhaps more general consideration of the experience of other professions might yield different insights.

THE EXPERIENCE OF THE LEGAL PROFESSION

Some relatively objective reportage might help to set the stage for further speculation and critical observations.

The CBA is a voluntary association which enjoys the participation of most Canadian lawyers, and in some provinces, of all of them. Its functions do not include regulation of the profession. Rather, regulation is the task of provincial law societies, in which membership is compulsory, and which enjoy statutory power to admit, discipline and otherwise control the qualifications and behavior of lawyers. None the less, in 1920, the CBA adopted a code of professional ethics which then, in effect, served as a model or map for provincial governing bodies.

From 1920 until it was replaced in 1974, this Code was never amended, never formally debated within the CBA, never formally interpreted by published advisory or adjudicative rulings, never – so far as the public record goes – quoted in connection with the discipline of a single lawyer.

It was occasionally referred to in after-dinner speeches, convocation addresses, continuing education panel discussions, and the self-serving propaganda issued by the profession for public edification. It was effectively a dead letter, except to the extent that it may have reinforced, in some inexplicit way, a professional culture that expressed itself in other formal and informal processes of governance and discipline.

A number of provincial law societies formally adopted the CBA Code, sometimes with local variations. However, adoption did not give the Code legal force. Professional discipline proceeded generally under open-ended statutory language proscribing "conduct unbecoming a barrister and solicitor" and "unprofessional conduct," supplemented by regulations dealing with trust funds. At best, the CBA Code seems to have been regarded as providing general guidance to those who had to administer, and those who wished to meet, the statutory standard.

However, one must speak with some diffidence about what standards were actually applied in disciplinary proceedings. Reasoned decisions in professional discipline proceedings were never published. Thus we do not know whether or not the 1920 CBA Code actually mattered in any practical sense. However, there is no secondary evidence to suggest that its vague and contradictory admonitions contributed to, detracted from, or even impinged upon, discipline processes: there is no record of any debate by the law societies concerning its meaning, no proposals that it be changed to reflect changing circumstances of practice, no public statements of how the Code actually worked in a given set of circumstances.

On the contrary, all the secondary evidence – which is scant enough – is to the contrary. The only published study of discipline in the legal profession showed that virtually the sole cause of disbarment was theft of clients' funds or similar forms of dishonesty; virtually no one was formally disciplined for violation of any of the matters with which the CBA Code was concerned: violations of rules concerning intraprofessional relations, conflicts of interest not involving funds, breach of duties owed to the administration of justice, etc.

In one critical area, moreover – that of professional competence – we know that the CBA Code could not have had any impact: it did not even mention the topic. Nor indeed did any governing body address the competence question without the benefit of guidance from the CBA: as near as can be known, across all of Canada no incompetents were disbarred except those who suffered a total collapse of personality due to mental illness, addiction, or other affliction.

It would be fair to say, then, that the 1920 CBA Code of Ethics had nothing practical to do with anything ethical. Ultimately this conclusion came to be shared by the CBA itself, which then faced a choice: it could either abandon altogether the project of professional ethics, or it could try again and from the beginning. It opted for the latter approach, and in 1969 it appointed a committee to make a fresh start.

As a member of that committee, I can testify to the considerable time and effort which went into the revision, which produced an entirely new and much more presentable document. The new Code of Professional Conduct was replete with principles, commentary and footnotes, offering a reasoned defense and instructive examples of its prescriptions. It took into account some of the vast changes which had occurred in legal practice and professional discourse over the fifty years since the first CBA Code was adopted. And the new 1974 Code was strenuously debated, and then with some fanfare adopted, and locally promulgated and published, by provincial law societies. Notwithstanding, it remains almost as much of a dead letter as its predecessor.

Professional discipline continues to be driven by the same

vague statutory standards I quoted earlier – "professional misconduct" and "conduct unbecoming" – and the Code serves largely rhetorical purposes. Moreover, discipline tribunals continue to be preoccupied with issues of honesty and the protection of clients' trust funds, although they have now begun to address other forms of patently improper behavior, including incompetence. And finally, very little, if any, serious discussion has developed around ambiguities or imperatives in the text of the new Code as it relates to the disposition of individual "hard cases." This suggests that the new Code neither challenges nor inhibits, neither empowers nor constrains, those who make operational decisions about standards of behavior in the legal profession.

ETHICAL CODES, ETHICAL CONDUCT, AND ETHICAL ENFORCEMENT

Codes of legal ethics thus do not seem to have much to do with the enforcement of standards of professional behavior, at least in so far as such behavior is enforced through formal discipline systems. Conversely, whatever purposes are served by formal discipline systems, they do not appear to exist primarily in order to enforce codes of professional discipline.

This is not to deny that there are in fact normative systems which govern professional behavior and what might be referred to as professional ethics. It is simply that these normative systems, these professional ethics, do not happen to be coextensive with the CBA Code which ostensibly occupies the field. Nor do I intend to suggest that formal discipline systems have no purpose or effect. They do; it is simply not the purpose and effect which one might assume if one's sole source of information was the CBA Code and its provincial variants.

If the operative ethics of the bar are not found in the CBA Code, where can we look to find them? I suggest that the existence and content of such norms can be discerned by observing the behavior of lawyers and of their governing bodies.

For example, the CBA Code has little or nothing to say about important behavioral norms such as: forms of dress and address which are conventionally observed in such native

96

habitats of lawyers as courtrooms and offices; respect for the "property" rights of lawyers who refer clients elsewhere for specialist services; abstention from overt criticism of other lawyers; and the preaching and practice of both collective and individual professional autonomy.

But if the CBA Code does not function as an ethical touchstone, why does anyone bother with it? Yet bother they do, in a peculiar way: despite the irrelevance of the Code to professional behavior, when adopted by the CBA and provincially it engendered considerable controversy within professional circles. For example, the profession debated hotly the provisions of the Code relating to advertising, and has since continued to debate those provisions as they have been radically amended over time. Or, to take another example, provincially adopted versions of the Code have been amended so as to signal the bar's concern with such diverse phenomena as the employment of paralegals and courtroom security risks.

Something of importance obviously was happening. However, that something, I suggest, was not so much the articulation of a moral imperative as it was the playing out of a political conflict involving forces within and beyond the profession.

Advertising again provides the example. Decisions of the United States Supreme Court had cast into doubt, on constitutional and anti-trust grounds, traditional "ethical" prohibitions against advertising. In Canada, consumer groups, newspaper editorials, and government committee reports had fastened on these traditional prohibitions as evidence of the profession's willingness to advance its collective economic interests over the public interest in information and competition. Within the profession, changing demographies and patterns of practice had put in question both traditional authority structures and well-established market structures, both of which had been reinforced by the ban against advertising.

The convergence of all these internal and external forces created an almost irresistible movement toward the liberalization of advertising rules. It is not surprising that even prior to its adoption, differences about the advertising provisions of the CBA Code had caused a deep schism within the committee; in the mid-1970s various provincial bodies modified its restrictions; and in the mid-1980s, a see-saw battle in Ontario finally culminated in the adoption of new rules which permit considerable freedom to appeal for clients by truthful, dignified and non-pejorative advertising.

The advertising provisions of the Code cannot be taken seriously as an authoritative ethical statement about the relations amongst lawyers, or between them and the clientele they serve. Rather these provisions must be read as the locus of a conflict between competing visions of society and economy, of law and of legal professionalism.

The new liberal version of the rules may serve symbolically to reassure the public that its interests are after all heeded, and that further legislative intervention to promote competition in the supply of legal services is unnecessary. It may provide evidence that the Law Society is still dominated by representatives of the elite, who are not concerned with competition for ordinary clients and can thus afford to be public-spirited. It may signal the arrival within the profession of a new, entrepreneurial spirit.

But the new rule will not actually guide the perplexed or fundamentally change the behavior of ordinary, rank-and-file lawyers. On the one hand, no one in living memory had actually been disciplined for advertising, and many lawyers had already found ways of peddling their wares before the rules changed to accommodate what they are doing. On the other hand, the experience in other jurisdictions suggests that the issue of advertising is less significant than it seems; relatively few people end up taking full advantage of the right to advertise.

Finally, I have raised the issue of why professional discipline seems to have so little to do with professional ethics.

Professional ethics – whatever their source or content, CBA Code or legal culture – are enforced not just in formally designated disciplinary bodies, but through other means, especially those involving informal sanctioning methods. Thus, the staff of the Law Society frequently "suggest" that lawyers abstain from certain conduct, even when it is not formally proscribed; they tolerate other conduct which is proscribed so long as it is kept within limited bounds and pursued by individual lawyers with otherwise good reputations; tutelary measures are undertaken in the bar admission course and during the articling period by established lawyers, in an effort to socialize new entrants into acceptance of the profession's value system; and local lawyers' organizations, with no formal disciplinary powers, manage to generate local normative regimes enforced by a system of social and economic sanctions and rewards.

I have, moreover, not yet mentioned the most important devices for securing voluntary compliance with the profession's real code of conduct: education and socialization. Here, perhaps, the CBA Code has the greatest potential. It may serve as an ideological statement, reinforcing – sometimes possibly obscuring – the belief system of the profession. It interacts, in the long run, with other ideological expressions – law school images of legal practice and its discontents, bar admission propaganda and the intense socializing pressure of articling, intrafirm reward systems and exhortation by after-dinner speeches.

The ambition of all of these is not so much obedience as belief, and not so much works as faith. The CBA Code is therefore important – and worthy of study – because it forms part of an overall strategy to create professional and public belief in the value of the legal profession itself.

TEACHING PROFESSIONAL ETHICS

This conclusion leads me to some final remarks about the study of professional ethics in law schools.

I do indeed believe that we should study professional ethics, study them closely and seriously. But a study of legal ethics must be embedded in a larger study of legal professionalism. Such study is an important feature of attempts by both lawyers and critics of the legal profession to understand it more completely.

On the one hand, uncritical acceptance of the Code of Professional Conduct, uncritical acceptance of the values and rhetoric, the ideology and symbols of the profession, does nothing to sensitize young recruits. It does not prepare them for the difficult practical choices they will have to make on a daily basis as they practice law. It does not prepare them to deal with controversial issues of professional policy which may confront them as members of the profession, its governing elites, or the wider political community.

On the other hand, uncritical preoccupation with the Code as an accurate representation and originating inspiration of the ethical sensibilities of the bar is a mistake made occasionally even by unfriendly commentators on the profession.

We would all do much better, I suggest, to study legal ethics in context, from an anthropological or sociological perspective, rather than as a form of moral discourse. I have personally taught legal ethics that way, and can hardly imagine doing otherwise.

I may say that the recurrent refrain of those who approach the Code from this perspective is that they are mesmerized by "the gap": the gap between the ideal and the actual, between the overt and the latent, between the formal agenda and the real business. The same could be said of those who study law itself.

I do wonder, though, whether the determinants of behavior and the range of moral quandaries are any different from those which lesser breeds without the law have also to consider. Is the old chestnut about defending a guilty person any different from the dilemma which is implicit in all role conflicts? Is the duty of fidelity owed to a client any different from the duty of fidelity to which we respond as teachers or scholars or administrators? Is the duty of candor owed by a barrister to a judge any different from that owed by a senior civil servant or a corporate vice president to the next person up in the hierarchy?

These are all hard cases, but the ready-made outcomes provided by professional codes are unlikely to stimulate ethical analysis. Rather they are likely to deflect or dilute it, to substitute easy answers for difficult questions, to shift attention from reason to rule and from essence to form. I say again, and in conclusion, study them by all means, but do not take them seriously in their own terms.

6

LEGAL ETHICS

2 Commentary: legal ethics – sociology and morality

LESLIE GREEN

Harry Arthurs's paper is both astute and pessimistic. He shows, to my mind persuasively, that there is more ideology than ideal in the implementation of a code of professional ethics for lawyers. But he concludes from this that as teachers and students we would do much better "to study legal ethics in context, from an anthropological or sociological perspective, rather than as a form of moral discourse." The message, I take it, is that moralizing is more or less inert and that, instead of teaching professional ethics or advocating such norms, we should adopt the stance of unmasker. Instead of legal ethics, we should study and teach the sociology of the legal profession. While there is much in this view that I agree with, I do want to dissent at one point. I very much doubt that the sociological perspective provides the right antidote, in either legal education or practice, to the dominant professional ideology.

I am on the whole persuaded by Arthurs's account of the impotence of the various CBA codes. His strategy is to draw our attention to what might be called (if I may commit a sociology) the distinction between the manifest and the latent functions of ethical codes. They purport, on the manifest level, to guide the behavior of those to whom they apply. But their deeper, latent function is one of legitimation. A code makes us feel better about a politically unaccountable class which has wealth, prestige, and power: "it forms part of an overall strategy to secure professional and public belief in the value of the legal profession itself." The real, operative, ethics of the bar have little to do with codes, but are rather the product of professional norms, socialization and so forth.

101

As a descriptive analysis, I think this is largely sound though partly incomplete, for it leaves unexplained at least one interesting fact about lawyers. Though I can offer in its defense nothing but the fruits of casual observation, I think it is a true proposition that, of all the liberal professions, lawyers are the least guided by their professional codes. Doctors, for example, appear to take professional ethics more seriously, and sometimes even find room for ethics review committees within their hospitals and research centers. Why should this be? Of course, I do not doubt that medical ethics may be subjected to the same hard-nosed sociological scrutiny with which Arthurs unmasks his colleagues. But while that may lessen the difference between the two it will not fully eliminate it. What is missing from the descriptive side of Arthurs's analysis is an explanation of why lawyers are so particularly immune to ethics.

Let me offer a suggestion. Lawyers are professional experts in a particular normative system: the law. Every legal system is a comprehensive framework of rights and duties which itself purports to guide behavior, and the study of law is the study of that. In contrast, the study of medicine is not the study of a normative system. Doctors therefore in their professional lives experience confrontation with normative standards which are external to their science. In a hard case about medical treatment or the distribution of health care, what they know about health technology can logically offer them no guidance whatever on the question of what they should do. They must, to make any decision at all, apply an external normative framework: they must ask what is legally required or what is morally required, but not what is medically required. Doctors can therefore never honestly indulge the illusion that their own area of expertise provides general answers about what to do. Lawyers, however, are in exactly the opposite position. They can survive and succeed in their professional aims, and they can settle practical problems, without ever looking beyond the fortress of their professional knowledge. The famous old questions about fidelity to one's clients, the propriety of defending the guilty, or conflicts between personal and professional interests all have *legal* answers, answers provided by the legal system itself. (Sometimes, it is only the answer that whatever is not prohibited is permitted.) These answers are not always clear – they are often highly controversial – but they are answers none the less. A lawyer is therefore generally tempted, given her professional habits, to look to law itself for guidance about how to resolve practical dilemmas. For a lawyer, the correct standard of professional behavior is normally the legal standard.

Consider a simple, but I think revealing, example which I draw more or less at random from a volume directed at the professional audience. In an article on Ontario's "Spills Bill," a lawyer lists a range of options available to a company seeking to control potential losses under the regime of absolute liability for damage caused by toxic substances. Many of his recommendations incorporate straightforward, sensible advice, for example, "Pollutants ought not to be buried on premises owned by the client." But among these somewhat obvious points, one somewhat more devious suggestion particularly struck me. The author writes, "If it is necessary to transport such goods, and if insurance is unavailable in the circumstances, title to the goods should be transferred to a subsidiary company without other assets" (Bates 1986: 48). That is, if you are a company and need to ship, say, dioxins from Toronto to Montreal, first transfer ownership to a fictitious, assetless subsidiary, which cannot therefore profitably be sued in the event of serious environmental disaster. Most non-lawyers reflecting on this advice would probably think that it crosses the line between avoiding liability and evading it. And, if they are like me, they will think that it is immoral deliberately to subvert the legitimate legislative aims of this bill. But when I put this to my legal colleagues, I almost invariably get one of two responses. First, most of them say that a lawyer has an absolute institutional duty to inform her client of anything which might work and might benefit him. Second, inasmuch as they are troubled at all by the example, their critical reaction is generally limited to the interesting *legal* question of whether the proposed strategy would in fact work, of whether or not the courts would pierce the corporate veil and hold the company liable after all. To the question of what one may legitimately do in response to the Spills Bill, they tell us what we may legally get away with.

This reaction, I suggest, is the product of legalism: the view that law is the most important normative order in our society and that, once behavior is certified as not illegal, no further criticism can be brought to bear on it. Law trumps ethics every time. Now, I deplore this attitude, and I am sure that Arthurs would join me in this judgment. Where we may part company, however, is on the question of the appropriate professional and pedagogical response to it. He suggests that since ethical codes are themselves part of the problem they cannot figure in a useful solution and that we should turn from the study of ethics to the study of legal sociology. Now, although the latter is a legitimate subject in its own right, I think that it is ill suited to depose ethics here. For sociology is not a prescriptive science. A callous though intelligent lawyer could, in her spare time or as a hobby, take up the sociology of the profession, without finding anything to mandate a change in her views about the lawyer's appropriate role. She might discover that lawyers are an elite who talk about ethics in order to legitimate their privileges, but nothing within sociology itself would tell her whether to approve or deplore their tactics. To challenge the hegemony of legalism, what we need is not merely a more accurate understanding of that ideology, but a competing normative theory. We need to confront law with a moral framework external to law. Moral reflection is more than an exercise in values-clarification or a ritual confession of bias preliminary to social science. Rather, it is the necessary driving force behind our practical and theoretical concern about how serious decisions should be made. Just as a doctor must, after mastering the technology of healing, face the further and different ethical question of how that art is to be used, the lawyer too must look beyond the fortress of law. My suspicion is that the teaching of legal ethics as if it were a branch of legal sociology will not provide this. We need, in my view, to study and teach it precisely as a branch of ethics and not some other thing. In doing so, of course, we will have to keep our eyes open to the reality which Arthurs so lucidly describes; and perhaps our ambitions should be modest. Above all, we must not simply lapse into what he rightly decries as the "uncritical acceptance of the Code of Professional Conduct, uncritical acceptance of the values and rhetoric, the ideology and symbols of the profession"; and we must not suppose that the professional codes can provide "ready-made outcomes" to hard decisions. But there is space between this uncritical, self-serving ritual and the distant, disengaged perspective of the anthropologist or sociologist. And, in my view, that is precisely the space occupied by practical ethics.

REFERENCE

Bates, T. P. (1986) "Defence Perspective and Loss Control," in S. M. Makuch (ed.) *The Spills Bill*, Toronto: Butterworths (citing an unpublished address by C. Lax).

7

ETHICS AND SOCIAL POLICY

Equality of opportunity: common ground for opposing ideologies

PETER PENZ

ACKNOWLEDGMENTS

This paper has gone through substantial transformation since its initial presentation. Comments at that time, especially from Don MacNiven, David Shugarman, and Leslie Green, were an important impetus for this transformation and are herewith gratefully acknowledged.

OPPOSING POLITICAL IDEOLOGIES, COMMON GROUND, AND DISTRIBUTIVE JUSTICE

The purpose of this paper is to make a case for argument across ideological boundaries. The issue of economic distribution is particularly suitable for this purpose since it involves conflicting interests and is highly contentious, both politically and philosophically. I will argue that it is possible to take seriously the moral concerns both of socialists for equality and needs, and of adherents to capitalist ideas about reward for contribution, incentives, and liberty. In particular, I propose that the time-honored, but inadequately developed, ideal of equality of opportunity is a principle that, although it lends itself to different interpretations, provides a common ground that accommodates the central concerns of these opposing perspectives. Within this common ground the different interpretations and the implications of the principle can be tested, contested, refined, and eventually realized. Moreover, equality of opportunity can lead to policy implications that may be more desirable from both perspectives than the current system of welfare capitalism. (Because this is addressed to a multi-disciplinary readership rather than exclusively or even primarily to philosophers, the discussion will draw on broad schools of thought rather than on the more particular positions of individual philosophers.)

The possibility for common ground for opposing ideologies stems from two considerations. One is that, normally, no simple principle captures all the moral positions of a thoughtful individual. Although we may start out with a simple moral principle, as we engage in moral discussion we are usually forced, by our notions of intellectual consistency, empirical realism, and moral impartiality, into recognizing either a plurality of moral principles or a complex set of qualifications to the simple starting point. This dynamic process of moving to increased adequacy of our moral positions both depends on and is conducive to openness to learning from others or from the exchange with others. The second consideration is that we are all bound together within the same social and political system and, if this system is not to operate on the basis of control through brute force and submission due to fear, it has to have popular support, which in turn requires moral legitimacy. Broadly based moral consent in a system with opposing ideologies requires inter-ideological dialogue, consensus at the level of ground rules, and at least compromise at the level of policy.

Why, however, should this lead to anything other than pragmatic compromises based on concessions in recognition of the power of the different partisans to destroy social peace and functioning? How is a *moral* understanding possible? At a relatively unsophisticated level, this occurs because ideologues or opinion leaders form minorities and have to persuade the relatively uncommitted majority that what they are proposing makes sense morally. (The latter is indicated by the fact that, even when interest groups pursue their self-interest, they typically do so by presenting the advocated policies as being in the public interest and impartially good.) The ideologues thus have to compete using their moral arguments. Moreover, the ideologues – and I am here including not just extremists, but also middle-of-the-road ideologues – presumably have a personal need for moral adequacy. This need may make them open to seriously considering points from opposing positions that the political contest exposes them to.

Openness to increased moral complexity and inter-ideological dialogue not only creates the opportunity for common ground, but also shapes the nature of this common ground. In the simplest terms, if we have two ideological starting points, A and B, and each of them represents a reasonable but partial moral sensibility, then, by introducing the considerations represented by B to position A, and vice versa, these qualifications of ideologies A and B will lead to certain forms of AB. While the relative emphasis of the different aspects of AB may still vary significantly, not only will common ground for dialogue have been attained, but the ideologies will have enriched each other as well as political action by the society as a whole.

How such common ground can be attained will be shown in the context of polar ideological positions concerning distributive justice. It is in this context that the problems of cross-ideological discourse are greatest. Specifically, I am contrasting capitalist and socialist conceptions of justice concerning the distribution of income. The capitalist conception can be boiled down to the principles of liberty and of contribution. As long as there is no state appropriation and property is not acquired by force or theft, then, according to the principle of liberty, as articulated within the capitalist-libertarian tradition, market exchange leads to a just distribution. The contribution principle may serve as a complement or an alternative to the liberty principle. It answers the question of what individuals are entitled to by referring to the contribution that they make to the welfare of others, with the value of this contribution being revealed through the willingness of the beneficiaries to pay for such contributions in the market. In that case poverty is a reflection of an inadequate contribution made to society. Thus, on the basis either of the principle of contribution or of liberty, although poverty is not something good, it does not constitute social injustice.

The core of the socialist conception can be represented by the distributive-justice principles of equality and need. On the basis of either of these socialist principles, poverty is unjust. In the case of the principle of equality, poverty is a manifestation of inequality and thus of injustice. In the case of the principle of need, poverty represents deprivation and, as long as there are others who are well off, it indicates that distribution is not in accordance with need. We thus have diametrically opposed perspectives on distributive justice.

My argument will be structured as follows: I will first take the socialist principle of need fulfillment and compare it with equality of opportunity to show why the latter is more persuasive to adherents to capitalist conceptions of distributive justice. I will then show that equality of opportunity, appropriately interpreted, can be at least as satisfactory from a socialist point of view as need fulfillment. Next, I will argue that the strong interpretation of equality of opportunity that a socialist would require should have considerable moral force for conservative liberals as well. Finally, I will indicate some of the policy implications, both consensual and disputed ones, that emerge from that interpretation of equality of opportunity and make the claim that the basic thrust of these policy implications should be morally more desirable to both sides than the current patterns of welfare capitalism. (It should be noted here, however, that I have not found it possible to deal with the issue of the private ownership of capital and income in the form of profits. I must thus admit that I have thereby omitted what some would claim to be the most contentious distributive issue. Whether it can be resolved by reference to equality of opportunity in the way that this principle is used here must be left for another occasion. In any case, I believe that the argument presented here applies as much to an economy with socialist ownership as it does to a capitalist economy. I have also had to leave aside consideration of the uncompromising libertarian position which is based on an extremely atomistic conception of society. But then the extremes are not the most promising starting points for inter-ideological dialogue.)

OPPORTUNITIES VS. NEEDS I: THE VIEW FROM THE RIGHT

Why should equality of opportunity appeal more to the ideological right than need fulfillment does? Apart from the fact that this appears to be true empirically (I am relying on impressionistic observation here), there are good reasons for this appeal. Those who hold that distributive justice is a matter of reward according to contribution see a complementarity between individuals' contributions to and benefits from society. The needs principle detaches benefits from such contributions. Equality of opportunity, on the other hand, refers to the opportunity to participate in this process of contributing to and benefiting from the division of labor and economic exchange.

Moreover, distribution based wholly or primarily on the needs principle entails either turning contribution into an obligation ("from each according to his ability") or relying on the very optimistic view of human nature according to which it is expected that individuals will want to contribute fully to the welfare of others, including the multitude of strangers in the society, without quid-pro-quo rewards. The capitalist position on distribution is to treat the willingness of individuals to contribute without either economic incentives or compulsion as unreliable. Compulsion, in turn, is rejected on grounds of liberty. Liberty is seen as requiring that contribution be voluntary so that it is up to individuals whether and to what extent they participate in the system of contributions and benefits. As a prescription, this again is compatible with equality of opportunity. Thus, the concern to steer between unrealistic idealism about human nature, on the one hand, and compulsion, on the other, leads to the strong connection between contribution and benefits, and this connection appears better protected by the principle of equality of opportunity than by the principle of need fulfillment.

Given the inferiority of the needs principle relative to the opportunity principle from the point of view of the ideological right, are there positive reasons for the latter to accept equality of opportunity as an ideal? Certainly there are reasons for protecting opportunities. Liberty implies a range of choice, that is, a range of opportunities. The contribution principle, too, requires that there are opportunities for making contributions. *Equality* of opportunity may not be of paramount importance in capitalist conceptions of distributive justice, but certain basic notions of equality are, in fact, accepted on the whole by adherents to this perspective. It needs to be recognized by socialists that the adherents of capitalist ideals are not opposed to equality as such, but only to certain strategies for pursuing equality. It is true that the latter qualification is important and will lead to a much weaker form of equality of opportunity than the socialist form, but common ground is attained when both sides accept the same general principle. Heated argument and sharp divisions are still possible over the interpretation of that principle, but at least the initial basis for discourse has been established. The discourse can then consist of the various ideological parties attempting to persuade each other (or the uncommitted audience) to take their respective concerns regarding equality of opportunity seriously, whether it is incentives, freedom or enabling conditions. (That there are compelling reasons for adherents to the capitalist conceptions of distributive justice to adopt the strong version of equality of opportunity is argued later on.)

LIMITS TO THE NEEDS PRINCIPLE

Having indicated briefly why equality of opportunity is an ideal that is potentially acceptable to adherents to capitalist conceptions of distributive justice, I will now develop the basis of the argument that socialists should conduct their public advocacy in terms of equality of opportunity rather than in terms of the fulfillment of needs. In particular, I will introduce various considerations that are taken to be important within the capitalist conceptions and show why socialists should take them seriously as difficulties for the needs principle. Eventually, I will also show that equality of opportunity is potentially at least as egalitarian an ideal as the needs principle and that it can point to a more radically egalitarian system of policies. (All this is not to say that discussions in terms of needs should be avoided. I myself am deeply involved in theoretical research on needs. What the position here means is that, since equality of opportunity and fulfillment of needs are closely related and since the conservative-liberal critics of the welfare state are more amenable to appeals to equality of opportunity, it is in terms of this principle that those concerned with the plight of the poor should conduct their efforts to persuade the critics. Moreover, a review of the traditional needs approach, in light of considerations that emerge from the criterion of equality of opportunity, will serve to improve that approach.)

Given the centrality of the ideal of equality to socialism, a quick clarification of the relationship between the principles of need and equality is in order. The two principles are to be seen as complementary. Needs are remediable deficiencies of individuals which are responsible for their falling short of some level of adequacy, usually with respect to living conditions, but also to productive capacity. Thus, varying needs are fulfilled (through varying provisions) in order to come as close to equality as possible. Once deprivation with respect to this level of adequacy is eliminated, either the principles of need and equality are held not to be the primary principles of distributive justice any more, or we adopt radical egalitarianism and thus go beyond the needs principle. Up to this point, however, the needs principle stands in the service of the principle of equality. Rather than elaborate the concept of needs here more fully, I will leave that to occur in the process of raising certain difficulties for the needs principle that bring in the capitalist considerations regarding distribution.

The first is a phenomenon that is occasionally labeled the "deprivation monster." It refers to needs that are so difficult to meet that the attempt to do so practically gobbles up all of society's resources. Certain disabilities, including some kinds of mental illness, simply cannot be remedied. While it may be possible in a number of cases to provide compensatory assistance, such as seeing-eye dogs, wheel-chairs, prostheses, and protective environments, such measures cannot bring all dimensions of the quality of life for such individuals to a level that we would consider adequate for ourselves. We could, of course, redeploy our resources such that at least minor improvements for such individuals are made, even if it means huge sacrifices for the rest of us. This is what would be required by a strict maximin (or "difference") principle of distribution, according to which it is the lot of the worst-off that is to be maximally improved. However, there are reasons why the strict application of this principle may not be appropriate.

If we use the thought experiment of a social contract to deal with this issue, then we could well conclude that the participants in the social contract, acting wholly impartially, would, in the face of the high social costs of reducing deprivation by small amounts, arrive at distributive rules that would stop short

112

of a complete maximin distribution. This could hold even when we allow the social contractors to be not only impartial but also benevolent to a considerable degree. Another consideration is the question of what a complete maximin distribution would do to another basic socialist value (although a non-distributive one), namely solidarity. Such a distribution might well strain the perception of many citizens that social arrangements are, in general, for everyone's benefit. This may reflect a certain element of selfishness and it may well be that the issue here is one of distributive feasibility rather than distributive justice. Nevertheless, these points do mean that some inequality, beyond what is most beneficial to the worst-off, may have to be accepted when needs that are impossible or extremely costly to meet are involved. This difficulty does not actually bring either of the two capitalist principles of distribution into play, but merely the general capitalist acceptance of inequality.

A difficulty that does call forth one of these principles is that the preference priorities of individual beneficiaries may not accord with the needs attributed to them. Needs are not the same as wants. Needs are those interests of individuals that society agrees constitute some form of entitlement *vis-à-vis* society. A fanatic hobbyist may insist that the materials for his hobby are more important to him than food or health care, but if the rest of us, collectively, recognize only the latter as needs and not the former, we have a divergence between recognized needs and first wants. This brings in the issue of liberty for the intended beneficiaries. Libertarian considerations suggest that individuals should not be coerced into receiving need provisions, so that the state is to provide only the *opportunities* for need fulfillment. Moreover, some needs should be met in convertible form, such as money, so that the beneficiary has some opportunity to use her or his own judgment about priorities.

Similarly, liberty can arise as an issue in the logistics of determining and providing for needs. Such determination and provision can be highly intrusive and constitute serious interference into the privacy of the intended beneficiaries. The more finely tuned the application of the needs principle, the more it will be necessary for state officials to assess, monitor and review the conditions of individuals. This, too, is a case for relatively general forms of both assessment of and provision for needs.

A third liberty issue arises with respect to the providers for needs. Does a doctor have an obligation to respond to every health need that she has appropriate skills for? Are even former doctors morally obligated to give "according to their ability" when faced with health needs? If there are no limits to such obligations, need-providers will have less choice (and perhaps less leisure) than those who select economic roles that cater to wants that are not needs. This would create an inequity with respect to liberty. It would also introduce an incentive problem in that it would create a disincentive to becoming a need-provider. The answer presumably is to make society as a whole, i.e. government, responsible for the provision of needs, including the creation of a fair system of opportunities and incentives for individuals to serve to fulfill these needs. The obligations of individuals then are limited to those more specific ones that they have contracted for (which may, of course, include the general professional obligation to provide emergency assistance). Without such limits, the principle "from each according to his ability" is equivalent to slavery, albeit slavery for the sake of distributive justice (when the ability principle is combined with the needs principle) rather than privilege.

Contribution considerations, too, limit the scope of the needs principle. First of all, there is the question of whether it is just to provide equally for two persons, one of whom makes no effort to contribute to the means for society to meet needs while the other gives her all to do so. In the first instance, this is an issue of desert or just reward. But it can also be treated as an issue of equality. Assuming that no other relevant differences are involved, the first person is better off than the second even though they have equal consumption. The inequality lies in the fact that the second person has less leisure than the first person.

Apart from the issue of justice regarding productive effort, there is also that of incentives. Society's capacity to provide for needs has to be protected and developed. This requires that there should be not only compensation for forgoing leisure but also reward for individuals who adjust to changing production

114

requirements caused by changes in needs or in production and service possibilities, for having equipped themselves to become more productive and for finding new ways of fulfilling needs. The requirement for such incentives will put a limit on how much society can distribute strictly and directly on the basis of need. There may also be a need for another kind of incentive, namely making available, on a voluntary basis, savings (i.e. entitlements to resources) for investment to extend or improve society's capacity to fulfill needs.

The extent to which such incentives have to be provided in the form of purchasing power depends, of course, on the pattern of motivation of the populace. The more altruistic producers are, the less need there will be for incentives; mere information about needs will suffice. How altruistic it is possible for us to become through appropriate socialization (upbringing, education, public appeals) is something I cannot say. Those socialist countries that have attempted this seem to have had limited success and have not been able to dispense with incentives altogether. After having reduced the magnitude of material incentives, some are now increasing it to stimulate the growth of productive capacity. Another alternative to material incentives is reward in a form other than purchasing power, such as pleasant and stimulating working conditions, conviviality in production, status, and power. Although that may be appropriate in particular instances, as a general solution it merely converts material inequality into another kind of inequality.

Incentives could, of course, be dispensed with, at least in principle, if we were to enforce the principle of "from each according to his ability." But that violates liberty in a particularly serious way. It is one thing to coercively redistribute purchasing power; it is quite another to require each of us to make productive contributions according to society's (in effect, the state's) understanding of the abilities of each of us and the consumption needs and preferences of all of us. Moreover, it would be extremely difficult to determine what people's abilities are and to make them turn them to productive use when they want to withhold them. Those difficulties mean that the supervisory and coercive apparatus has to be very elaborate and socially costly, and even then productivity will remain far below potential because of popular resistance. Wholesale coercion of productive contribution can thus be expected to impair society's capacity to provide for needs.

OPPORTUNITIES VS. NEEDS II: AN ARGUMENT ADDRESSED TO THE LEFT

It is now clear that distribution according to needs has to be constrained by considerations of liberty, of just reward (with respect to compensation for sacrifices for production) and incentives, all of them central considerations in the capitalist conception of distributive justice. There is, however, still the question of the relationship between the needs principle so constrained and the principle of equality of opportunity that I have put forward as the candidate for common ground between socialist and capitalist perspectives. There are two aspects to the relationship. One is that needs can be satisfactorily presented in terms of equality of opportunities. The other is that needs arise from society's failure or inability to fulfill equality of opportunity.

The relationship between the principles of need and of equality of opportunity becomes apparent when we consider the relationship of each to equality of well-being. The needs principle, it was mentioned on pp. 108–9, refers to what is required by each individual to bring her or him to a level of adequacy with respect to well-being. Equality of opportunity will, for the time being, be discussed exclusively in its strong version, defined as the equalization of unequal productive endowments and opportunities for which we as individuals cannot be held responsible. Equalizing productive endowments and opportunities means that everyone is equally enabled to reach a certain level of well-being, even under a system that rewards according to contribution. Thus, what the needs principle requires can be achieved by fulfilling the principle of equality of opportunity. Needs can be defined as what is required for equality of opportunity.

Rather than weakening the needs principle, this definition actually makes it more demanding. The reason is that the strong version of equality of opportunity does not confine itself to the elimination of deficiencies with respect to necessities or an "adequate" level of well-being, but goes beyond it. Everyone is equally entitled to the productive endowments and opportunities necessary for whatever level of affluence is generally possible in the particular society.

It is true that social efficiency may require compromises with the strong version of equality of opportunity. If the problem of the deprivation monster applies to well-being needs, it applies with even greater force to the equalization of productive capacities. Such equalization may simply be impossible, or it may be socially inefficient, in the sense that bringing particularly disadvantaged individuals to a level of productivity equal to that of others would take more from society's resources (both material and human) than it would eventually add in production. The morally responsible solution is to convert entitlements with respect to equality of opportunity to entitlements with respect to consumption. Does this mean sacrificing justice to efficiency? The answer is no, in that justice is protected by maintaining the entitlement of the individual. At the same time efficiency is protected by converting the entitlement from one form to another.

Does it then still make sense for a socialist to make her case in terms of the liberal principle of equality of opportunity? The reason it does is that meeting well-being needs as such can now be treated as an obligation of society to the individual resulting from its failure to meet the requirements of equality of opportunity. In other words, it is compensation for societal failure. This seems to me to be a stronger claim than a direct need claim. Moreover, need claims are constrained by standards of adequacy, whose political determination may turn out to be quite ungenerous, while equality of opportunity is conceptually not constrained in this way.

WEAK VS. STRONG VERSIONS OF EQUALITY OF OPPORTUNITY: AN ARGUMENT ADDRESSED TO THE RIGHT

A question that may have been nagging the reader is whether the common acceptance of a very general principle by two politically contesting sides is an advance over competition between different principles, when the alternative versions of the general principle can be as different as the weak and the strong versions of equality of opportunity. So far I have discussed only the strong version. The weak version confines itself to equalizing the opportunities external to individuals; it does not include the equalization of individuals or of individuals' capacities. What I will argue is that, in order to overcome the inherent weaknesses of the weak version, it is necessary to move to the strong version. This argument can be made in terms of the general pattern of considerations of the adherents to the capitalist conception of distributive justice.

There are at least three important versions of the principle of equality of opportunity. Version (1) refers to equal opportunity to *compete on the basis of capacity and willingness to be productive* in a particular economic role. This version has two further variants whose distinction is important. One is that, given a set of productive roles, such equality of opportunity must prevail. Here the principle creates obligations of fairness only with respect to the filling of productive roles, not with respect to their creation. The other, stronger variant is that equal opportunity to be productive requires society to ensure that such opportunities are available. As a minimum, it requires the full employment of all those able to be productive. Beyond that, it can be taken to require that the pattern of productive opportunities is such that individuals are not underemployed, in light of their skills and the interests of consumers. A good argument can, I believe, be made for the second variant, but the focus here will be less on the issue of whether the range of choice should be part of the criterion of equality of opportunity; it will rather be on the issue of the source of a person's productive capacity.

Version (2) of equality of opportunity refers to the equal opportunity to *acquire productive capacities*. In the first instance, this means equality of educational and training opportunities. Again there are weaker and stronger variants. The weakest takes the educational and other skill development opportunities as fixed and merely requires fair competition for them on the basis of intellectual merit. A stronger variant is that, even though the more talented may receive different education and training from the less talented, they do not get more education and training. This variant can be further strengthened by referring more broadly to environmental conditions that affect the conversion of innate capacities and propensities into skills and requiring compensatory discrimination in education to equalize overall environmental opportunities for individuals by providing advantages that compensate for other environmental disadvantages, such as cultural deprivation.

Version (3), the strongest version of the principle, is equality of opportunity *to be productive* as such. This means that everyone has the opportunity to be as productive as everyone else. Inequalities in rewards then are due merely to individuals' choices about how much leisure they are willing to sacrifice in order to employ their productive capacities in contributing to society's production. Since it requires the actual equalization of productive capacities – capacities that do not need to be the same but have to be equivalent in terms of earning power (or, more generally, the power to reap benefits, including attractive working conditions) – it goes beyond equal opportunities to acquire such productive capacities. In fact, it requires compensatory discrimination in favor of those with innate disadvantages regarding productive capacities, certainly at the level of environmental opportunities to convert talent into skills and perhaps even at the level of the structure of and access to jobs.

Which of these conceptions of equality of opportunity is morally to be preferred? If society's goods and services are to be distributed according to the contributions of its members to the production of these goods and services, then that is presumably because it is up to each individual to decide to what extent and in what manner to make such a contribution. It is up to each person in the sense that each person is responsible for the decision. That means it has to be under the person's control. What is not under the individual's control is not something that he or she can be held responsible for. What then is it that the individual can be held responsible for regarding productive contributions? They can be held responsible for what they do with their productive capacities and, at the developmental stage, perhaps also for what they did with their innate talents in terms of skill development. But they cannot be held responsible for their innate talents or for the component in their productive capacities which is due to their

119

innate talents or to environmental influences beyond their control.

Which conception of equality of opportunity fits this image of personal responsibility? Actually, none of the versions spelled out does so entirely. Certainly, version (1), equality of opportunity to compete, neglects all those factors influencing earnings that were mentioned as being beyond the control of individuals. Version (2), equality of opportunity to acquire productive capacities, is also too weak because it does not recognize the innate component in productive capacities, while version (3), equality of opportunity to be productive, is too strong because it neglects the fact that productive capacity depends in part on individuals' prior choices about acquiring skills.

This suggests a principle that is a kind of hybrid of versions (2) and (3). It is the equal opportunity to become productive. This is stronger than version (2) in that it requires overcoming inequalities in innate capacities, but it is weaker than (3) in that it allows inequalities due to differential effort to acquire skills. In other words, it stipulates inequality with respect to whatever is not under the individual's control. This is what I will refer to as the *responsibility version of equality of opportunity*.

With respect to past decisions to acquire skills, it is important not to overemphasize individual responsibility. First of all, many skill acquisition choices, or at least choices about prerequisites to skill acquisition, are made at an early age, when the individual cannot be expected to be fully responsible for his or her choices. Either they do make their own choices but their lack of maturity makes it morally improper to hold them fully responsible for them or they are made, on their behalf, by parents or, in the case of compulsory education, by the state, in which case they are not under the control of the individual. Secondly, even where skill acquisition decisions are made at a more advanced level of maturity, the level of uncertainty about the future earning power of prospective entrants to alternative occupations is normally quite high and depends on the general social and economic conditions that society's economic management generates. There is thus a case for joint individual and collective responsibility for the productive capacities and the resulting earning power that individuals come to hold.

Moreover, society may inadvertently fail to provide equal opportunity to become productive or decide it is socially too costly to do so. This places the responsibility for differences in productive capacities on society and is, as I argued earlier, the basis for consumption entitlements on the part of those who are thus disadvantaged.

BASIC POLICY IMPLICATIONS: COMMON GROUND AND RESIDUAL DISAGREEMENT

At the policy level it is also possible to establish common ground, but at this level the disagreements that remain within the common ground become more clearly apparent. Here I will merely make some general points regarding the general direction of policy development based on equality of opportunity and then raise some more particular policy issues and try to indicate what could be considered to be common ground and what would be grist for the mill of political debate within the area of general agreement. In particular, I will focus on the policy implications of, respectively, the egalitarian concerns of socialists and the liberty and incentive concerns of those committed to the market system.

The focus on equality of opportunity has a particular implication for the relationship between social efficiency (roughly the maximization of living standards) and equity (their distribution). In welfare capitalism, on the whole, efficiency is pursued first in the economic sphere, which generates a distribution of living standards, to which equity corrections are then made through what can be conceived of as a second stage of social policy. In other words, efficiency is pursued first and only then equity. The requirement of equality of opportunity is the reverse. Individuals are first equitably equipped to participate in the process of production, which is then to be pursued in an efficient manner. The reason is that equality of opportunity, interpreted in the strong sense of equality with respect to whatever is not under the control of individuals, establishes an entitlement that is much more basic than mere entitlement to welfare assistance, whether in the form of means-tested and closely monitored payments to the poor or, alternatively, entitlements in the form of social

121

insurance benefits or guaranteed income payments. It goes beyond such welfare measures in that the entitlements are not merely minimum-consumption rights, but are rights to preparation for and participation in the productive system, which then pursues efficiency on the basis of incentives aimed at freely choosing individuals. Only when society finds it impossible or inefficient to satisfy (all or part of) the productivity entitlement is (all or part of) it converted into equivalent consumption rights.

The following brief elaboration of the basic policy implications will be to make three points. (1) The broad implications for labor market policy are relatively straightforward and conflict free. (2) More contentious, but not without reasonable prospects for convergence toward consensus, are the issues of entitlement to educational resources as the basis for productivity and of entitlement to income supplementation as compensation for failures with respect to equality of opportunity. (3) The most serious problems arise with respect to the conflict between freedom and incentives for *families* and equal opportunity for *individuals*.

(1) The first requirement is a strong commitment to full employment. Although concessions with respect to other policy goals may be necessary, full employment should be important to a conservative-liberal position, as long as it is a moral one and not merely a matter of defending class interests. Substantial unemployment makes equality of opportunity impossible in anything but the weakest sense, namely the equal opportunity to compete for limited opportunities to be productive. Workers in general will be disadvantaged in their ability to bargain with employers on working conditions and those who are unemployed have no actual opportunities to be productive, let alone equality with respect to such opportunities. A concern for efficiency, productivity, incentives, and liberty, if it is to be impartial with respect to social classes, must put the highest priority on full employment.

In addition, labor market policy must make earnings differentials its target. It is true that equal opportunity does not lead to equality of earnings as such; full-time workers are entitled to more remuneration than part-time workers.

122

Moreover, even with respect to hourly earning rates, inequalities constitute incentives for performance effort, for skill acquisition and for adjustment to changing demand and supply conditions. For that reason, the morally appropriate policy to implement equality of opportunity is not legislation on equality of earning rates, but a more qualified and indirect egalitarian policy.

It might be referred to as a *structurally egalitarian* labour market policy. It would consist of taking inequalities of earning rates as signals of the need for government action. To be justified in terms of equality of opportunity, in its responsibility version, these inequalities must be justified on the grounds that they reflect more onerous working conditions or more onerous education and training. Inequalities so justified do not violate equality with respect to a broader conception of personal welfare, namely one that includes working conditions and extends over a longer period of time, including educational and training preparation. On the other hand, differences in earning rates may reflect sluggish market adjustment to changing patterns of demand and supply for labor, including failures or limits of government policy with respect to equipping workers for the new patterns. For that reason, they should be treated by the government as signals that the market incentives may not be sufficient and the government may have to step in to make it easier for workers to move from sectors (occupations, industries, areas) with surpluses to sectors with shortages. Both the provision of services such as vacancy information, mobility assistance and training programs, and regulatory policies that serve to prevent and tear down barriers to mobility resulting from monopoly power by the privileged, whether they are professional associations, labor unions or enterprises, are needed for such a strategy.

Such a policy strategy cannot be expected to produce complete equality, but it can certainly limit inequalities. The differences in earnings between janitors and managers, for example, would be contained by keeping the supply of janitors limited relative to demand, and by offering actual and potential janitors opportunities to equip themselves to move into more remunerative lines of work, while an effort would be made to keep the supply of potential managers relatively plentiful, by aiming productivity improvement services also at potential managers. This is a strategy that maintains freedom of choice regarding productive roles as well as price signals that indicate where labor is particularly valuable in production and ultimately to consumers, while it constantly works to reduce inequality.

(2) Another level of policy that shapes the distribution of earnings is that of education. Educational resources can be distributed between children according to either of the following principles: (i) the principle of efficiency, according to which educational resources should go to those children who will benefit most in terms of productivity improvements; (ii) the principle of equality of educational resources, according to which each child is entitled to the same level of educational resources; (iii) the principle of equality of opportunity to become productive, according to which children are entitled to the resources necessary to bring them to some productivity norm. According to the argument I have presented on pp. 118–20, justice requires principle (iii). That principle would ensure that reward according to contribution would not be affected by differences in ability and would instead be for that part of a contribution which is under the individual's control, namely his or her effort.

At the same time, I argued on p. 117 that allocation of resources according to the efficiency principle is justified as long as the resulting violations of equality of opportunity are compensated for by equivalent entitlements. This constitutes a synthesis of efficiency and justice. It allows access to education on the basis of the ability to benefit from it in terms of productivity. (Other purposes of education come, of course, into play as well and may make education more egalitarian than what would follow from the efficiency principle alone. For example, participation in and preparation for production is to be assessed not only in terms of productivity and the resulting consumption, but also in terms of the sense of belonging and personal usefulness that it gives individuals.)

While it provides scope for efficiency considerations, this synthesis of principles also sets up entitlement to income supplementation of earnings, not on the basis of need, but on

124

the basis that society has failed to provide, or has set aside, equality of opportunity. What does this mean for the redistribution of earnings? If all inequalities in earning rates were attributed to inequality of opportunity, such redistribution would have to eliminate all earning inequalities. Two considerations weigh against such a policy. One is that not all earning inequalities are due to inequality of opportunity; some could be due to unequal effort to make use of educational and training opportunities, to adjust to changing demand and supply conditions or to perform on the job. The second is that such radical redistribution would destroy all incentives. At the same time, the fact that educational policy involves deviations from equal opportunity to become productive means that there is certainly some inequality of opportunity. This in turn means that there should be at least some income supplementation, but less than fully egalitarian redistribution. Conservative liberals and socialists will probably differ on the extent of redistribution, but, recognizing each other's legitimate moral concerns, both groups must reject the extremes.

(3) So far, I have discussed policies as though individuals, including children, were solitary students, workers, and consumers not living within families. The introduction of the family unit creates important complications and, in particular, conflicts between liberty and incentives for families, on the one hand, and social justice for individuals, in the form of equal opportunity, on the other. The following are some forms that this conflict can take. Liberty for individuals and families presumably should include the freedom of parents to abstain from consumption for the sake of an inheritance for their children; this is also an incentive for saving and contributing to society's ability to accumulate capital. Yet this is one of the most serious sources of inequality of opportunity. Similarly, liberty and efficiency incentives are arguments for parents' freedom to choose how much consumption to forgo in order to help their children to develop and acquire skills and to choose among different educational institutions, thereby also creating incentives for those institutions to do their best. Unequal ability and willingness of parents to make sacrifices for their children and to assess educational institutions is another source of inequality

of opportunity. Finally, equality of opportunity may require various forms of state assistance to families with children, such as income support or day care; yet this may be deemed to undermine incentives for couples to restrain their procreation to a level commensurate with their earnings.

As far as incentives are concerned, this is in the first instance an empirical question. To what extent is family size a function of state support? To what extent does the opportunity to transmit material wealth to the next generation affect saving? But it is also a moral question. Is it moral to make the opportunities of children dependent on the capacities and preferences of their parents? Should the incentives apply to parents on behalf of their children, or should the incentives apply to the children themselves, once they are mature enough to respond to them? Similarly, is the liberty of parents more important than equality of opportunity among the next generation?

Here, I fear, the divergence in policy positions between the right and the left will be particularly great. An emphasis on the primacy of equality of opportunity will lead to close to 100% taxation of inheritance, access to education on the basis of the ability to benefit from it (rather than familial conditions), state support for families with children and, if necessary, the state assuming a role in generating savings for capital growth. An emphasis on liberty and incentives, on the other hand, will legitimize inheritance, provide for greater familial choice regarding education, and emphasize familial responsibility for the needs of children. The two positions represent fundamentally different views about the nature of parenthood. According to the first view, parenthood is a form of social contribution entitled to reward, while in the second view it is a form of consumption chosen over other possible forms of consumption, such as traveling or expensive entertaining. The latter view reflects a rather atomistic conception of society and represents a willingness to let the conditions of the next generation and thus of the continuation of the society hinge on individual choices as opposed to collective choices. On this set of issues, I suspect there is no apparent ideological convergence, and their resolution, if it is not forestalled by the exercise of power, may have to depend on the moral persuasiveness to the citizenry at large of the alternative positions in the dialogical contest.

CONCLUSION

At the beginning of the paper I argued that common moral ground between opposing ideologies can be found by doing something that ought to be done in any case to make the moral positions satisfactory. The proposed process is that the initially simple ideological position be exposed to the central concerns of opposing ideological positions. As a result one should expect some degree of moral convergence, which may then be sufficient to provide the basis for dialogue and even some degree of policy consensus. With respect to distributive justice, equality of opportunity offers a basis for such convergence, but it has to be interpreted in a strong sense, i.e. equality of opportunity to become productive. The equal-productivity requirement is relaxed for the sake of efficiency only by converting that entitlement into a compensatory consumption entitlement. The policy implications, which point to an egalitarian economy that also emphasizes liberty and incentives, should be more attractive to both sides than the prevailing welfare capitalism. This common ground, however, still provides considerable room for moral disagreement, especially with respect to the conflict between familial self-reliance and equality of opportunity for the next generation.

8

MEDICAL ETHICS
The basis of medical ethics

H. A. BASSFORD

Most texts in medical ethics begin with a survey of ethical theory. They either elaborate the various "isms" (Kantianism, utilitarianism, etc.), or examine important general moral principles (autonomy, non-maleficence, etc.). These principles and outlooks are then used to analyze moral problems arising in the practice of medicine. Discussions of this sort are often very useful, for there are many moral problems in medicine resolvable by direct application of universal moral considerations. But they are not sufficient to provide an ethics of medicine, for they do not capture those important moral considerations which are generic to medicine and which arise from the nature and goals of medical practice itself. In this essay I shall begin to develop the "role-specific" norms of medicine, and to analyze the way in which they interact with general moral norms. My goal is to start providing a basis for what could properly be called a medical ethics.

PROFESSIONAL ETHICS IN GENERAL

Before talking specifically about medical ethics, however, I wish to look generally at the notion of any professional ethic. It is worth noting first why morality is important in a professional setting. The key factor is that any professional practice involves complex knowledge and highly developed technical skills. The traditional professions, such as law, medicine, and engineering, all have long study periods, needed to allow the mastery of difficult material. This knowledge and skill refer to matters considered crucially important to the members of a society,

128

either because they deal with basic human needs or because they are crucial to providing some of the benefits of technological society. Thus, for example, physicians tend to the sick and engineers make it possible to build safe bridges.

These facts suggest three reasons why it is important that the professional have a high level of morality. First, because of the complexity of their skills, we, as laypeople, are extremely dependent upon their good will. We go to professionals because they provide services crucial to our well-being, which we cannot provide for ourselves. If such dependencies are to be socially decent and productive, they cannot proceed on the basis of *caveat emptor*. Rather, professionals must see themselves as accepting a fiduciary obligation.

Second, more than a morally proper attitude is needed. Because of the complexity of the technical skills, there will have to be complex decisions made, which will require more than technical competence. Think of the neo-natal unit. Very premature children can now be saved, but often at high cost in terms of physical and mental handicaps. In these cases decisions about whether and how to treat have extremely serious moral implications. Technical complexity is often accompanied by moral complexity, and because of this it is important for professionals to have highly developed moral skills.

Third, because of the importance of their skills to society, and because of the dedication required to learn and maintain them, professionals receive economic rewards and positions of power and authority. They therefore have the potential for providing great benefits or great harms in social planning and policy.

Given this, it is appropriate to investigate what sorts of ethical knowledge professionals should have. This can be schematized by distinguishing between what I term "general" and "role-specific" moral considerations. A general moral problem is one which is most appropriately solved by the application of universal moral considerations. Take the case of a physician who has several patients who are candidates for kidney transplant, all of whom meet the requisite medical criteria. If an adequate number of kidneys are not available, then the physician faces the dilemma of deciding who should receive the transplant. This is a complex and agonizing decision to make, but at this point it does not require any further considerations specific to medicine. Rather it is an example of a general problem of distributive justice, namely the question of what criteria are appropriate for distributing scarce resources. Ethics classes have traditionally discussed this problem through the example of whom to save in the lifeboat. They could bring the discussion closer to current reality, but invoke the same philosophical considerations, by looking at questions of the allocation of organs for transplant.

Many ethical dilemmas which arise in professional settings are of this general sort; they are problems in a profession, but not from the profession. Accordingly, it is important that professionals have a thorough general moral knowledge if they are to successfully solve many of the moral problems which will arise in their practice. This knowledge is not different in kind from that which any concerned citizen should have, nor will decisions based upon it differ in kind in professional settings from those which any reflective member of society will be able to make, no matter what that person's station happens to be. It is worth noting, though, that gaining general moral knowledge may be an especially difficult problem for some professionals. In many cases their whole lives are devoted to technical training, and are lived in hybrid environments. They often do not have the life experience of normal reflective citizens, and so do not have the practical basis for good moral intuition that others do. Because of this it is most important that professions see to it that their educational programs be imbued with a moral dimension.

General moral knowledge is not enough, however, for the practice of each profession will give rise to moral norms specific to that profession. These are what I call "role-specific" norms. They arise from the social role which the profession plays or from the nature of the profession itself. Given their conceptual tie to the nature or role of any given profession, role-specific norms play a central part in a profession's moral prescriptions. Let me elaborate upon this. All professions are role-oriented. They exist in order to play certain social roles and to further certain social purposes. They are in fact defined in terms of their purposes. As a teacher of philosophy, for example, my role is to help students learn the history, skills, and relevance of the discipline. This not only describes what it is for me to be a teacher, it also provides the basis for determining my value as a teaching professional. It sets up the role-specific norm which I should use to guide and evaluate my work; i.e. something like: "provide accurate philosophical information in such a way that students can learn it and benefit from it."

This of course is only a bare beginning toward developing the role-specific norms of education, but it illustrates how to go about generating an ethic for any given profession. One should first study the practice of a profession to determine its basic purposes. This will allow the statement of the basic role-specific norms of that profession. One should then look and see whether there are subsidiary role-specific norms necessary to accomplish the goals expressed by the basic norms. For example, to teach philosophy to students it is necessary that I be highly knowledgeable about philosophy, which implies the need for rigorous training and evaluation procedures for philosophers. Finally, it is important to see how the given profession's values fit into the general scheme of human values, and to look at how the role-specific norms of the profession should interact with general moral norms. For example, as I shall discuss in detail later, health professionals must decide what to do when their concern for their patient's health suggests a certain procedure, but their patient does not comply. Here the general norm of personal autonomy is in conflict with the medical norm of patient health, necessitating discussion about how the health professions should rank these values. These discussions will undoubtedly be protracted and complex. Indeed discussions of this sort will regularly arise, given the ongoing evolution of society and professions. It would be illusory to think that the norms of any profession could be completely and finally stated. None the less, the steps I have outlined will allow the development of an organic, integrated core of a profession's ethics, which will allow clear evaluation of much behavior in professional practice, and which will provide a useful basis for discussion of newly arising dilemmas. In the rest of this essay I shall begin this undertaking with respect to medical ethics, and in particular with respect to the ethics of the practicing physician.

THE PATIENT-HEALTH NORM OF MEDICINE

The basic role-specific norm of medicine is quickly derivable from the idea of medicine itself. The primary purpose of medicine is, to quote from the *Oxford English Dictionary*, "the restoration and preservation of health." This quote does not, of course, do more than begin to characterize the richly textured concept of medicine, and a much more detailed analysis would be required to develop all of the role-specific norms of medicine.[1] None the less it is clear that the goal of health preservation and restoration is central to the concept of medicine, which is why it has been placed in the forefront of considerations in professional statements of medical ethics, from Hippocrates to the present time.[2]

Now of course having the goal of promoting health does not qualify a person to truthfully claim to be a medical practitioner. Unless one has a certain minimum (and the minimum is pretty high) of technical knowledge about the means of and proficiency in preserving and restoring health one cannot accurately be called a health provider. One is rather a crackpot or a charlatan. Beyond this minimum the question is not whether one is a doctor or not, but whether one is a good or bad doctor. Those physicians who have great knowledge and skill, and who use it to promote the health of their patients, are good doctors. Those who have lesser knowledge and skill, or who do not consistently promote the health of their patients, are poor doctors. What is to be noted here is how evaluative terms become appropriate as one gives a description of the nature of medicine.

Having evaluative terms does not mean the discovery of a role-specific norm for medicine, however, for normative language need not involve moral evaluation. It takes considerable skill to be a good safe-cracker, but being a good safe-cracker is hardly a morally good thing. In the case of medicine, however, there is no doubt that the promotion of health is a moral good. First, health is a value in itself. It would appear on most people's lists of basic human values. Second, health is of value as a means to the attainment of the good human life. It would be at least very difficult for most people to obtain their life goals without the possession of health. Third, individual health is important in terms of general social goals. Healthy individuals will, generally, be better able to contribute to building a society than unhealthy ones. Accordingly, we can say that the good doctor is more than a proficient technician. The good doctor is acting in accordance with a basic moral norm for medical practice: "So act as to promote the health of your patient." The patient-health norm, which physicians have historically seen as their core moral obligation, is thus seen to be immediately derived from the nature of medicine itself.

Before proceeding it is necessary to consider a conceptual challenge to the meaningfulness of the patient-health norm. Varieties of the argument have appeared in recent books by Ivan Illich (1977), Ian Kennedy (1981) and Thomas Szasz (1977), all well-known critics of the over-medicalization of society. They argue that the terms "illness" and "health" are inherently vague, and not capable of precise definition. In conjunction with this, they argue that the criteria for applying the terms "health" and "illness" vary from culture to culture, or from one historical period to another, and reflect changes in social values rather than developments in scientific knowledge. This is thought to imply that "illness" is not "a descriptive term, applied to a set of objective facts," and that when doctors judge someone to be ill or well, they are not making an objective judgment, but are rather engaged in an exercise of power involving at most the application of social mores (Kennedy 1981: 7). If this argument is sound, then the role-specific norm of patient health is empty of meaning and the medical profession has been seriously in error in giving it pride of place in its moral thinking.

In fact, however, the argument is not sound. Consider first the claim that the operative terms are vague. In a sense this is true, but only in the way it would be true about most general empirical terms. Most such terms have many central cases, instances to which the terms clearly apply, and many contrary cases, instances to which the terms clearly do not apply. Further, most terms also have many borderline cases, and in such cases it is difficult to decide whether or not the terms should be used. But the fact that general terms have indistinct borders does not imply that they do not have perfectly objective empirical meanings.

H. L. A. Hart (1961: Chapter 7) has argued this point decisively. Take the straightforward by-law, "No vehicles are allowed in public parks." Now, if I drive my car into a park for a picnic out of the trunk, I am clearly violating the by-law, and if I walk into a park, I am clearly not violating the by-law. But what if I ride my bicycle into a park, or land in a helicopter, or come in by ambulance to care for a heart-attack victim? These are borderline cases, which must be compared with the central and contrary cases in order to see whether or not there are sufficient similarities to justify applying the term "vehicle" in the context of the by-law. But, and this is the important point, this fact does not in the least imply that the term "vehicle" is not a descriptive term, or that it is not normally used objectively.

The case is the same for the terms "health" and "illness." Consider the case of a physician who is asked to certify that a student is ill so that he or she can be excused from an examination. Often the physician will have no difficulty making a determination. Sometimes, however, the symptoms may be unclear or conflicting. In such cases it will be difficult, if not impossible, to decide whether the student is ill, and the physician will have to decide what to do based on other considerations. While the existence of such borderline cases makes the physician's professional moral life more difficult, they do not imply that the concepts of illness and health are without descriptive application.

It is worth noting that the application of the patient-health norm to borderline cases would usually produce results contrary to that which concerns Kennedy and his associates, namely that doctors would act so as to enforce the values of the prevailing power groups in society, and so issue "sick-notes" only when the patient is clearly unable to work because of illness. But the patient-health norm requires the physician to make the patient's health the primary consideration. If it cannot be clearly determined whether or not the patient is ill, then there is a reasonable possibility that the patient is indeed not well. To require the patient to work would be to risk damage to the patient. In other words, the patient-health norm would suggest giving the benefit of the doubt to the patient. Borderline cases should, from the point of view of medical ethics, be given their "sick-note."

None the less, the patient-health norm will not be very satisfactory if it is true that the concept of health is culturally relative, and is basically just an embodiment of social mores. The argument for this claim proceeds either (a) by trying to show how in fact health norms vary from culture to culture, or from time to time, or from class to class within a culture, or (b) by trying to show that the very meanings of "health" and "illness" embody this relativism. I shall consider each of these in turn.

Ascriptions of health and illness do vary as claimed in (a). We consider epilepsy to be an illness, but at other times it has been considered to be evidence of witchcraft. Or again, nervous tension among middle-class Victorian women was thought indicative of a frail physical condition, and thus thought to be an illness, while among working-class women it was thought only an immoral attempt to escape from work. Further examples of these sorts could be added virtually indefinitely, but to do so would not demonstrate the relativist conclusion.

Examples of the first sort show different levels of scientific understanding, with correspondingly different ascriptions of health or illness in some cases, but this does not imply a different concept of illness. The "witches" of Salem were thought not to be ill because a mistaken metaphysics led to a mistaken analysis of the cause of their symptoms. But a proper appreciation of an organic cause would, even then, have resulted in a judgment that they were ill rather than evil.

Examples of the second sort show at best an inconsistency in the application of standards. If the cases in the example were significantly similar, then the Victorian doctors who judged them to be different were morally culpable. They were letting their class bias stand in the way of their objective medical judgment. But inconsistency in the application of standards is not evidence for variance in the meaning of terms.

Accordingly, it remains only to examine form (b) of the argument. The clearest statement is given by Ian Kennedy. He explains (1981: 3) the general agreement that someone is ill who has an inflamed appendix:

What we have is certain facts about the physical condition of a person. We all agree that these are illnesses because we accept two propositions. The first is that there is a normal state in which the appendix is not inflamed and breathing is easy while resting. Second, it is appropriate to judge someone who deviates from this norm as ill.

The problem with the argument is that "the normal state against which to measure abnormality is a product of social and cultural values and expctations." Kennedy gives many examples, including the results of a study in South Wales showing "how tiredness was taken for granted as a normal state of everyday life by members of the working class, but was likely to be seen as a sign of illness by those in the middle class." Similarly, either because of natural endowment or training, the middle-class Victorian woman's constitution would be considered a much more delicate one, and the symptoms of nervous tension more easily accepted as evidence of ill health.

The problem with Kennedy's argument is his taking the operative concept to be "normal state," whereas the appropriate idea is the Aristotelian one of "function." A look at the *Oxford English Dictionary* (1971) will confirm this. There health is defined as:

1. Soundness of body; that condition in which its functions are duly and efficiently discharged.
2. By extension, the general condition of the body with respect to the efficient or inefficient discharge of functions: usually qualified as good, bad, weak, delicate, etc.

No extended analysis of bodily functions is necessary here. No one will be confused when told that one of the functions of the liver is to manufacture bile, and that bile works in the intestine to break down fat globules. Nor will anyone who knows this doubt that a liver which is not adequately producing bile is an unhealthy liver. More important, the question of a liver's health is not culturally relative. If one culture thinks a certain organic state healthy while another thinks it diseased, then one of the cultures has made an error of scientific analysis.

It is understandable that a normal state analysis should be substituted for a functional analysis. The normal state of most bodily organs is usually the same as the properly functioning state of the organs. A person usually knows there is something wrong with an eye when it does not work as well as usual, or with a leg when it hurts to walk. But what is normal for a person, group, or whole society can be malfunctional. Third-century Roman patricians, for example, might have thought the symptoms of those suffering from mild lead poisoning were normal, and not have realized that they were ill. Or, again, a whole culture suffering from a dietary deficiency might not realize their normal state is not a healthy one. But no one who realizes how the relevant proper functioning is being inhibited in these cases would doubt that the two groups were not well.

It has accordingly been shown that the conceptual challenge to the patient-health norm fails. The argument has been useful for furthering understanding of the norm in several ways. First, there are many borderline cases, wherein the norm cannot be simply and straightforwardly applied. Medical ethics, as is the case with the law and most other practical human activities, is not just a matter of the deductive application of rules. Physicians need practical wisdom as well as theoretical wisdom, which requires a history of reflective moral practice and the ability to draw upon others' experiences to supplement their own.

Second, physicians must take great care not to have their decisions biased by their social, economic or gender status. Given that most physicians are male, upper-middle class, and not at all trained to reflect upon the potential bias this produces, there is much potential for misapplication of the patient-health norm. This poses a great challenge for medical selection and education, and requires an ongoing dialogue about medical ethics on the part of many members of society.

Third, the discussion shows the conceptual centrality of scientific rigor to the practice of good medicine. The requirement that physicians develop and maintain scientific competency is a crucial subsidiary norm to the patient-health norm, as has been properly emphasized by medical codes of ethics. At the same time, however, the discussion shows that while scientific rigor is a necessary condition for the practice of proper medical ethics, it is not sufficient. Together all of these considerations show that a proper development of a medical ethics requires attention to much more than the patient-health norm. None the less, it can be concluded that the patient-health norm has a proper conceptual foundation and should be seen as serving as the fundamental role-specific norm of medicine.

ROLE-SPECIFIC AND GENERAL MORAL NORMS

In much, and perhaps in most, everyday practice of medicine, the patient-health norm or those role-specific norms subsidiary to it provide the answer as to what morally proper practice should be. Surgeons who do not perform well because of taking on too many patients in order to make a greater income, physicians who do not keep upgrading their knowledge, medical researchers who think of their research more than their patients can all be seen to be morally culpable by a direct application of the norm. The health of the patient provides the goal of medical practice and overrides most other concerns, personal or otherwise, which physicians may have. In most cases the problem is not in sorting out what should be done, but in having the will, the character and the institutional mechanisms to do what is correct.

Difficulties arise, however, in two kinds of cases. The first kind occurs when it is not clear how the patient-health norm applies in a given instance. The previous section began an exploration of the part of this problem that arises from the open texture of moral rules, but a proper investigation would require an analysis of practical wisdom in medicine which is beyond the scope of this chapter. The second kind of problem arises when the patient-care norm clearly does apply to a particular case, but still does not mandate a moral course of action because a significant opposing ethical principle also applies to the case. This is the problem of what to do when a role-specific norm of medicine conflicts with a general moral norm; of how role-specific considerations should be integrated into general ethical considerations. This problem is the topic of the remainder of the chapter. I shall look at it mainly by concentrating upon possible conflicts between a patient's health and personal autonomy.

In recent years one of the primary criticisms of physicians has been that they often do not provide sufficient information to their patients.[3] It is claimed that they do not fully explain to patients what is wrong with them, that they do not adequately inform patients of the risks of treatment, or that they do not sufficiently explain the pluses and minuses of possible alternative treatments. In such cases patients are not able to make informed choices, and so cannot properly exercise their right to self-determination.

In many cases these situations arise out of physicians' concern for their patients' health. In a landmark Canadian case on informed consent this point was made clearly.[4]

Q. When you come down to specific procedures would you agree with me that you are under an obligation to tell your patient about specific risks?

A. Yes, it might vary a bit with the patient but generally, yes.

Q. Why do you say it would vary a bit with the patient?

A. Some patients are certainly very nervous, anxious.

Q. Frightened?

A. Frightened, yes.

Q. You have had the experience very often where you have explained the specific risks attendant upon a particular procedure that you feel should be done for the patient's benefit and the patient has refused the surgery?

A. Yes.

Q. Too nervous or too scared, or whatever it is?

A. Yes.

Here the physician considered the patient's right to self-determination, but believed it should be overridden by the role-specific patient-health norm, which was here the competing consideration.

This paternalistic attitude has been the dominant one among physicians. In his 1961 study of 219 doctors, Donald Oken reported that almost 90% withheld from their patients the information that they were terminally ill of cancer, basing their decision mainly "on the anticipation of profoundly disturbing psychological effects." Recently, however, the tendency seems more to reverse the ordering. A recent study (Novak *et al.* 1979), using the same questionnaire as Oken, showed 97% of the respondents preferring to inform their patients that they have cancer, with 100% thinking "that the patient had the right to know." The question is which of the orderings is the correct one.

The key is to look again at the moral basis of any profession. Professions exist in order to provide human services, to help make the quality of human life better. This is the context in which its role-specific norms are developed, and it is the context which must be kept in mind whenever they are applied. Normally, when it is applied the patient-health norm furthers this goal. But in some cases, its application could undermine a patient's self-respect and sense of dignity, which are crucial to being able to live a satisfying and properly human life. In such cases, the patient-health norm must yield.

This can be usefully elaborated by considering the practice of slavery. The moral odiousness of the practice does not derive *only* from the horrible suffering usually inflicted upon slaves. An enlightened slave owner might provide excellent care: good housing and nutrition, ample opportunity for recreation, etc. Such benevolent concern would exhaust the moral obligation of the pet owner, but it clearly does not exonerate the slave owner. Human beings have the ability and need, if they are either to have any self-respect or to be able to achieve their human potential, to decide how they are to structure their lives. In denying slaves the chance to exercise this ability, the slave owner deprives them of an essential element of human dignity, and so treats them as less than human.

In their book, *The Individual and the Political Order*, Bowie and Simon (1977: 78) express this point very well in arguing for their view of human rights.[5]

Rights, we are suggesting, are fundamental moral commodities because they enable us to stand up on our own two feet, "to look others in the eye, and to feel in some fundamental way the equal of anyone. To think of oneself as the holder of rights is not to be unduly but properly proud, to have that minimal self-respect that is necessary to be worthy of the love and esteem of others." Conversely, to lack the concept of oneself as a rights bearer is to be bereft of a significant element of human dignity. Without such a concept, we could not view ourselves as beings entitled to be treated as not simply means but ends as well.

To respect persons as ends, to view them as having basic human dignity, seems to be inextricably bound up with viewing persons as possessors of rights; as beings who are *owed* a vital say in how they are to be treated, and whose interests are not to be overridden simply in order to make others better off.

Nor even, we can say, to make that same person better off.

The goal here is not to put forward a theory of rights, but to show the basic importance of allowing people to be self-determining. This importance remains even when people are deciding to undertake dangerous activities. Mountain climbers and race-car drivers are allowed to follow their chosen vocations even though the risks to their lives are very great. When a Jehovah's Witness decides not to have a blood transfusion, recognizing and accepting the extreme risk this involves, then we must respect the decision, and cannot properly invoke the patient-health norm to justify administering a transfusion against the patient's wishes.

Of course the decision will not always be so straightforward. When people are incompetent or under very great stress, it is often thought best to have someone else decide at least temporarily what is in their best interest. And this might be thought more often appropriate in the case of the sick than in other social circumstances. The sick are in an especially vulnerable state.[6] Their bodies do not function properly. They experience acute anxieties about mortality or their future modes of living. Their cognitive functioning is often diminished. In such cases the doctor may feel that the right of self-determination does not have its usual grounding, and that the only truly operative principle would be the patient-health norm.

This is sometimes the case, though even then it is morally vital that the patient be treated in as dignified a manner as possible. But usually the vulnerability of the sick imposes a greater than normal burden on the physician to protect self-determination rather than giving grounds for overriding it. The problem is not that the ill cannot make meaningful decisions about themselves, but rather that they need a more than usually supportive environment, along with a fuller and more careful provision of information, in order to be in a semblance of the cognitive and emotional state in which they normally make their self-determinations. Self-respect and sense of dignity require that people have control over how their lives are conducted. When people are ill their sense of control over their lives is lost and with it is lost much of their sense of dignity. But if patients are respectfully and carefully given information about their conditions and the possibility of treatment, some degree of control is re-established and a fundamental sort of anxiety is diminished. This conclusion is reinforced by the few empirical studies which have been done (Gerle *et al.* 1960; Cassem and Stewart 1975; Gray 1978). These all agree that even when the news is very bad, patients who are informed appreciate the information and have fewer difficulties (including a lower complication rate) than patients who are not informed. Physicians claim (undoubtedly honestly) to withhold information because of a concern over its traumatic effects. But moral theory and empirical study both suggest an error has been made about where the greatest potential for trauma lies.

The conflict between patient health and patient autonomy need not arise as often as is thought. Meeting the requirement of the role-specific norm will, in other words, usually entail meeting the requirements of the general norm. This is to be expected given the placement of the goals of medicine in the general human value scheme. However, in some cases the requisite treatment will conflict with values which have a more basic placement in a patient's goal structure than the value of health. In these cases the medical profession's role-specific norm must take a subordinate place. Even though this makes the moral task of the physician more complex, it should not be seen as a cause for despair. The reflective physician will know that this limitation upon the role-specific norm flows from the same considerations that make the technical goal of medicine into a morally significant one.

NOTES

1. One useful and detailed version of such an analysis, and a moral argument with a similar grounding to the one presented here, can be found in Pellegrino and Thomasma (1981).

2. For a good review of historical codes see D. Konold (1978) "Codes of Medical Ethics – I. History," in *Encyclopedia of Bioethics, Vol. I*, New York: The Free Press.
3. This criticism is not restricted to patients' rights groups, but occurs regularly in the popular press. It was the subject, for example, of an article in *Homemaker's Magazine*, which is "published 10 times a year ... and is delivered at no charge to 1,336,400 homes in pre-selected areas in 28 of Canada's largest cities." See C. Kelly "What's Up Doc?", *Homemaker's Magazine*, March, 1983, pp. 62–72c.
4. *Reibl v. Hughes* (1980), *Dominion Law Reports* 114 (2d), 1.
5. The authors quote from Joel Feinberg (1970) "The Nature and Value of Rights," *Journal of Value Inquiry* IV (14): 137–44.
6. For an excellent statement of patient vulnerability see Pellegrino and Thomasma (1981: 207–19).

REFERENCES

Bowie, N. and Simon, R. (1977) *The Individual and the Political Order*, Englewood Cliffs, NJ: Prentice Hall.

Cassem, H. H. and Stewart, R. S. (1975) "Management and Care of the Dying Patient," *International Journal of Psychiatric Medicine* 6: 293–304.

Gerle, B., Lundun, M. S. and Sandblom, P. (1960) "The Patient with Inoperable Cancer from the Psychiatric and Social Viewpoints," *Cancer* 13: 1206–17.

Gray, B. H. (1978) "Complexities of Informed Consent," *Annals of the American Academy of Political Science* 4337: 37–48.

Hart, H. L. A. (1961) *The Concept of Law*, Oxford: Oxford University Press.

Illich, I. (1977) *Limits to Medicine*, London: Penguin.

Kennedy, I. (1981) *The Unmasking of Medicine*, London: George Allen & Unwin.

Novak, D., Plumer, R. and Smith, R. L. (1979) "Changes in Physicians' Attitude Toward Telling the Cancer Patient," *Journal of the American Medical Association* 241: 897–901.

Oken, D. (1961) "What to Tell Cancer Patients: A Study of Medical Attitudes," *Journal of the American Medical Association* 175: 1120–8.

Pellegrino, E. D. and Thomasma, D. C. (1981) *A Philosophical Basis of Medical Practice*, Oxford: Oxford University Press.

Szasz, T. (1977) *The Theology of Medicine*, Baton Rouge: Louisiana State University Press.

9

ETHICS AND HUMAN REPRODUCTION
The bias of bioethics

THELMA McCORMACK

"Men and women of full age, without any limitation due to race, nationality or religion, have the right to marry and to found a family."

Article 16, *The International Bill of Human Rights*

The Trobriand islanders, according to Malinowski (1929), did not understand the connection between coitus and reproduction. This curious finding which has long engaged scholars raised formidable questions about the interpretation of information from another culture. Did the Melanesians really not understand the relationship, or was this a case of denial based on sexual repression? Or was it, as Malinowski suggested, a functional myth that served a system of matriliny? And what did it say for the distinction in western thought between mythological and scientific explanation? These and many other questions have been the subject of extensive discussions on the meaning of sexuality, the nature of preliterate knowledge, and beliefs about causality.

But at long last, a half-century later, Malinowski's "savages" have had their revenge. For reproduction without coitus has become a reality in our culture, and may, at some future time, become a statistical norm. The last laugh, then, is theirs as we fumble in our efforts to understand this strange phenomenon and create the appropriate myths. Even the story of the stork, long maligned by enlightened parents and sex educators, makes more sense than today's sex manuals for children since the stork is only a metaphor for reproductive technology.

The term "reproductive technology" covers a group of medical strategies including in-vitro fertilization ("test-tube babies"), artificial insemination by spouse or donor, the development of sperm banks and of techniques for predetermining the sex of a fetus, as well as surrogate parenting. Its primary objectives are to increase the effectiveness of contraception, overcome infertility, and reduce the risk of genetically transmitted deformities.[1] At present, only a small proportion of the population has any reason to use these services, but in the future as the methods improve – the risk of side-effects is reduced, the cost lowered and the success rate increased – many more persons may want to take advantage of them. Single women, lesbian women and others who would normally be deprived of the experience of childbirth can do so.

However, the pressure to hasten development comes not from single persons but from couples who would normally have dealt with infertility through adoption. A combination of factors including more access to abortion, better contraceptive information and use, and a trend among teenage women to keep their babies has made adoption increasingly difficult, a prolonged, agonizing process which more often than not ends in failure. Under the circumstances, couples have turned to fertility clinics which offer some hope and where the probability of bringing a baby home although still low is better than an adoption agency offers. Whether these clients are being misled by our symbolic idealization of motherhood, whether they are hostage to our naïve belief in technology as a solution to all problems, or whether they are rationally weighing the costs – the physical inconvenience, the time and the money spent – against a desired outcome is seldom studied. But there is no shortage of experts to tell us.

For one group the new science and technology represents progress, a step forward toward greater management of fertility and less dependence on the randomness of chance. It is an enlargement of freedom for couples, especially those with some history of genetic impairment, and empowerment for women who, for a variety of reasons, including their spouse's low sperm count, are unable to conceive without assistance.

For another group the terms are reversed: reproductive technology represents a reduction of freedom for couples and the empowerment of specialists at the expense of women. The Vatican views non-coital reproduction as a cynical disregard of human dignity, part of the erosion of our traditional and humanistic values, while secular critics, including many feminists, claim that the new technologies exploit women for research and, at best, manipulate their anxieties about motherhood (Vatican 1987, Wikler 1986). Most people, however, are undecided, curious but unsure; they recognize that reproductive technology and the scientific research related to it raise serious questions about sexuality, family life, and gender relationships for which we do not have answers; indeed, we may not even have the right questions.

The questions fall into two groups; first, those which are related to the boundaries of permissible scientific research and experimentation on embryos; and, second, those which are connected with clinical applications.[2] Somewhere between them is a third category of practical questions which must be decided by physicians, genetics counsellors, judges, social workers, legislators and others who are on the spot, people who are acutely aware of how little they know of the life sciences in the post-DNA era, yet feel, and are, in some instances, compelled to act. But on many of the issues there is no consensus.

Surrogacy is a good illustration. The Ontario Law Reform Commission (1985) recommended that surrogacy be regulated but not prohibited. More recently, Liberal MP Sheila Copps introduced a Private Member's Bill (C-284) that would effectively prohibit it. Others have proposed that surrogate contracts, even those that are privately arranged and non-commercial, be declared unenforceable. Although the unenforceable contract is intended to protect the surrogate mother who may wish to change her mind, it would also give the biological father and his wife the right to change theirs. Britain, influenced by the Warnock Report, made commercial surrogacy criminal but many persons who initially favored it appear now to have misgivings about the decision (Brahams 1987). In Frankfurt, Germany, a surrogate motherhood center was closed by court order as "contrary to the country's adoption laws and to basic moral principles" (*New York Times*, January 7, 1988). Meanwhile, there is confusion among clients who insist they have a moral and legal right to have children and who may not feel the need to be protected from commercial entrepreneurs. Above all, they do not understand either the logic or ethics of groups who are "pro-choice" where abortion is concerned and anti-choice when the issue is infertility; pro, Dr Morgentaler; anti, Dr Steptoe.

Many of the contradictions and paradoxes that plague us in the discussions of reproductive technology occur in other contexts as well. But reproductive technologies are unique in one respect: they have a special impact on women. And, because they do, it is from the perspective of women that any rules, principles, concepts or policies must start and ultimately be judged. Not all women share the same opinions; there are strong and well-publicized ideological differences on many of the particular issues. But the range of questions (legal, philosophical, religious, political) that have been generated are first, and foremost, women's questions; they cannot be treated as if they were disembodied decontextualized abstractions (Sherwin 1984–5). Thus, the discourse is a feminist one in the broad sense of giving privilege to the perspective of women. This is not to suggest that men have no stake in reproductive decisions or cannot contribute wisely to the discussions, but rather to suggest that women have a more compelling interest and a special knowledge.

The answers women give or the directions they indicate will be influenced by history, religion, science, philosophy, law, and art; and, in so far as women scholars will be dealing with relationships, heterosexual and homosexual, rather than individuals, men need not fear a crude woman bias. In addition, the generalizations will be more universal than the here and now, and more cross-cultural than western societies. In short, there will be no less objectivity than we presently have in philosophy and social science, while the gain may be in a more comprehensive and holistic paradigm. However, for better or for worse, the primary and fundamental premise, the a priori proposition, is that matters of reproduction belong to the special domain of women whose knowledge overlaps with men's but is informed by their own subjectivity, and whose "ways of knowing" have been both devalued and marginalized by a patriarchal social order. In short, the issues surrounding reproductive technology are correctly described as applied ethics, but they are more properly and precisely feminist applied ethics.

Beyond a genre, method, and style grounded in gender, there is a distinct feminist position based on a substantive critique of the private/public dichotomy in social organization, the nuclear family, the division of labor, and the subordinate and dependent status of women by virtue of gender. The goal of the feminist movement is social change to achieve structural equality (a redistribution of power) and liberation or self-determination. It is not only the opportunity-structure that must be changed, but women's minds, language, imagination, and consciousness. It is from this more specific feminist perspective that the literature in bioethics is found unsatisfactory, for the bias of bioethics is not just its abstract argumentation, but its conservative stance which criticizes individual behavior and individual motives rather than the social order; in particular, there is an uncritical acceptance of the traditional nuclear family and the more general pattern of gender inequality.

> Properly understood, the largely universal taboos against incest, and also the prohibition against adultery, suggest that clarity about who your parents are, clarity in the lines of generation, clarity about who is whose, are the indispensable foundations of a sound family life, itself the sound foundation of civilized community.
>
> (Kass 1979)

Contemporary feminists contest the centrality of the family and no longer measure the efficiency of social practices by it. The implication is that feminists go beyond a feminist applied ethics; in their view it ought to be a critical feminist ethics as well.

USING WOMEN TO MAKE SOCIAL POLICY

Reproductive technologies do not exist in a vacuum; their cultural context is our beliefs about motherhood and the family that are, in turn, enforced by moral judgments. These judgments which assume individual accountability constitute a system of social control based on law and on conscience or the internalization of norms. The inequities built into institutions and social policy are invisible and seldom analyzed. So, for example, birth rates may be influenced by the economy, medical insurance, the availability of day care and other structural and cultural factors, but the judgment is on the person, the woman in this case, who is stereotypically described as preferring a career and a high standard of living to selfless motherhood, or "careless" or a nymphomaniac or some other invidious variant in the good/bad girl syndrome. Like other powerless groups, women are the "Patsies," the scapegoats in a no-win system of ethical discourse.

This process of making judgments is not random; it is a ranking order and patterned to maintain a system of female dependency. A case in point is our attitudes toward abortion. Every public opinion poll conducted in Canada on abortion shows strong support for abortion. But there are different degrees. We are most sympathetic when the pregnancy is the result of rape or incest, and the woman is truly a victim; least, where a woman decides on her own to terminate a pregnancy for economic reasons. The first is labeled tragic; the second selfish, but a woman who decides to terminate a pregnancy when she learns from amniocentesis that there is evidence of fetal damage which would lead to a severely handicapped child gets no clear-cut signal. Similarly, in the case of artificial insemination, we are most supportive when the infertility is medically caused, e.g. by blocked fallopian tubes; least, when the decision is based on life-style and described as frivolous. Convenience, the Warnock report (1984) said, is "totally ethically unacceptable." Necessity, according to Mady, is the only justifiable basis for surrogacy. "To permit convenience to justify use of a surrogate mother subjects the arrangement to the criticism that it treats human lives as capable of manipulation at personal whim" (Mady 1981).

The key to this normative code is that women have the greatest sympathy and support when they are passive, when they are acquiescent to male authority as they typically are in the "sick role"; the least, when they are acting freely, independently, taking charge of their own lives without appeals to the milk of human kindness. An agential role is described pejoratively as opportunistic and undeserving of what may be

149

scarce resources. Concealed in this modern economic language with its concern about the allocation of resources is a Victorian stereotype of a weak and fragile female based on Victorian biology.

By introducing "motives" women are asked to do what the society is unwilling to do. Judgments provide the pressure to conform while, at the same time, no blame is attached to social institutions. For example, the failure to provide good services for the handicapped means that women are expected to adapt their lives to children who may require full-time and life-long care (Lapham 1981; Finger 1984). When amniocentesis indicates a deformed fetus, the result is a predictable process of conflict followed by an abortion and subsequent guilt. Criticism by handicapped groups compounds the injury (Tait 1986). Cumulatively these are profoundly disturbing experiences that can result in depression; at best, they are alienating experiences which leave their residues of regret and bitterness. Either way they silence women and, in the long run, depoliticize them.

Current debates about abortion and the viability of a fetus similarly make women responsible for decisions the society wants to avoid. The right of a woman to have an abortion is one question; what to do about a viable fetus is a separate question. They are related temporally, not logically. Ideology has joined them by means of an anti-abortion scenario that endeavors to make the legality of an abortion contingent upon the status of the fetus. The connection is false whether the fetus is ten weeks or twenty, whether the technology required for the delivery is harmful to the fetus or not (Fost *et al.* 1980). If we as a society are morally disturbed by the deliberate destruction of a viable fetus, it is our collective responsibility to make other arrangements – either to maintain the fetus through heroic nursing measures and high-tech neonatal units or to let it die with dignity – but it is sexist in the extreme to turn our backs and refuse to make these important and difficult decisions, to let women bear the consequences of our failure of nerve.

ELIGIBILITY

In theory artificial insemination by husband (AIH) should pose no problems for ethicists or, indeed, public opinion. Apart

150

from religious injunctions against masturbation, there appears to be very little reason not to expect insemination-on-demand. Nevertheless, as long as physicians act as gatekeepers, any number of reasons may be given for refusal. It is their prerogative to make decisions on medical and psychiatric grounds. But, in fact, social criteria may be introduced. When physicians in Ontario were asked about the conditions for carrying out the procedure, a third required some proof of marriage, and all insisted on the husband's approval. Single persons and lesbian couples were excluded. The Warnock report does not require the partners to be married, but defines a couple as heterosexual.

The donor arrangement (AID) is more threatening to the family since the biological father is an outsider and questions are raised about adultery and the legitimacy of the offspring. In an age of single parenting, in an age where marriages dissolve and both partners remarry so that children have many sets of parents and siblings, the concern with questions of adultery is a good example of the wrong question. Nevertheless, writers frequently go to great lengths to point out that AID differs from adultery and carries with it none of the consequences to a marriage of adultery. "AID procreation of a child does involve an exception, a profound and weighty exception," Roy writes, "to the normal structure of a marital relationship." But, he says, "the donor *does not*, by reason of his communication of genetic material to this marriage, obtain rights over the body, much less over the person of the wife" (Roy 1980: 507; his emphasis). The test of adultery is based on the woman's body as property over which her husband alone has rights. But, "even if technical adultery and illegitimacy are not involved," according to a Conservative Jewish theologian, the surrogacy arrangement is unacceptable because "the family bond is shattered" (Berenbaum 1987).

Consistent with this concept of marriage as a husband's exclusive right to his wife's body is the concept of the family as having two parents. Any woman who would bring a child into the world where there is no parenting father is, according to one philosopher, inflicting harm; it is "the equivalent of mutilating her child" (Ribes 1978: 132). "[A]s a general rule," the Warnock report (1984) says, "it is better for children to be born into a two-parent family with both father and mother." Snowden and Mitchell (1981) insist they be married as well.

If a single parent is undesirable, three can create other problems detrimental to the welfare of the child. A mother who arranges to have her daughter's child through in-vitro fertilization using the son-in-law's semen may offer a fine gesture of motherly love, but can only do the child harm "by contradictory values about genetic ties, by confusion over who may claim the child and who is responsible for it (and whom the child may claim and be responsible to)" (Tiefel 1985). Traditional kinship lines which are more honored in the breach are too important to be tampered with even by rare exceptional acts of concern by a mother for her infertile daughter.

The donor must be screened to match the couple's physical appearance. "Experience with adopted children has shown," Snowden and Mitchell (1981) write, "that a physical likeness to the adoptive parents helps the child to identify with the parents and the parents with the child." In short, the treatment for infertility may be bizarre, but it does not in any way challenge the nuclear family which under ideal circumstances was a source of oppression for women. More myth today than reality, it is oppressive in a different way, for the two-parent nuclear family lives in the imagination and nostalgia of men. Like the image of the old west, the classical nuclear family can't be restored but it can be used as a measure of the "good old days" and what ought to be a "haven in a heartless world."

DISTANCING THE DONOR

The integrity of the nuclear family is reinforced by excluding all other persons who might have some claim. The donor, whether it is the man who supplies the sperm or the woman who provides the ova, is distanced psychologically by creating an impersonal commercial transaction; that is, the payment of money for something "money cannot buy." The payment is usually defended as it is with blood donation: a necessary, though not a desirable, incentive to find enough and appropriate volunteers (Titmus 1971; McCormack *et al.* 1959). But another and more important function of the payment is to define kinship, to establish and limit family boundaries and kinship obligations (Simmel 1978). Indeed, a donor who refused payment would create an awkward situation. What are his motives? Semen donation is not, after all, like blood donation where there is a life-and-death surgical crisis or the acute need of a haemophiliac patient. In this situation, there is strong suspicion of some form of self-interest that could come back to haunt us. Because of our disbelief in something for nothing, and our distrust of this form of altruism, it is important to maintain the fiction of a cash nexus. The demarcation is to the advantage of both parties, donor and receiver, who can assume that there are no hidden bonds of reciprocal obligation based on favors or gifts, no outstanding IOUs that could be called in. The couple who have the baby are secure that it is truly theirs, while the donors, male or female, cannot be accused of infidelity, of tampering with their own marital bonds.

The same principle applies to the recommendation by Snowden, Mitchell and Snowden that male donors should remain anonymous (1983; see also Snowden and Mitchell 1981). We are told it is better for all concerned: the donors since they might be deterred from donating if their identities were known; better for the couple since there might be an element of rivalry between the two men; and better for the child who knows only the social father. All of this is based on some kind of "common sense" knowledge since no evidence is offered that donors want their actions hidden; no evidence, apart from Freud's *Totem and Taboo*, of this fratricidal rivalry; and no evidence that children are unable to accept having two fathers.

The surrogate mother has no chance of being anonymous, and, indeed, from what little we know about the women who volunteer to be surrogate mothers she may not wish to be (Parker 1983: 1). From her perspective, and from the perspective of a male donor, there is pride and satisfaction in helping a childless couple. Yet the price of maintaining the two-parent family is to reduce them to being mere providers of biological services. In their minds it may become a stigma of low esteem.

It is not surprising, therefore, that from time to time donors protest, especially surrogate mothers who have developed an emotional attachment to the fetus they are carrying. The origin of this bond may be in the gestation process itself, but it is made stronger by the emphasis we put on the experience of childbirth (Romalis 1981). In a society where families have become smaller and where the education and socialization processes are no longer the major responsibilities of parents, a woman can afford to be sentimental about child-bearing and the phenomenology of gestation. Childbirth becomes a Maslovian "peak" experience (Maslow 1968). In addition, there are a group of child-development experts who regard the bonding between the fetus and woman during pregnancy and between the neonate and mother in the post-partum phase as critical to the child's personality development. A psychiatrist who testified in a recent surrogate case said that a child taken from its natural mother and given to its natural father might eventually view the world "as a hostile place," a world "that doesn't allow things to happen according to nature" and which could lead to "alienation from society and its institutions."[3] Considering that women have turned their newborn babies over to wet nurses for centuries, there is very little historical evidence to support the prediction of radical protest, but one way or another, women are encouraged to keep babies regardless of the quality of care they can give them, a message that is not lost on women who enter into surrogate contracts. If they don't change their minds, they ought to.

Philosophers and others, then, who believe it is necessary to protect the family from threats created by the outsider are protecting a family that is increasingly more fiction than fact, and are doing so at the expense of the outsider who loses an identity. For the modern surrogate mother who is not obeying a command of God, not following a biblical tradition, this experience may create an emotional trauma; her own justification is cheapened by the exchange of money, while her protective emotional indifference to the fetus which she must surrender is treated as pathological by those who think bonding is both necessary for her and the future mental health of the child. Male donors may feel the same way to a lesser degree. Both want a recognition and a status that they are denied by a literature which proposes an anonymity for them.

To summarize then, the literature of bioethics has been anti-feminist. In general, it treats women's questions as if they were universal questions; it imposes judgments on women that are more properly imposed on social institutions; it opens its arms to women when they are in dependent roles, and shuts them out when they are acting independently; it protects the nuclear family by creating a system of eligibility which excludes single persons, and which distances all third parties who serve as donors or surrogates.

The alternative to this model is to restore the dignity of the donor by recognizing that donors are performing a social service rather than a biological one. In France, the model is a gift relationship (David and Lansac 1980). Male donors are not paid for the semen. And it is understood that the sperm is a gift to a couple, not an individual. The couple who receive it are obliged to find another couple who can replace the semen, so that, in effect, a network, partly visible, partly invisible, is created. Donors do not know which children they father but they are recognized as fathering.

The French approach answers some of the objections made by social critics who question the concept of Biological Man (the "stud") or Economic Man (the indigent medical student looking for a fast buck) or Psychological Woman like the woman in Penelope Mortimer's novel, *The Pumpkin Eater* (1962), who has some deep obsessive need to be pregnant but is not interested in children.

Other suggestions have been to regard surrogacy as a form of organ donation (Simmons *et al.* 1977). The recent example we have had of a mother who knew her baby would be born anencephalic and insisted on carrying the child to term so that its heart could be given to another infant provides one model (*Globe and Mail*, October 19, 1987). At the other end of the continuum, going from the sublime to the crass, is the physician who planned to market body parts which would be bought and sold as needed. Surrogacy, then, can be seen as either a gift or a transaction. If it is the former and the contract is made between the women (one who conceives easily and enjoys pregnancy and another who is yearning for a child but is unable to bear one), it can be properly called a *feminist surrogacy contract*.

Within the feminist movement there is strong opposition to any form of surrogacy based on the assumption that the contracts are made by men and that the surrogate woman is at an economic disadvantage. More generally, surrogacy is understood as the ugly result of a fusion between capitalism and patriarchy. In a non-patriarchal society, Overall (1987) says, there would be no surrogacy. The view taken here is that surrogacy is an independent variable; it may or may not be exploitative, and it may or may not be patriarchal. The effects of gender and class inequality must be addressed but they should not be confounded with surrogacy. Surrogacy is similar in this respect to adoption. When couples adopt babies from the Third World they are benefiting from the poverty of underdeveloped countries. No one would suggest that adoption be made criminal. The problem is poverty not adoption.

Ultimately, then, the problems of reproductive technology are a subset of population policies. This is more clearly seen in India than it is in Canada where we prefer to drift and vacillate between pro- and anti-natalism. Meanwhile, the gift ethic offers an approach to these very difficult and emotionally complex sets of problems.

To summarize, the new reproductive technology has created its own science fiction. There are predictions that men will become extinct (Cherfas and Gribbin 1984); other predictions that women will become redundant (Guttentag and Secord 1983). In addition there is the specter of Nazi eugenics balanced by the joy of the many loving persons who become parents. The late Paul Ramsey, a distinguished bioethicist, looked into the future and saw the possibility of women being forced to abort a handicapped child, a loss of freedom to the woman and a loss of life to the child. Some feminists have seen this as a new scam perpetrated on women, further attempts by men to control the reproductive lives of women (Corea 1985); others have seen it as motherhood without coercive hetero-sexuality (Robinson and Pizer 1985). But societies do not undergo abrupt radical transformations, and values, not technology, still direct history. Philosophers have the most to tell us about values and how to examine them, but the bioethicists who have commented on these new technologies have failed to examine their own biases and presuppositions about reproduction. They have marveled at the new technology and been shocked by it, they have said "yes," "no" and "maybe" but have left intact the androcentricity of a western ethical tradition. To reiterate, reproductive decisions and policies rest on what we have defined here as feminist ethics. The answers to questions we seek will not be forthcoming until the method and models are applied. Nevertheless, we can differentiate between theories that are close to a feminist perspective and those which are so distant as to be properly described as anti-feminist. We have indicated here that the subtext in many of the discussions is the nuclear, two-parent heterosexual family. Kass (1979) uses this idealization of the family to oppose many of the uses of reproductive technology; other philosopher-scientist-lawyers disagree with him about the technology, but accept his assumption about the family (Benditt 1983). For those who do not make this explicit, it is implicit in their discussions and recommendations on eligibility and donor choice. Under the circumstances, the approach which moves us along toward a feminist model is the concept of reproductive technology as providing a social service, and the concept of organ donation in the AID case, a gift relationship where surrogacy is involved; that is, a gift exchanged between two women.

In our comments here there are a number of related issues we have not touched upon. The ethical problems raised in genetic counselling, the use and abuse of sex-determination technology, problems of "informed consent" when the scientific information is itself equivocal and subject to random error – all of these and many others belong to the new area of bioethics and reproductive technology. There are distinctive questions relating to each, but some of the principles we have tried to outline here concerning gender relationships and the family can be extended to these areas. We have not attempted either to look at social policy which is caught between the Scylla of over-regulation based on patriarchal principles, and the Charybdis of under-regulation based on the same ideas. "In Liberal society," Robertson writes (1986: 939), "the invisible hand of procreative preference must be allowed to flourish, despite the qualms of those who think it debases our humanity." Critical feminist applied ethics can offer a different, more sensitive and imaginative direction.

NOTES

1. It also includes abortion, amniocentesis (a procedure that detects fetal deformities in the amniotic fluid), chorionic villus sampling (an examination of cells cut from projections on the membrane surrounding the fetus; it can be done earlier than amniocentesis making any subsequent abortion less of a risk), the storage of frozen sperm (cryopreservation), the development of artificial wombs and specially designed nursery environments which make it possible to maintain a fetus removed from the womb in the first trimester.

2. In March, 1988 the Medical Research Council of Canada approved research on embryos up to 17 days in gestational age, but forbade "the creation of test-tube factories to use embryos solely for research purposes" *Globe and Mail*, March 5, 1988, p. A6. See also Kass (1979).

3. Dr Steven L. Nickman testifying in the Baby M case. Nickman is identified as a psychiatrist who teaches child psychotherapy at Harvard Medical School. *New York Times*, February 27, 1987.

REFERENCES

Benditt, Theodore (1983) "Surrogate Gestation. Law and Morality," in James M. Humber and Robert F. Almeder (eds) *Biomedical Ethics Reviews*, Clifton, NJ: Humana.

Berenbaum, Michael (1987) "Jewish Views of Hi-Tech Birth," *Moment* (November).

Brahams, Diana (1987) "The Hasty British Ban on Commercial Surrogacy," *Hastings Center Report*, New York: Hastings-on-Hudson.

Cherfas, Jeremy and Gribbin, John (1984) *The Redundant Male*, London: Bodley Head.

Corea, Gena (1985) *The Mother Machine*, New York: Harper.

David, Georges and Lansac, Jacques (1980) "The Organization of the Centers for the Study and Preservation of Semen in France," in Georges David and Wendel S. Price (eds) *Human Artificial Insemination and Semen Preservation*, New York: Plenum.

Finger, Anne (1984) "Claiming All of Our Bodies: Reproductive Rights and Disability," in Rita Arditti, Renate Duelli Klein and Shelley Minden, *Test-Tube Women: What Future for Motherhood?*, London: Pandora.

Fost, Norman, Chudwin, David and Wikler, Daniel (1980), "The Limited Moral Significance of 'Fetal Viability'," *Hastings Center Report*.

Freud, Sigmund (1950) *Totem and Taboo*, trans. James Strachey, London: Routledge & Kegan Paul.

Guttentag, Marcia and Secord, Paul F. (1983) *Too Many Women?*, Beverly Hills: Sage.

Kass, Leon R. (1979) "'Making Babies' Revisited," *The Public Interest* 54.

Lapham, Virginia Shepard (1981) "Living with an Impaired Neonate and Child. A Feminist Issue," in Helen B. Homes, Betty B. Hoskins and Michael Gross, *The Custom-Made Child?*, Clifton, NJ: Humana.

McCormack, Thelma, Elkin, Frederick and Westley, William A. (1959) "Anxiety and Persuasion," *The Public Opinion Quarterly* XXIII (1).

Mady, Thereasa (1981) "Surrogate Mothers: The Legal Issues," *American Journal of Law and Medicine* 7 (3).

Malinowski, Bronislaw (1929) *The Sexual Life of the Savages*, New York: Harcourt.

Maslow, Abraham H. (1968) *Toward a Psychology of Being*, New York: Van Nostrand.

Mortimer, Penelope (1962) *The Pumpkin Eater*, New York: McGraw-Hill.

Ontario Law Reform Commission (1985) *Report on Human Artificial Reproduction and Related Matters, Vols I, II*, Toronto.

Overall, Christine (1987) *Ethics and Human Reproduction*, Boston: Allen & Unwin.

Parker, Philip J. (1983) "Motivation of Surrogate Mothers: Initial Findings," *American Journal of Psychiatry* 140: 1.

Ramsey, Paul (1973) "Screening: An Ethicist's View," in Bruce Hilton, Daniel Callahan, Maureen Harris, Peter Condliffe and Berkley Burton, *Ethical Issues in Human Genetics*, New York: Plenum.

Ribes, Bruno (1978) *Biology and Ethics*, Paris: Unesco.

Robertson, John A. (1986) "Embryos, Families and Procreative Liberty: The Legal Structure of the New Reproduction," *Southern California Law Review* 59: 939.

Robinson, Susan and Pizer, H. F. (1985) *Having a Baby Without a Man*, New York: Fireside.

Romalis, Shelly (ed.) *Childbirth, Alternatives to Medical Control*, Austin: University of Texas.

Roy, David J. (1980) "AID: An Overview of Ethical Issues," in Georges David and Wendel S. Price (eds) *Human Artificial Insemination and Semen Preservation*, New York: Plenum.

Sherwin, Susan (1984–5) "A Feminist Approach to Ethics," *Dalhousie Review*.

Simmel, Georg (1978) *The Philosophy of Money*, London: Routledge & Kegan Paul.

Simmons, Roberta G., Klein, Susan D. and Simmons, Richard L. (1977) *Gift of Life. The Social and Psychological Impact of Organ Transplantation*, New York: Wiley.

Snowden, R. and Mitchell G. D. (1981) *The Artificial Family*, London: George Allen & Unwin.

Snowden, R., Mitchell, G. D. and Snowden, E. M. (1983) *Artificial Reproduction: A Social Investigation*, London: George Allen & Unwin.

Tait, Janice J. (1986) "Reproductive Technology and the Rights of Disabled Persons," *Canadian Journal of Women and the Law* 1 (2).

Tiefel, Hans O. (1985) "Commentary on 'When Baby's Mother is also Grandma – and Sister'," *Hastings Center Report*.

Titmus, Richard M. (1971) *The Gift Relationship. From Human Blood to Social Policy*, New York: Pantheon.

Vatican (1987) *Instruction on Respect for Human Life in its Origin and on the Dignity of Procreation: Replies to Certain Questions of the Day*.

Warnock report (1984) *Report of the Committee of Inquiry into Human Fertilization and Embryology*, Cmnd 9314, London: Her Majesty's Stationery Office.

Wikler, Norma Juliet (1986) "Society's Response to the New Reproductive Technologies: The Feminist Perspectives," *Southern California Law Review* 59 (4): 1043–57.

10

ETHICS AND PLANETARY ENGINEERING

1 Ecce ecopoiesis:[1] playing God on Mars

ROBERT H. HAYNES

ACKNOWLEDGMENTS

I thank my fellow Martians for inspiration and discussion, in
particular Elise Boulding, Philippe Garigue, Helena Groot de
Restrepo, Geraldine Kenney-Wallace, Jim Lovelock, Lynn
Margulis, Gary McCarron, Ann Montgomery, Rod Park, and
Gunther Stent. I remain deeply grateful to my wife, Jane
Banfield-Haynes, for her persistent, but I fear futile, attempts
to improve my morals.

FROM THE FANCIFUL TO THE POSSIBLE

Toward the weary end of a National Aeronautics and Space
Administration (NASA) committee meeting in 1967, I suggested,
only partly in jest, that the feasibility of establishing some form
of life on Mars should be examined seriously. I argued that
there were unlikely to be any living things currently inhabiting
the Red Planet. I based this surmise, weakly to be sure, on the
superficial resemblance between the Martian and lunar sur-
faces that had been revealed for the first time in the 1965
Mariner 4 flyby mission. If, upon further exploration, Mars did
indeed prove to be a barren planet, surely there could be no
philosophical objection to my admittedly quixotic proposal. A
jocular discussion ensued. After the predictable jokes about
founding a Celestial Panspermic League, we concluded, a trifle
more soberly, that any such undertaking would be rejected on
ethical grounds, even by politicians: Would it not be wicked for
anyone to "play God" on such a cosmic scale? And didn't Mars

161

have "rights," which would not necessarily include the "right to life"?

Today, the notion of constructing an ecosystem on Mars is much less of a whimsy than it was in 1967. In recent years, a few knowledgeable scientists have thought seriously about this far-out proposition which, for most people, still lies securely in the realm of science fiction. Thus, it may not be entirely idle to ask if there is an ethical dimension to ecopoiesis which would interest philosophers. Perhaps in 1967 a harmless fantasy was inhibited by the over-heated moralizing attitudes of the times. Would not modification of the Martian atmosphere, climate and surface be as amoral as the change of seasons, the building of mountains by volcanic eruptions, or the tectonic drift and collision of continents on our mobile, ever-changing, Earth (Wilson 1963)? Note, however, that the breezy quodlibets which did arise two decades ago were based on the element of human contrivance and construction. The changes envisaged would be engineered deliberately; they would not be expected to arise in the natural course of planetary history if Mars really is a biologically "dead" planet with an atmosphere close to chemical equilibrium (Lovelock 1975).

In this chapter I first outline in general terms what would, and what would not, be entailed technically in ecopoiesis. I then comment on some basic philosophical questions that arise; in an accompanying text, pp. 184–97, C. P. McKay continues the discussion in the context of current thinking on environmental ethics.

The first detailed appraisal of the prospects for propagating life on Mars was prepared for NASA by Melvin Averner and Robert MacElroy in 1976. Their report was completed after the four Mariner flyby and orbiter missions, but just prior to the landing of two Viking spacecraft in June and August of 1976. They concluded that there seemed to be no fundamental reasons of scientific principle which would make it impossible for Mars to support some form of life. This basic conclusion remains unchanged today, even in light of the extremely harsh environmental conditions discovered during the very successful Viking missions.

Recently, a small "organizational" meeting, involving about a dozen interested scientists, drawn from universities and NASA staff, took place in January, 1988 at the NASA Ames Research Center, Moffett Field, California. Those attending had two general goals: first, to evaluate the rationales and practicability of terraforming Mars, based on current technology and available information, and also on projected future technologies and the possibilities for gathering specific classes of information about the planet's composition and dynamics. And second, to evaluate the usefulness of developing a special project in this area as a possible focus for the manned and unmanned scientific exploration of Mars during the coming century.

In light of these developments, it seems timely to alert philosophers, and the general public, to the fact that the idea of fabricating some form of indigenous life on Mars is not completely crazy, and that a feasibility study of ecopoiesis might be initiated within the next few years. In this regard, it is worth remembering that we habitually underestimate the rate of technological advance. For example, as late as 1933 Lord Rutherford, the first person to effect the disintegration of atomic nuclei, publicly stated at a meeting of the British Association that "anyone who looked for a source of power in the transformation of atoms was talking moonshine." Similarly, at the 1963 International Congress of Genetics, the renowned geneticist and polymath, J. B. S. Haldane, declared that the deliberate genetic modification of *Homo sapiens* must surely be millennia away. Yet today transgenic laboratory animals and biologically engineered livestock are commonplace; practical techniques for gene therapy in humans are virtually in hand. Interestingly enough, the first experimental trials of these latter procedures have been delayed as much on ethical as medical grounds.

Philosophers have the admirable trait of wanting to know precisely what is intended, and what would be involved, before moralizing on novel technical proposals. In this case, unfortunately, only a general outline can be provided. Therefore it would be premature for anyone to try to form any final judgment today on the ethics of ecopoiesis. The reasons for this are twofold. First, our basic knowledge of Mars still is quite limited. In particular, we cannot be sure that there are no "road-blocks" to ecopoiesis associated with unrecognized

163

geochemical or geophysical features of the planet. If such obstacles exist, the technologies needed to overcome them might be unavailable in the foreseeable future or impractical in the extreme. In this case, questions of practical ethics would become moot. Secondly, there exists no single, obvious method for carrying out such a project, even though several scenarios have been suggested (Oberg 1981; Allaby and Lovelock 1984). Thus, we cannot rule out the possibility that, even if the objective is desirable, the means required to achieve it might be judged inadmissible. Clearly, much more detailed exploration of the physical, chemical, geological, and climatological features of Mars is essential, and indeed is being planned both by the USA and USSR, in cooperation with other countries (see, Solar System Exploration Committee of the NASA Advisory Council (1986.)

FROM ECOPOIESIS TO TERRAFORMATION

The notion of "terraformation" is well-known to, and originated in, science fiction (Williamson 1969, 1968; Heinlein 1950; Allaby and Lovelock 1984). As implied by the Latin root *terra*, the word denotes the programmed fabrication of an *earthlike* ecosystem on a presumably lifeless planet (Oberg 1981). The goal of terraformation would be to endow the planet with an oxygen atmosphere, hydrosphere and biosphere similar to their earthly counterparts. A terraformed planet would be stocked with normal terrestrial microorganisms, plants and animals. Biogeochemical cycles, driven by solar energy, as in the great "mill-wheel" of life on earth, would allow long-term survival and development. An originally sterile, desolate planet could become a frontier in space for human habitation and exploitation: *Terranova* is the obvious name for this new land in the sky. People could live and work there much as they do on Earth. They neither would require the bulky protective space suits used by contemporary astronauts, nor would they be dependent on imported supplies of air, food, and water. Ultimately, the Terranovan biota, including human colonists, might evolve along paths quite different from those on earth.

The objective of ecopoiesis need not be to achieve climatic and biological conditions as they now exist on earth. If the present Martian environment could be altered to support the growth and proliferation of *any* biota, however exotic, then the more modest goal of ecopoiesis would be attained: *Vitanova* is a suitable name for the strange garden in the sky that would result from this effort. In the case of Mars, present scenarios suggest that the most readily achievable, biocompatible atmosphere would contain a high concentration of carbon dioxide, but little oxygen. With some moisture in the soil, a variety of microorganisms could grow under such conditions. If the atmosphere was sufficiently warm and thick, human explorers could live and work outside their spacecraft in something akin to scuba gear. Furthermore, a prolific microbiota could provide a valuable local resource of biomass for food, energy and other purposes. Astronauts, based in enclosed habitats, might be able to remain on the planet long enough to begin, if deemed desirable, the further transformation of *Vitanova* to *Terranova*.

It is important to distinguish ecopoiesis from biopoiesis. The latter is a technical term for the abiotic formation of biochemical systems, and the emergence of "protocells," in the primordial "organic soup," thought to have been formed photochemically on the primitive earth. It is the basic script for the orthodox Haldane-Oparin picture of the spontaneous generation of life on Earth from inorganic precursor molecules (Pirie 1937; Oparin 1957; Miller and Orgel 1974).

Ecopoiesis differs also from the ancient notion of *panspermia*. In the fifth century BC, Anaxagoras taught that organisms grow from "slimy earth" when fertilized with "ethereal germs" (spermata) which he assumed to pervade the cosmos (Furley 1987). A modern version of this idea was proposed in 1906 by the celebrated Swedish chemist Svante Arrhenius, shortly after the discovery of bacterial spores (Oparin 1957). He argued that spores were sufficiently small and light to be ejected randomly from their planets of origin, and resistant enough to remain viable in space during long interplanetary transits, propelled by the radiation pressure of starlight. Note, however, that panspermia does not explain the origin of life, it merely gives an account of how it could have arrived fortuitously on a sterile, but receptive Earth.

Recently, Francis Crick (1981), one of the founding-fathers of molecular biology, devoted an entire book to putting again the case for panspermia. However, in Crick's view, it was no accident that brought the first bacterial colonists to these shores. Rather the whole affair was directed by some extra-terrestrial intelligence (ETI) seeking to impregnate a nice warm pot of primordial soup: truly a latter-day version of Special Creation by an avatar of ETI. This spooky idea is difficult, if not impossible, to disprove, especially in light of current interest in ecopoiesis! However, as we shall see, a simple "Johnny Appleseed" approach to propagating even "plastic" spores would not work on Mars because of its presently hostile environment.

FROM EARTH TO MARS

There exists a "continuously habitable zone" around the sun. It is the region of space where a planet of sufficient size and suitable atmosphere could maintain a moderate climate long enough for a biosphere to develop over evolutionarily signifi-cant periods of time. Recent calculations indicate that this belt is wider than once thought. It is now considered to extend from just inside the orbit of earth to just beyond the orbit of Mars (Kasting *et al.* 1988).

McKay (1982a) has drawn a useful distinction between what he calls biocompatible and biogenerative planets. The latter are cosmic bodies whose physical and environmental parameters lie within the limits necessary for life to originate locally through biopoiesis and then evolve to a high level of cellular complexity. Biocompatible planets are those whose purely physical para-meters would allow the existence of a stable atmosphere and climate suitable for life. On the Haldane-Oparin hypothesis, Earth is not only biocompatible but also biogenerative.

The biological sensors carried on the Viking spacecraft found no evidence of life on Mars (Horowitz 1986). However, the existence of drainage networks and outflow channels on its surface is consistent with erosion by large water flows in the past. Thus, it is possible that Mars was once a biogenerative planet and that extinct forms of early life may be found there. Mars remains today a biocompatible planet, even though its small size (diameter 53% of Earth) could impose temporal constraints on the longevity of any biosphere that might be established there (Kasting *et al.* 1988). None the less its unalterable planetary features, in particular its size, rotation rate and axial tilt, make it seem almost "custom-made" for ecopoiesis, and perhaps even terraformation (McKay 1982b, 1987). All of this is good news; now we must consider some bad news.

Present environmental conditions on the Martian surface are extremely hostile to any known form of carbon-based life. At temperate latitudes in summer, the average temperature is about −60°C. The Viking landing sites revealed extreme diurnal variations ranging from a low of −83°C to a high of −30°C. The atmospheric pressure also is very low, less than one-hundredth of that on earth. What little "air" exists is 95% carbon dioxide (CO_2) and 3% nitrogen (N_2), with only a small amount of oxygen (0.13% O_2) and water vapor (0.03% H_2O). Despite the substantial amount of water which is likely to be tied up in various geological sinks, the low atmospheric pressure and temperature mean that its soil is highly desiccated. The thin atmosphere, and lack of a protective ozone layer, allow biologically dangerous levels of solar ultraviolet and ionizing radiations to penetrate to the surface. The interested reader can find further information on the physical and environmental properties of Mars in Carr (1981) and in the convenient summary provided by NASA Technical Memorandum 82478.

Perhaps the most surprising discovery made by the Viking Landers was the absence of even trace quantities of organic compounds. The surface material sampled at the two landing sites, Chryse Planitia and Utopia Planitia, proved to be highly oxidizing and therefore destructive to organic molecules (Biemann *et al.* 1977). It was expected that even if no chemical evolution or biopoiesis had ever taken place, there would still be found some organic material derived from meteoritic impact. It has been suggested that any organic substances arriving on Mars are destroyed as a result of reactions stimulated photochemically by solar radiation (Chun *et al.* 1978; Hunten 1974, 1979). Indeed, Oro and Holzer (1979) have shown in laboratory experiments that the half-life of a large number of organic compounds irradiated with ultraviolet light under conditions approximating those found on Mars ranges from a few hours to a few days. Thus, any organisms, even the most resistant bacterial spores, casually sprinkled on Mars, would not only fail to reproduce for want of water and proper nutrients, they would be degraded utterly to dust.

Mars is an extremely cold, dry and even toxic planet. However, all is not lost for ecopoiesis. There is good reason to believe that the near-surface layers of the planet do possess substantial quantities of the basic materials needed to support life, in particular such critically important volatiles as water and carbon dioxide. Unfortunately, the global availability of nitrogen remains problematic, and much of the carbon dioxide might be tied up in carbonate deposits from which it could be released only with difficulty.

If future exploration does reveal the existence of sufficient and accessible quantities of volatiles and other essential materials, then a general scenario for ecopoiesis would include two main phases. First, planetary engineering designed to produce a warm, thick atmosphere; and second, biological engineering to design, construct and implant a suite of symbiotic species capable of proliferation and functioning as a primitive ecosystem in the newly salubrious Martian environment produced in the first phase (McKay 1982a). If the structure, function and early evolutionary history of Earth's biosphere can provide any precedent at all, it is clear that the first permanent residents of Mars would have to be microorganisms (Krumbein 1983; Margulis and Sagan 1986; Schopf 1978). The great chemical and biochemical versatility of microbes in exploiting unusual nutrients and energy sources makes them obvious candidates for a pioneering role on Mars. Thus, ecopoiesis could be defined more specifically as the establishment of a *microbial* ecosystem on a sterile planet.

FROM STERILITY TO VITALITY

According to McKay's (1987) preliminary calculations, Mars is capable of supporting a warm, stable, largely CO_2 atmosphere, at a pressure about twice that on earth; the ambient temperature would be above freezing, probably averaging 15°C. A small amount of oxygen would be produced from the dissociation of CO_2 by sunlight.

To produce this atmosphere some practical engineering technique(s) would have to be devised to warm the planet. A small rise in temperature could stimulate the release of CO_2 absorbed in the soil and thereby increase further its concentration in the atmosphere. Since CO_2 is a greenhouse gas, a positive feedback effect would ensue: the more CO_2 released into the atmosphere, the warmer still it would become through the greenhouse effect. This in turn would stimulate further releases until all available CO_2 was cycling through the atmosphere. The concomitant liberation of water vapor from the permafrost also would contribute to the warming effect. As the temperature and vapor pressure of water in the atmosphere passed the appropriate threshold levels, rainwater would once again fall on the Martian surface. However, on the basis of present knowledge, the atmosphere would contain only trace amounts of nitrogen. McKay estimates that if this process could utilize about 1% of the solar energy incident on Mars, about 200 years would be required to achieve the atmosphere described above. Environmental changes would have to be monitored during this period in order to determine as accurately as possible planetary conditions at the start of the second, biological, phase of ecopoiesis.

Methods proposed to achieve the warming of Mars range from focusing solar energy on the polar regions with giant space mirrors, and lowering the reflectivity of the ice caps by spreading suitable absorbing material over them, to introducing into the atmosphere highly efficient greenhouse gases, such as chlorofluorocarbons (Oberg 1981; Allaby and Lovelock 1984; McKay 1982a, 1987). Despite the appealing simplicity of the positive-feedback system for CO_2 release described above, it must be pointed out that it depends crucially on the amount of CO_2 accessible for release by warming. If this inventory is too small it might not be possible to achieve a sufficient rise in planetary temperature to produce liquid water through this process. Furthermore, the temperature of the polar caps would have to be increased to prevent the condensation of the newly liberated CO_2 gas into CO_2 frost in these "cold traps". If this could not be achieved the atmospheric pressure would not build up to any significant degree (Murray *et al.* 1981).

Obviously the technological problems, cost, and political

commitment involved in initiating and carrying through a 200-year planetary engineering project would be enormous. However, relative to the resources of contemporary society, such a megaproject would not be any more taxing than were some of the great engineering feats of the past, for example the construction of the pyramids at Giza or the Great Wall of China. Certainly it would not cost as much as the dangerous scheme known as "Star Wars."

The biological component of ecopoiesis is much more difficult to delineate at present. We know very little about the workings of our own biosphere, let alone how to construct, *ab initio*, a stable ecosystem in an alien environment. Here the problem is lack of basic knowledge, or even good theory, on biospheric structure and function.

Once detailed knowledge of the new Martian environmental conditions became available, it would be necessary to marshal an appropriate constellation of microorganisms capable of proliferation and symbiotic interaction as a stable ecosystem. It would not be enough to put down a single species and just "let it grow." The optimal nature, number, relative population sizes, arrival sequence, and geographic distribution are only some of the factors which would have to be considered. Some of these organisms might be found among the many exotic species that already live in extreme environments on earth, for example the chemoautotrophs (Clark 1979). These bacteria have simple, purely inorganic nutrient requirements and can obtain energy by the oxidation of reduced *inorganic* compounds, for example, *Thiobacillus denifriticans* which utilizes sulphur or thiosulphate as an oxidizable substrate. (Clark 1979). If even exotic earth organisms proved inadequate, there exists a large repertoire of unusual biochemical adaptations which might be drawn upon for ecopoiesis (Hochachka and Somero 1984). The genes responsible for the required features could be brought together in unusual combinations, using genetic engineering techniques, to produce artificial organisms suitable for the new Martian environment.

Unfortunately, present speculation on the biogeochemical properties of possible Martian ecosystems is not strongly constrained by hard facts. It is likely that a variety of different kinds of microbial ecosystems, utilizing chemically different sources of metabolic energy, could be constructed. These could vary not only in the vigor with which they produce biomass, but more particularly in their ability to add oxygen to the atmosphere. If the ultimate goal was to be terraformation, then obviously a primitive, oxygen-producing biota would be essential. As the concentration of oxygen in the atmosphere increased, ozone would be formed photochemically, especially at high altitudes. This, of course, would provide a gradually increasing degree of protection against the genetic effects of solar ultraviolet light incident on the planet. However, it is important to realize that such an ecosystem might not in fact be "optimal" with respect to Martian resources and conditions (Clark 1979), especially if the first objective was the local production of biomass of *some* kind.

McKay (1987 and personal communication) has argued that Mars also could support an earth-like atmosphere of oxygen and nitrogen. On the basis of present knowledge it could be produced most readily by an appropriately designed Martian biota capable of converting atmospheric CO_2 and soil nitrates to the desired oxygen-nitrogen mixture. Although this would be a thick atmosphere which animals could breathe, it would be very cold, about $-40°C$. However, its temperature could be raised to more tolerable levels by the addition of trace amounts of chlorofluorocarbons which would have a "greenhouse" effect. He estimates that the time required to produce this atmosphere could be as long as 100,000 years, a long time for all of us, but not long on geological or evolutionary time scales. Nor are such time frames long with respect to those currently being discussed for the safe, geological containment of high-level fuel wastes from existing nuclear power reactors (Dormuth and Nuttall 1987)!

FROM GOLDILOCKS TO GAIA

In the familiar childhood fable, Goldilocks is the little girl who finds the porridge of Father Bear too hot, that of Mother Bear too cold, but Baby Bear's is just right. In Greek mythology, Gaia is the Goddess of Earth, honored as the mother of all, who nourishes her children and gives them rich blessings.

These two ladies also loom large in the imagination of certain climatologists and students of Earth's biosphere.

For climatologists, the Goldilocks problem is to understand just why, from presumably similar starting points 4.5 billion years ago, Venus has become much too hot for life ($\sim460°C$) and Mars has become too cold ($\sim-60°C$), while Earth has remained just right ($\sim15°C$): this despite an initially low output of solar energy around the time these planets were formed (about 30% less than today), and a gradually increasing solar luminosity ever since. One answer is that the three planets have dramatically different climates because they differ in their ability to cycle carbon dioxide between their crusts and atmospheres (Haberle 1986; Kasting *et al.* 1988). On Earth, this CO_2 cycle is thought to provide a thermostatic negative-feedback loop which prevents both the runaway (or moist) greenhouse effect which occurred on Venus and the global deep-freeze which overtook Mars. The cycle has the effect of increasing or decreasing atmospheric CO_2 as the surface temperature falls or rises respectively. On this theory, Mars cooled down because its small size and high surface-to-volume ratio meant that it lost its initial internal heat at a rather rapid rate. After an early warm period, lasting perhaps one billion years, it became so cold that it could no longer release CO_2 from its interior carbonate sediments to replace that being lost from the atmosphere in the form of carbonic acid rainfall. Thus, the regulatory CO_2 cycle between crust and atmosphere was severed, and concomitantly with this, the planet cooled through loss of the CO_2 greenhouse effect. If the level of atmospheric CO_2 is maintained only, or primarily, through a purely geochemical re-cycling mechanism of this kind, then any new biosphere established on Mars might also be short-lived. Goldilocks would consume Baby Bear's porridge and the story would end once again.

The Gaia hypothesis suggests that the presence of life provides an additional cybernetic regulatory system which acts homeostatically to maintain the climatic and geochemical conditions of Earth within the relatively narrow range required for organisms to survive (Lovelock and Margulis 1974; Lovelock 1979; Lovelock and Watson 1982; Kerr 1988). On this theory, life itself plays a significant role in keeping the chemical composition of the atmosphere well removed from that of a purely abiological equilibrium state. Living organisms are not lonely actors on an inert stage of earth physics and chemistry. Rather the biosphere, atmosphere, lithosphere and hydrosphere are viewed as integral parts of a single dynamic system of planetary regulation and evolution. If this theory has merit, then it is possible that ecopoiesis on Mars could generate a born-again Gaia on our sister planet.

In this area of planetary science there seem to be more questions, and conflicting opinions, than answers and well-confirmed theories. None the less, it should be evident that much important research would be stimulated even by a feasibility study of ecopoiesis, quite independently of whether such a project was ever launched. The knowledge gained would be of inestimable value to future generations in tending the biosphere we do know, and thereby perhaps in putting off or avoiding for Earth the heat death of Venus or the cold death of Mars.

FROM SPECULATIONS TO ASSUMPTIONS

The basic scientific and engineering elements of ecopoiesis and terraformation, as presently conceived, can be summarized in a series of general assumptions for purposes of philosophical discussion and analysis. The list is not intended to be exhaustive and all assertions remain subject to alteration in light of future scientific and/or technological advances. However, they do provide a useful framework of hypotheses on which we can fix ideas and raise several philosophical questions. Therefore, I will state the assumptions as simply as possible:

a   Mars is the only biocompatible planet in the solar system, other than Earth.
b   There is no presently existing life of any sort on Mars; it is indeed a sterile planet.
c   Present environmental conditions on the Martian surface are actively hostile, not only to all known forms of life, but even to the existence of the simple organic molecules which form the basic building-blocks of cells.

d   There are no reasons of scientific principle why ecopoiesis on Mars is impossible.

e   A substantial number of exploratory missions to Mars, both robotic and manned, would have to be launched in order to provide the additional basic knowledge of the planet needed for any decision to proceed with the project.

f   If no technical road-blocks exist, the first phase of ecopoiesis would require a massive, long-term program of planetary engineering designed to increase the average temperature of Mars to produce a thick CO_2 atmosphere and a substantial amount of liquid water on the surface. If, for any reason, the project was aborted during this phase, physical conditions on the planet would revert ultimately to something similar, if not identical, to their present state.

g   The second phase of ecopoiesis would involve the seeding of Mars with a suite of symbiotic microbial species capable of forming a primitive ecosystem. Some of these organisms might be "artificial" products of genetic engineering. We will call this the "primary microbial ecosystem," to distinguish it from later evolved or engineered ecosystems.

h   To achieve terraformation, an oxygen/nitrogen-producing biota would have to be introduced on the planet.

i   As far as possible, all aspects of the project would be tested first on Earth, both in detailed computer simulations and "pilot plant" trials in specially constructed "Mars Environment" laboratories.

j   The cost of the project would be large, but not beyond the economic capacity of the industrialized world.

k   A large-scale program of manned missions to Mars, leading to the development of enclosed human habitats in "field stations" is likely to be launched by the USA and the USSR early in the next century (Wilford 1988).

In addition to these basic assumptions, there are many strategic and tactical questions which would have to be addressed if the overall feasibility of the project was confirmed as a result of further planetary exploration and laboratory trials, for example:

A.   Should ecopoiesis be carried out on a full-scale global level, or rather be confined to some appropriate "oasis," for example on a very broad and deep valley specially engineered for the purpose?

B. Should the ecosystem be "tended" by regular monitoring and further intervention, if necessary; or should it be left "untended" and allowed to develop "on its own"?

C. Should terraformation be the ultimate objective of ecopoiesis?

Obviously there are many other important issues that would have to be addressed, especially in the economic, socio-political and legal areas. However, it is possible to raise some basic philosophical questions in light of the foregoing set of assertions and questions.

FROM NATURAL PHILOSOPHY TO MORAL PHILOSOPHY

There are at least two questions that merit attention. First, is there any ethical dimension to ecopoiesis at all? If the answer is affirmative then a second follows: does ecopoiesis present novel issues that could open up hitherto unexplored reaches of practical ethics and axiology? My response to the first question is indeed affirmative; to the second, it is a definite "maybe."

I base my positive response to the first question primarily on the fact that there is a significant number of people who do claim that important ethical questions are raised not only by terraformation but also by the entire space program. (Ecopoiesis seems to have been discussed so far only under the assumption that its ultimate objective is terraformation.) Recently, an entire symposium, involving space scientists, social scientists, phil-osophers, theologians, and lawyers, was devoted to wide-ranging discussions of environmental ethics in the context of solar system exploration and exploitation (Hargrove 1986). Even if one subscribes to emotive, personalist or relativist theories of ethical judgments, it seems to me that the sober reflections of informed people, whatever their perspective, command respect. On this basis the issue must be joined by philosophers and scientists alike.

If it could be argued successfully that ecopoiesis *per se* is ethically neutral, the policy question of whether we should proceed with it would raise further ethical questions regarding its indirect "opportunity costs": would not such a venture inevitably erode the level of public funding that otherwise might be devoted to more immediate earthbound priorities for which most of us do sense a categorical imperative, for example the alleviation of disease, poverty and famine? Moral permission does not entail moral obligation. However, ethical questions of this latter kind are by no means novel. Unfortunately, they have little force in affecting public policy, as so amply demonstrated in the enormous amounts of money that even poor countries lavish on their military establishments.

The answer to the second question is far less clear and for this reason I consider it to be the most interesting aspect of ecopoiesis for philosophers to ponder. The notion that ecopoiesis might indeed pose fundamentally new questions in philosophy emerges from two presuppositions, generally unstated, that seem to inform most ethical discourse: homocentrism and geocentrism. That is, ethical principles and theories of value are widely assumed to have application only in the relations between people living on this planet. However, it is interesting to note that Michael Ruse (1985) has argued, along both Kantian and utilitarian lines, that there are indeed "universal" ethical principles that we follow and which would be followed by sentient extraterrestrials, if they are the products of biological evolution as we know it. On his view we would find that rape is wrong also on Andromeda.

Prominent Judeo-Christian philosophers have adopted an extreme personalist view of values. For example, Emil Brunner (1947) has asserted flatly that there are no intrinsic values and that value exists only in reference to persons. Martin Buber has claimed that value is always value for a person rather than something with an absolute, independent existence (Friedman 1955). If one adopts this homocentric bias, then, *a fortiori*, one also must be a geocentrist for we know of no other sentient beings in the universe (*pace Deo*).

Albert Schweitzer (1933) was a prominent critic of the homocentric position. He argued that

Man is ethical only when life, as such, is sacred to him, that of plants and animals as well as that of his fellow men....

176

> The ethic of the relation of man to man is not something apart by itself: it is only a particular relation which results from the universal one.

The rise of environmental ethics and the "animal liberation" movement is a further manifestation of Schweitzer's basic view. Particularly relevant to ecopoiesis is Tom Regan's (1982) argument that ecosystems may be of "direct moral significance" to us. Holmes Rolston (1986) has carried this line of thinking to its logical conclusion and would grant value, and (I infer) moral considerability, to all objects of "formed integrity" in the cosmos, i.e. landscapes, seascapes, rocks, moons, planets, indeed anything "worthy of a proper name." Clearly such an ethic is neither homocentric nor geocentric. However, its strict application would prohibit not only the planetary engineering phase of ecopoiesis, but also much civil engineering here on Earth. It also raises the specter of a possible moral obligation to prevent catastrophic collisions in space between, say, other planets and asteroids, should we acquire the technical capacity to perform such feats.

These considerations suggest to me that we need from philosophers a new "cosmocentric" ethics, and perhaps a revised theory of intrinsic worth, if we are to evaluate the moral pros and cons of proposals for ecopoiesis in an intelligent and sensitive way. As I see it, the first objective of such an ethic would be to resolve the dialectical contradiction that commonly arises between superficial views of "evolutionary progress" and "ecological harmony." If pushed to their obvious extremes these conflicting myths could lead to the grossest kind of human environmental imperialism on the one hand, or to the destructive elimination of all technology, including modern medicine and agriculture, on the other. For me, a cosmocentric ethic would allow scope for human creativity in science and engineering throughout the solar system, but also recognize that at present we depend utterly on the vitality of the Earth's biosphere for our very existence. It would recognize also that the physical artifacts of humanity are as much a part of the universe as are stars, planets, plants and animals. In this connection, I would urge environmentalists and devotees of the cult of the "natural" to remember Thomas Browne's observation in the *Religio Medici* (1643) when he said "all things are artificial for Nature is the Art of God."

Westermarck (1932) has argued, from his position of ethical relativism, that moral judgments, by disinterested observers, consist simply in labeling acts as "good" or "bad", according to "certain obvious characteristics which they present in common with other acts belonging to the same group." If this analysis is exhaustive and persuasive, then there would seem to be yet another reason for thinking that ecopoiesis presents issues which fall outside the range of traditional ethical theories. For what is the "reference group" of acts to which ecopoiesis might be compared? Irrigation of deserts for purposes of agriculture comes to mind, but the analogy is not a good one because species indigenous to the area cultivated (e.g. "weeds") normally are displaced or eliminated.

Recall that the second assumption above is that Mars is indeed a sterile, lifeless planet. On the basis of environmental ethics, McKay (pp. 184–97) concludes that if, and only if, there are no indigenous forms of life on Mars should we attempt to alter its global environment to accommodate immigrant species from Earth. However, this requirement could present a serious ethical block to ecopoiesis if absolute proof were required for the initial sterility of the planet. Organisms have been found on Earth which are well-adapted to extraordinary microniches in macroenvironments once thought to be sterile, the most notorious being the cryptendolithic lichens which live a few millimeters below the surface of sandstone rocks in Antarctic dry valleys (Friedmann 1982). Short of totally ransacking the planet searching for indigenous biota, an undertaking as damaging as it would be costly, it is difficult to see how one ever could convince uncompromising critics that the planet is totally sterile everywhere. Thus, it seems possible that rigorous adherence to the second assumption could forestall the project. The facts that human activities have already led to the extinction of species on Earth, and that in the historic course of evolution many more species have been eliminated through natural selection, can hardly be expected to carry much weight with environmental extremists.

A similar problem arises from the fifth assumption. It is reasonable to suppose that the scientific community would make a strong and cogent case for extensive exploration and study of the geophysical, geochemical and possible paleontological features of Mars in its pristine state before agreeing to any large-scale program of planetary engineering to alter it. Such studies would be costly and require a great deal of time. Again, if carried to extremes, even this important research could delay indefinitely any program of planetary engineering.

Let us suppose that some means are found to rule out any significant probability of life presently existing on Mars, at least to the satisfaction of reasonable, well-informed individuals. Let us suppose further that the planetary engineering phase of ecopoiesis is successful and that a primary microbial ecosystem is established. This microbiota would now be "indigenous" to the planet, and on the basis of the position advocated by Regan (1982), would have to be accorded some "right" to its own natural evolutionary trajectory. Now chance events and various stochastic processes, at the levels of mutation, genetic drift and natural selection, play crucial roles in determining the directions and rates of natural evolutionary change (Haynes 1987). The theory of evolution does not allow detailed predictions to be made of future speciations and extinctions. In particular, we could not be sure that any oxygen-evolving microorganisms (if these could be included in the primary ecosystem) would not become extinct at some future date. Thus, if terraformation was to be the ultimate objective of an ecopoiesis project, it seems likely that the Martian biota would have to be tended or nurtured in such a way as to ensure the development of the desired oxygen atmosphere. This would compromise the ecosystemic "freedom" of the primary microbial ecosystem to evolve "naturally." Clearly, on the basis of Regan's (1982) environmental ethic it would appear that terraformation would be morally objectionable even if ecopoiesis were not.

I will not rehearse here the various philosophical and socio-political arguments that have been put forward in support of terraformation as these are to be found in the writings of Oberg, McKay and others. It is interesting to note, however, that the ecologist Frank Golley (1986) has argued that the space programs of the superpowers, including the development of extraterrestrial ecosystems, if feasible, will proceed apace for the simple reason that such endeavors are consistent with the dominant myths and metaphors of western civilization. He can see no turning back from this great adventure of humankind because to do so would require a fundamental reorientation of our culture.

I suspect we will never adequately understand the workings of our own biosphere until we have made a serious attempt at least to design, if not actually to generate, another one. The science that would emerge from a feasibility study of ecopoiesis might never be used to do anything for Mars, though it could provide the knowledge and insight necessary to sustain our earthly habitat.

Immanuel Kant concluded his "Critique of Practical Reason" with the famous line: "Two things fill my mind with ever-increasing wonder and awe – the starry heavens above me and the moral law within me." If indeed morality has roots in the very nature of things, then it is unlikely that ecopoiesis can take place if it violates any ultimate moral principle of the universe. At any rate, if Crick is right about directed panspermia, it is obvious that his Promethean ETI discerned no profound ethical prohibition in sowing the seeds of life on Earth.

NOTES

1. *Ecopoiesis* is my neologism. The term refers to the fabrication of a sustainable ecosystem on a currently lifeless, sterile planet, thereby establishing a new arena in which biological evolution ultimately might proceed independent of further human husbandry. *Terraformation* is a specialized form of ecopoiesis which refers to the development of specifically earth-like conditions culminating in the transfer of suitable earth organisms to the target planet. In either case, the new ecosystem might be confined physically to some suitable planetary oasis, or it might be global in extent, in which case it would be called an "ecosphere" or "biosphere". The expression ecopoiesis is derived from the Greek roots οἶκος, an abode, house or dwelling-place (from which we also derive "ecology" and "economics") and θοίησις, a fabrication or production (from which we derive "poesy," as well as a variety of other biological terms such as biopoiesis, hematopoiesis, etc.). The word already has been given some currency in publications of Margulis and Sagan (1985) and Lovelock (1987).

REFERENCES

Allaby, M. and Lovelock, J. E. (1984) *The Greening of Mars*, New York: St. Martin's/Marek.

Averner, M. M. and MacElroy, R. D. (1976) *On the Habitability of Mars. NASA Report SP-414*, Springfield, Va: National Technical Information Service, US Department of Commerce.

Biemann, K. (and twelve others) (1977) "The Search for Organic Substances and Organic Volatile Compounds on the Surface of Mars," *Journal of Geophysical Research* 82: 4641–62.

Browne, Thomas (1643) *Religio Medici*, reprinted in *The Works of Sir Thomas Browne*, ed. G. Keynes, London: Oxford University Press, 1964.

Brunner, E. (1947) *The Divine Imperative*, Philadelphia, Pa: Westminster Press.

Carr, M. H. (1981) *The Surface of Mars*, New Haven and London: Yale University Press.

Chun, S., Pang, K., Cutts, J. A. and Ajello, J. M. (1978) "Photocatalytic Oxidation of Organic Compounds on Mars," *Nature* 274: 875–6.

Clark, B. C. (1979) "Solar-Driven Chemical Energy Source for a Martian Biota," *Origins of Life* 9: 241–9.

Crick, F. H. C. (1981) *Life Itself*, New York: Simon & Schuster.

Dormuth, K. W. and Nuttall, K. (1987) "The Canadian Nuclear Fuel Waste Management Program," *Radioactive Waste Management and the Nuclear Fuel Cycle* 8: 93–104.

Friedman, M. B. (1955) *Martin Buber: The Life of Dialogue*, Chicago, Ill.: University of Chicago Press.

Friedmann, E. I. (1982) "Endolithic Microorganisms in the Antarctic Cold Desert," *Science* 215: 1045–53.

Furley, D. (1987) *The Greek Cosmologists, vol. I*, Cambridge: Cambridge University Press.

Golley, F. B. (1986) "Environmental Ethics and Extraterrestrial Ecosystems," in E. C. Hargrove (ed.) *Beyond Spaceship Earth: Environmental Ethics and the Solar System*, San Francisco, Calif: Sierra Club Books.

Haberle, R. M. (1986) "The Climate of Mars," *Scientific American* 254: 54–62.

Hargrove, E. C. (ed.) (1986) *Beyond Spaceship Earth: Environmental Ethics and the Solar System*, San Francisco, Calif: Sierra Club Books.

Haynes, R. H. (1987) "The 'Purpose' of Chance in Light of the Physical Basis of Evolution," in J. M. Robson (ed.) *Origin and Evolution of the Universe: Evidence for Design?*, Kingston and Montreal: McGill-Queens University Press.

Heinlein, R. (1950) *Farmer in the Sky*, New York: Ballantine Books.

Hochachka, P. W. and Somero, G. N. (1984) *Biochemical Adaptation*, Princeton, NJ: Princeton University Press.

Horowitz, N. H. (1986) *To Utopia and Back: The Search for Life in the Solar System*, New York: W. H. Freeman & Co.

Hunten, D. M. (1974) "Aeronomy of the Lower Atmosphere of Mars," *Rev. Geophys. Space. Phys.* 12: 529–35.

—— (1979) "Possible Oxidant Sources in the Atmosphere and Surface of Mars," *J. Mol. Evol.* 14: 71–8.

Kasting, J. F., Toon, O. B. and Pollack, J. B. (1988) "How Climate Evolved on the Terrestrial Planets," *Scientific American* 258: 90–7.

Kerr, R. A. (1988) "No Longer Willful, Gaia Becomes Respectable," *Science* 240: 393–5.

Krumbein, W. E. (ed.) (1983) *Microbial Geochemistry*, Oxford: Blackwell Scientific Publications.

Lovelock, J. E. (1975) "Thermodynamics and the Recognition of Alien Biospheres," *Proceedings of the Royal Society of London*, B 189: 167–81.

—— (1979) *Gaia*, Oxford: Oxford University Press.

—— (1987) "The Ecopoiesis of Daisy World," in J. M. Robson (ed.) *Origin and Evolution of the Universe: Evidence for Design?*, Kingston and Montreal: McGill-Queens University Press.

Lovelock, J. E. and Margulis, L. (1974) "Atmospheric Homeostasis by and for the Biosphere," *Tellus* 26: 1–6.

Lovelock, J. E. and Watson, A. J. (1982) "The Regulation of Carbon Dioxide and Climate: Gaia or Geochemistry," *Planetary and Space Science* 30: 795–802.

McKay, C. P. (1982a) "Terraforming Mars," *Journal of the British Interplanetary Society* 35: 427–33.

—— (1982b) "On Terraforming Mars," *Extrapolation* 23: 309–14.

—— (1987) "Making an Earth of Mars," *Planetary Report* 7: 26–7.

Margulis, L. and Sagan, D. (1985) "Biospheric Concepts," in *The Biosphere Catalogue*, London: Synergistic Press.

—— (1986) *Micro-cosmos: Four Billion Years of Microbial Evolution*, New York: Simon & Schuster.

Miller, S. L. and Orgel, L. E. (1974) *The Origins of Life on Earth*, Englewood Cliffs, NJ: Prentice-Hall.

Murray, B., Malin, M. C. and Greeley, R. (1981) *Earthlike Planets*, San Francisco, Calif.: W. H. Freeman & Co.

NASA Technical Memorandum 82478 (1983) *Mars* (by C. P. McKay), reprinted from *Space and Planetary Environmental Criteria Guidelines for Use in Space Vehicle Development 1982 Revision* (vol. I), compiled by R. E. Smith and G. S. West, NASA Scientific and Technical Information Branch, Washington, DC.

Oberg, J. E. (1981) *New Earths*, Harrisburg, Pa: Stackpole Books.

Oparin, A. I. (1957) *The Origin of Life on Earth*, London: Oliver & Boyd.

Oro, J. and Holzer, G. (1979) "The Effects of Ultraviolet Light on the Degradation of Organic Compounds: A Possible Explanation for the Absence of Organic Matter on Mars," in R. Holmquist and A. C. Strickland (eds) *COSPAR, Life Sciences and Space Research*, New York: Pergamon Press.

Pirie, N. W. (1937) "The Meaninglessness of the Terms Life and Living," in J. Needham and F. Green (eds) *Perspectives in Biochemistry*, Cambridge: Cambridge University Press.

Regan, Tom (1982) *All that Dwells Therein: Animal Rights and Environmental Ethics*, Berkeley: University of California Press.

Regis, E. (ed.) (1985) *Extraterrestrials: Science and Alien Intelligence*, Cambridge: Cambridge University Press.

Rolston, H. (1986) "The Preservation of Natural Value in the Solar System," in E. C. Hargrove, *Beyond Spaceship Earth: Environmental Ethics in the Solar System*, San Francisco, Calif.: Sierra Club Books.

Ruse, M. (1985) "Is Rape Wrong on Andromeda? An Introduction to Extraterrestrial Evolution, Science and Morality," in E. Regis (ed.) *Extraterrestrials: Science and Alien Intelligence*, Cambridge: Cambridge University Press.

Schopf, J. W. (1978) "The Evolution of the Earliest Cells," *Scientific American* 239: 110–38.

Schweitzer, A. (1933) *My Life and Thought, an Autobiography*, trans. C. T. Campion, London: George Allen & Unwin.

Solar System Exploration Committee of the NASA Advisory Council (1986) *Planetary Exploration Through the Year 2000: an Augmented Program*, Washington, DC: US Government Printing Office.

Westermarck, E. (1932) *Ethical Relativity*, New York: Harcourt, Brace & Co.

Wilford, J. N. (1988) "Destination: Mars," *New York Times Magazine*, March 20, 1988.

Williamson, J. (1968) *Seetee Ship*, New York: Lancer Books.

—— (1969) *Seetee Shock*, London: Mayflower Books.

Wilson, J. T. (1963) "Continental Drift," *Scientific American* 206: 86–100.

GENERAL BIBLIOGRAPHY

Boston, P. J. (ed.) (1984) *The Case for Mars, Vol. I*, Science and Technology Series 57, San Diego, Calif.: The American Astronautical Society.

Carr, M. H. (1981) *The Surface of Mars*, New Haven and London: Yale University Press.

McKay, C. P. (ed.) (1985) *The Case for Mars, Vol. II*, Science and Technology Series 62, San Diego, Calif.: The American Astronautical Society.

Matsunaga, Senator Spark M. (1986) *Journeys beyond the Cold War*, New York: Hill & Wang.

National Commission on Space (1986) *Pioneering the Space Frontier*, New York: Bantam Books.

10

ETHICS AND PLANETARY ENGINEERING

2 Does Mars have rights? An approach to the environmental ethics of planetary engineering

CHRISTOPHER P. MCKAY

INTRODUCTION

It is becoming increasingly clear that the activities of humans can be, and are, a factor capable of altering environments on a planetary scale. We are presently engaged in both inadvertent and deliberate modifications of the global environment of Earth. The most immediate example of the global impact of human technology is the increase in atmospheric CO_2 due primarily to the burning of fossil fuel.[1] Serious proposals for deliberate planetary-scale engineering projects include:[2] altering the flow of rivers in western Russia, flooding the Sahara Desert, and damming the Amazon Basin. All of these projects would have global environmental repercussions. Altering the environment of Earth raises many valid concerns which, for the most part, fit into the context of current discussions of environmental ethics.

The same basic technological capability that has extended the reach of human activity to global dimensions could also be used to alter the environments of other planets. Typically, it has been assumed that the objective of such alteration would be to provide an environment suitable to unprotected humans. However, a more general consideration can be construed. I have defined *terraforming* as the use of planetary engineering techniques to

> alter the environment of a planet in order to improve the chances of survival of an indigenous biology or to allow habitation of most, if not all, terrestrial life forms. The

184

resulting system should be stable and should require no, or a minimum of, continued technological intervention.

(McKay 1982a)

Excluding the Earth, the most likely planet in the solar system on which terraforming, as defined above, might apply is Mars. The reasons for this have been discussed in detail elsewhere (McKay 1982b) and are only briefly summarized here. Currently the surface of Mars is too cold and dry to support life. However, all the elements necessary for life have been detected in some accessible form. Indirect evidence suggests that there are adequate supplies of these biogenic elements and compounds (e.g. CO_2, H_2O) to allow for a planetary-scale biosphere. Although the amount of nitrogen in the atmosphere appears inadequate to sustain life its concentration in the soil is unknown.

My own calculations and those of J. Lovelock (Lovelock and Allaby 1984) suggest that present levels of technology are capable of instigating processes on Mars which would alter the Martian climate resulting in an atmosphere of a composition that is suitable for life and within habitable temperature and pressure limits. It appears that humans have (or will very shortly have) the ability to terraform Mars. Thus, terraforming Mars is an issue for current consideration and is not necessarily relevant only to future more technologically advanced societies.

In the past, technologists have been heavily criticized for equating what can be done with what ought to be done. The procedure for determining whether terraforming Mars can be done is based on our understanding of the general principles of planetary climate and on a detailed knowledge of the present mineral state of Mars. The procedure is difficult due to incomplete data and insufficient theories, but it is conceptually straightforward. Considerable progress in the relevant fields coupled with new prospects for *in situ* studies of Mars bode well for the further clarification of the technical problems associated with terraforming Mars.

If we assume that terraforming Mars can be done, how can we determine whether terraforming Mars ought to be done? One possible approach to this issue is to analyze the results of the environmental movement and to see how the principles

185

and ethics developed there can be applied to extraterrestrial situations. The primary difficulty with this approach is that virtually all of the serious considerations of environmental ethics have been embedded within the context of the Earth, with at most a passing reference to the fact that some day these issues would be relevant to other planets. This is nicely illustrated by the recent collection of essays in environmental ethics, entitled, appropriately enough, *Earthbound*. The closing paragraph of the wrap-up essay, written by E. Johnston, is

> As we leap into the rest of the universe, these questions, questions of environmental ethical theory, become more and more pressing. Already scientists are talking about transforming the environments of *other* planets. For good or evil, we will not be earthbound forever.

> (Johnston 1984: 359)

In this chapter I have attempted to apply current environmental ethics to the problem of terraforming Mars. In order to do this it has been necessary to attempt to isolate the essence of the various ethical principles in a form that is not specific to the Earth but provides a general statement that can be universally applied. When this difficult task is completed it is straightforward to examine the implications of these principles for terraforming Mars.

FUNDAMENTAL PRINCIPLES OF ENVIRONMENTAL ETHICS

Environmental thinking developed in many aspects in response to crisis. Because of this approach many of the early statements of the principles of environmentalism are merely recognition of the facts of this crisis[3] or clever pedagogical statements about the properties of terrestrial ecosystems.[4] These concepts did provide the basis for action on environmental issues facing society but they did not elucidate the underlying principles that form the basis for the action of humans in the environment.

In his classic paper "The Shallow and the Deep, Long-Range Ecology Movements" (1973), Arne Naess attempts to go beyond these "shallow" ecological considerations to more fundamental precepts.[5] Other ecologists have similarly investigated the underlying dogmas of ecology in attempts to derive universally valid principles on which to base environmental action. It is to these studies that one must look for fundamental axioms of environmental ethics that can be applied to the question of terraforming Mars.

However, even "deep" ecology has focused, somewhat justifiably, on the study of the Earth. The interaction of the biological and physical components of Earth's environment are referred to as nature (or Nature) and the connection to extraterrestrial events is often neglected. It is clear that this is a simplification in many respects. Besides the obvious role that sunlight plays, cosmic rays are a pervasive reminder that Earth is not alone. More dramatically, the impact of extraterrestrial objects onto the Earth may have played an important role in the evolution of biological systems. Our view of ecology has been shaped by the fact that Earth is the only planet on which we know life to exist. None the less, to use the basic principles of eco-ethics we must first cast them in a form independent of Earth, independent of Nature.

Consider, for example, Leopold's egalitarian ecosystem ethic: "A thing is right when it tends to preserve the integrity, stability, and beauty of the biotic community. It is wrong if it tends to do otherwise" (1966: 262). There is no unequivocal way to apply this axiom to the question of terraforming Mars since it presupposes a healthy global-scale biota. There almost certainly is no "biotic community" on Mars. Does this principle then compel us to transplant a biotic community from Earth? Or to leave Mars alone? Leopold's classic "Land Ethic" is developed around a concept of land which he described as "not merely soil; it is a fountain of [biological] energy flowing through a circuit of soils, plants, and animals" (ibid.: 253). On Mars the land is merely crushed rock.

The task of distilling the fundamental principles of ecological ethics is further complicated by the fact that most of the emphasis in ecology has been on the operational implications of a particular point of view rather than the moral or ethical roots. This is to be expected due to the "lifeboat" situation of the environmental movement in which general awareness of the environment has come largely in response to serious problems.

Despite these difficulties, I have attempted to canvass the broad perspective of environmental thought and identify the various general principles on which it is based. For the purposes of this chapter I suggest that virtually all of the various ecological views have as their fundamental basis one, or a combination of the three following basic principles.

- *Anti-humanism*. Humans must live in accord with the rhythms of Nature in a simple pastoral setting free of technology. Humans have no special rights or needs and do not determine the value of the environment. This principle is closely linked to the principles of humility and "original sin."
- *Wise stewardship*. The bounty of nature is ours to use in a wise and constrained manner. The measure of value in the environment is ultimately tied to the present or future needs of humans. This principle is closely linked to the principle of utility.
- *Intrinsic worth*. There exists a set of objects that have intrinsic worth. Choices for this set are: humans, human and non-human animals, all life, all of Nature. Humans have a responsibility to respect and support the interests of members of this set. This principle is closely linked to the principle of the value of life.

These principles establish the underlying dogma from which secondary principles and operational conclusions are derived. In many works all three of these principles appear in various forms and with varying emphases.

Anti-humanism is based on the belief that humans are not privileged, being merely one part among many equals, and should not change the ecology of the planet. An intrinsic component of this view is the notion that the world-ecological system is too complex for human beings to understand, much less direct, and the ultimate goal and good of humankind is passive contemplation of nature. David Ehrenfeld in his book *The Arrogance of Humanism* provides a clear statement of the anti-humanism perspective. He concludes that humans have "defiled everything, much of it forever, even the farthest jungles of the Amazon and the air above the mountains, even the everlasting sea which gave us birth" (1978: 269). Ehrenfeld decries the global impact of human technology and suggests

188

that only by relinquishing it and subjugating our interests to Nature can balance be achieved. The underlying theme of the anti-humanism perspective is a mistrust in the capabilities of humans to make the choices that are in keeping with the harmony and balance of Nature. This leads to the suggestion that humans simplify their lives and eliminate the technology that gives such weight to their intrinsically faulted choices. The emphasis on simplification is evident in the following passage from *Deep Ecology*:

> Our vital material needs are probably more simple than many realize. In technocratic-industrial societies there is overwhelming propaganda and advertising which encourages false needs and destructive desires designed to foster increased production and consumption of goods. Most of this actually diverts us from facing reality in an objective way and from beginning the "real work" of spiritual growth and maturity.
>
> (Devall and Sessions 1985)

Perhaps the principle most prevalent in eco-ethics is that of *wise stewardship*. In this view the steward is not just interested in obtaining short-term profit from the system but has the wider perspective as suggested by René Dubos. The steward realizes that there are good economic reasons for preserving a diverse and stable biota and that it is to her advantage to study nature and approach change cautiously. The many economic reasons for valuing apparently non-useful biological resources include:[6] recreational and esthetic values, future values, ecosystem stabilization, examples of biological adaptive strategies, use in environmental baseline and monitoring studies, scientific research, educational, habit reconstruction. The list is sufficiently complete and diverse for the wise-stewardship principle to form the basis of a range of environmental policies, covering the political spectrum from liberal to conservative. The concept and arguments of wise stewardship are compelling and virtually all analysis of environmental ethics includes some appeal to the principle of utility. It is probably the only fundamental principle of ecological ethics that has universal appeal. This universal appeal may stem from the clear human need for the goods and services that nature can provide and the desire to maintain these benefits.

The principle of *intrinsic worth* seeks to establish that the non-human components of the biosphere have intrinsic value. Closely related to this assignment of intrinsic worth is the concept of extending the sphere of moral consideration and rights. Historically the progression of moral rights in the western world has extended from free white males to include all humans.

The principle of intrinsic worth is well summarized by the first two tenets of the deep ecology movement (Naess 1984):

1. The well-being of non-human life on Earth has value in itself. This value is independent of any instrumental usefulness for limited human purposes.
2. Richness and diversity in life forms contribute to this value and is a further value in itself.

On this view the concept of moral patients[7] no longer includes all and only humans. Animals are to be included either for fundamentally utilitarian reasons as suggested by Singer in *Practical Ethics* (1979) or because they have rights (Regan 1983; Singer 1980) on account of the fact that they have interests and suffer pain. In his book, *Should Trees Have Standing?*, Christopher D. Stone extends the concepts of rights to all life and in fact to the environment in general. He states: "I am quite seriously proposing that we give legal rights to forests, oceans, rivers and other so-called 'natural objects' in the environment – indeed to the environment as a whole" (Stone 1974: 9).

In a penetrating critique of the environmental ethics movement Richard Watson summarizes a serious argument against wholesale extension of the moral patient:

> ... a considerable amount of what goes on in the inner worlds of environmental ethics is either in ignorance of or in outright defiance of much that has been accomplished in philosophy since the Enlightenment. Ignored are such things as the value and responsibility of self-conscious individual actors, the vacuousness of equating what is good or right with what happens to be or to exist, the arbitrariness

(although not necessarily uselessness) of basing rights on the possession of this or that natural feature.

(Watson 1985: 13)[8]

IMPLICATIONS FOR MARS

Anti-humanism is clearly in conflict with the concept of planetary engineering. In fact, the suggestion that humans purposefully alter the environment of another planet in the belief that they can "improve" it would fuel the argument of the anti-humanists. They would suggest that the technology that enables humans to have global effects is inappropriate and must be dismantled. The question of dealing with an indigenous Martian biota is moot.

Wise stewardship, essentially equivalent to utilitarianism, would support the development of a planet that would be of use to humans, even if only in the distant future. Dealing with indigenous life is more problematical in this perspective. If the Martian biology can provide useful information or goods it should be cultivated. However, there is a conflict between leaving the Martian biota unchanged, assisting the Martian biota, and introducing Earth life forms.

The principle of intrinsic worth provides two radically opposed solutions to the question. Which solution applies depends on the nature of the set of objects which have values and deserve moral consideration. We consider this in two cases: 1) Only life is included and 2) Inanimate objects are also included. Under case 1 there is an explicit statement that life is better than non-life. There is also an implied responsibility to enhance the biological potential of the natural life forms and to resist overriding or replacing these forms. In this case, if there is an indigenous Martian biota we have a moral duty to maximize its biological potential. If there is no life on Mars then we have an obligation to introduce life to Mars and to strive to make that life "natural" under Martian conditions. This may result in a planet that is not habitable to humans.

Under case 2 in which even inanimate objects are moral patients we cannot alter Mars under any circumstances. If there is an indigenous Martian biota we cannot encourage its expansion at the expense of the rocks and regolith (loose surface materials) of Mars. Furthermore we cannot introduce life to alter a lifeless Mars since life has no precedence over non-life.

DOES MARS HAVE RIGHTS?

Can C. D. Stone's expanding circle of rights apply to the planets? Does Mars have rights? Certainly Mars in its present state is beautiful in its own way and useful to humans as it is. It is beautiful in the same sense that the rings of Saturn, the moons of Jupiter and the phases of the moon are beautiful. It is useful to humans in that it provides a planet for study that in many ways is similar to Earth. Much remains to be learned about comparative planetology from studies of Mars. Of particular interest is the possibility that life may have originated in an early Mars and subsequently gone extinct.

Although the Viking experiments suggested that there are no extant life forms on Mars, there is considerable evidence that some time in the past conditions on Mars were quite different. Large valley networks and outflow channels attest to the fact that copious amounts of liquid water once flowed on the Martian surface. This in turn implies that the surface temperature was considerably warmer than it is today with concomitant high pressures. Some of these fluvial features occur in terrain that is heavily cratered, indicating that this warmer climatic regime probably dates back over four billion years.[9]

This view is supported by theoretical considerations which suggest that during the first 500 million years after the formation of Mars and Earth, the surface conditions of both planets were more similar than they are today. During this time period the atmospheric composition and pressure on these planets was determined primarily by outgassing of juvenile material and the surface may have been dominated by the processes of crust formation.[10] In fact, Earth, Venus, and Mars may have all undergone initial periods of outgassing and crust formation that resulted in similar surface conditions on all three planets. We know from the fossil record that life on Earth evolved and reached a fair degree of biological sophistication in the first 500–700 million years. This time interval was probably much shorter but the absence of a suitable fossil record prevents a more accurate determination (Schopf 1983). It is entirely possible, then, that life also arose on Venus and Mars during an early clement epoch on these planets. Subsequent planetary evolution, however, seems to have favored only the Earth. The record of the origin and early evolution of life on Earth, and certainly on Venus, has been obscured by extensive surface erosion, while on Mars the situation is quite different and large fractions of the surface date back to this early time period. Hence, it is entirely possible that while no life exists on Mars today, it holds the best record of the chemical and biological events that led to the origin of life. Understanding this duplicate record of our own origins may, in the long term, be more valuable than another habitable planet.

There are equally cogent arguments that planets without life are unfulfilled and humans have a moral obligation to allow Mars to realize its potential as a biotic planet. Our desires to understand the present Mars and to search for the origin of life can be viewed as denying Mars's right to life in order to further our own interests.

An important caveat here is that life on a terraformed Mars is not necessarily human life. The planetary conditions on Mars may preclude any long-term stable environment suitable to humans. The "natural" biota of Mars may be bacteria, plants, and simple animals, living in an O_2-poor, CO_2-rich atmosphere. One can argue that Mars has a right to its own natural, stable, and unique biota.

AN APPROACH TO TERRAFORMING MARS

In this section I suggest one approach to the ethical issues involved in terraforming Mars. Fundamentally humans should terraform Mars: they should undertake the technological activity that will enhance the survival of any indigenous Martian biota and promote global changes on Mars that will allow for maximizing the richness and diversity of these Martian life forms. If, and only if, there is no indigenous Martian life then humans should alter the global environment of Mars so that the maximum diversity of Earth life can be accommodated there, consistent with the requirement that the resulting system be stable and require little, or no, constant human intervention.

I suggest that the primary motivation for this scenario is rooted in the intrinsic value of life principle. Life has precedence over non-life, life has value. A planet Mars with a natural global-scale biota has value *vis-à-vis* a planet with only sparse life or no life at all.

However, there is an issue of moral consideration to indigenous Martian life. In the approach to terraforming that I am proposing, Martian life has rights. It has the right to continue its existence even if its extinction would benefit the biota of Earth. Furthermore its rights confer upon us the obligation to assist it in obtaining global diversity and stability.

There are two operational implications to the approach to terraforming Mars suggested above. First and foremost is a requirement that the rights of any indigenous Martian life be respected. This necessitates that before humans land on Mars there is a thorough search for life and that the search continue after the establishment of a research base.

In approaching this question we must realize that the absence of life cannot be conclusively demonstrated by robotic missions, and possibly not by human biologists on the surface. The possibility that life could exist in an undiscovered cryptic niche will continually plague those who desire absolute answers from biology. The resolution of this dilemma will have to be in a two-step process. First, defining the biological impact of a localized human presence on Mars, and then determining what level of search is required to insure that any undiscovered cryptic Martian community of organisms is sufficiently well-hidden that it is unlikely to be affected by such a presence (McKay forthcoming).

The second guideline that can be gleaned from the ethical discussion above is that any terraforming effort be conducted in an extremely slow and conservative manner. A conservative approach would allow for maximum study of the present Mars and of all the intermediate stages. We have learned that biological alterations are often irreversible and that caution is warranted in any attempt to alter, and by analogy to construct, an ecosystem.

194

DISCUSSION

The perspective of *Deep Ecology* and the vast (and recent) literature on the rights of animals, plants, and objects fails to provide unambiguous guidelines when applied to environmental rights of Mars. This is because ecological ethics has been inextricably intertwined with the existence of life on Earth and the properties of that particular life; a result of the pervasive nature of life on this planet. Discussion of even such remote and seemingly lifeless places as the ocean bottom and the Antarctic land mass involve ecosystems. Furthermore, the recognized global interconnection of life through the biogeochemical cycles prevents one from rigorously treating any single object or collection of inanimate objects independently from the biological perspective. Thus the extension of rights from life to "mere things" may have no practical implications on Earth.

Mars is probably the first extraterrestrial object that will be utilized by humans. This utilization will occur as part of the human exploration of the planet. In fact current plans call for striving for self-sufficient bases on Mars based on utilization of the atmosphere and soil minerals in life support systems. It is timely and important that the lessons of environmental harmony learned with great effort here on Earth be generalized and applied to Mars, before we go.

NOTES

1. For a discussion of the buildup of carbon dioxide and its consequence, see *Climate Change*: *Report of the Carbon Dioxide Assessment Committee* Washington, DC: National Academy Press, 1983.
2. For a serious collection of essays on planetary engineering applied to Earth, see F. P. Davidson, L. J. Giacoletto and R. Salkeld (eds) (1978) *Macro-Engineering and the Infrastructure of Tomorrow*, Boulder, Colo.: Westview Press.
3. For example, William T. Blackstone, "Ethics and Ecology," in William T. Blackstone (ed.) (1971) *Conference in Philosophy and Environmental Crisis*, Athens, Ga: University of Georgia, p. 21, defines the "Ecological Attitude" with four points: 1) the acknowledgment that man can in fact cause irreversible changes in nature; 2) the awareness that our environmental resources are finite; 3) the recognition that our environment has a limited

capacity to absorb waste; 4) the acknowledgment that a finite
world with finite resources cannot support an infinitely expanding
population.

4. Commoner's often quoted laws of ecology provide an example of
this type of oversimplified ecology. In *The Closing Circle*, New
York: Knopf, 1971, he lists his four laws: 1) everything is
connected to everything else; 2) everything must go somewhere;
3) nature knows best; 4) there is no such thing as a free lunch, or
everything has to go somewhere.

5. See also: Arne Naess (1977) "Notes on the Methodology of
Normative Systems," *Methodology and Science* 10: 64–79; and Arne
Naess (1979) "Self-realization in the Mixed Communities of
Humans, Bears, Sheep, and Wolves," *Inquiry* 22: 231–41.

6. This list of suggested uses for environmental resources is from
Ehrenfeld 1978.

7. Johnston (1984: 337) defines Moral Patients as "those beings who
are members of the moral community, who deserve, or are owed,
direct moral consideration."

8. See also Richard Watson (1983) "A Critique of Anti-Anthropocentric
Biocentrism," *Environmental Ethics* 5: 245–56.

9. For a review of the geological conditions of Mars and the
implications for Mars's past history, see Michael H. Carr (1981) *The
Surface of Mars*, New Haven, Conn.: Yale University Press.

10. The early evolution of planetary atmospheres is reviewed in James
B. Pollack and Yuk L. Yung (1980) "Origin and Evolution of
Planetary Atmospheres," *Annual Reviews of Earth and Planetary
Science* 8: 425–87.

REFERENCES

Devall, Bill and Sessions, George (1985) *Deep Ecology*, Layton, Utah:
Gibbs Smith.

Ehrenfeld, David W. (1978) *The Arrogance of Humanism*, New York:
Oxford University Press.

Johnston, Edward (1984) "Treating the Dirt: Environmental Ethics
and Moral Theory," in Tom Regan (ed.) *Earthbound*, Philadelphia:
Temple University Press.

Leopold, Aldo (1966) *A Sand County Almanac*, New York: Ballantine
Books.

Lovelock, James and Allaby, Michael (1984) *The Greening of Mars*, New
York: St Martin's/Marek.

McKay, Christopher P. (1982a) "On Terraforming Mars," *Extrapolation*
23: 309–14.

—— (1982b) "Terraforming Mars," *Journal of the British Interplanetary
Society* 35: 427–33.

—— (forthcoming) "Exobiology Issues and Experiments at a Mars
Base," NASA publication.

Naess, Arne (1973) "The Shallow and the Deep, Long-Range Ecology Movement: a Summary," *Inquiry* 16: 95–100.

—— (1984) "A Defence of the Deep Ecology Movements," *Environmental Ethics* 6: 265–70.

Regan, Tom (1983) *The Case for Animal Rights*, Berkeley: University of California Press.

Schopf, J. William (1983) *Earth's Earliest Biosphere*, Princeton: Princeton University Press.

Singer, Peter (1979) *Practical Ethics*, Cambridge: Cambridge University Press.

—— (1980) "Animals and the Value of Life," in Tom Regan (ed.) *Matters of Life and Death*, New York: Random House.

Stone, Christopher D. (1974) *Should Trees Have Standing?* Los Altos, Calif.: William Haufmann.

Watson, Richard (1985) "Eco-ethics," *Whole Earth Review*, March.

ETHICS AND POLITICS
The use and abuse of politics

DAVID P. SHUGARMAN

ETHICS AND POLITICS

Historians since Thucydides have been recording instances of governments dissolving and regimes overturned because significant elements of respective populations refuse to tolerate what are perceived as corrupt practices. Today one has only to glance at a daily newspaper or listen to the evening news to find that a local or national politician has been implicated in some kind of scandal, or that some would-be emperor has committed his nation to a war he promised to avoid. Generally such practices have involved either transgression of the responsibilities of office in pursuance of personal gain or the use of office to further a cause or broad interest in a manner which violates normal understandings of moral conduct. In the first category politicians lie, take bribes, authorize murder, with their personal bank accounts in mind; in the second, they lie, give bribes, authorize murder, with their nation's or party's destiny in mind. The two forms or categories of corruption are not mutually exclusive: corrupt politicians seem to be adept at linking the national interest with their own. Moral politicians seem to be few in number. We are accustomed to leaders who treat words like cheap glass, there for breaking, and treat people little better. The impression is that corrupt practices are present not only in the fall but in the rise and ongoing success of those whose profession is the exercise of power.

The present essay addresses a question raised early this century by Max Weber in his musings on the nature of politics and politicians: in what sense are politics and ethics compatible, if at all? In practice, can we expect political actors to be good politicians, in the moral sense of good? Are there ways to avoid being corrupted by the trappings of power? Such considerations have often been central to issues in the history of western political thought. And they have long been central in practical politics. Weber held that ethics and politics could be combined but only within a context of the fundamentally corrupt nature of politics.

Much of what follows is concerned to show that Weber's approach to answering the question and his answer itself are unsatisfactory. In the next section, pp. 200–3, I introduce some key considerations of the nature of corruption and the relationship between ethics and politics by contrasting certain features of the tradition of political thought with twentieth-century political realism. Inasmuch as Weber and what I shall call the dirty hands advocates direct attention to what they claim is a necessarily corrupting *use* of power they not only reject the classical approach to the relationship of ethics and politics. They also draw attention away from a more classical understanding of corruption as the *abuse* of power. What is remarkable is that there has developed in Weber's train a justification for unethical uses of power as the norm in politics, such that lying, cheating, and killing can be treated as not just expectable, but acceptable. In the section "Dirty hands," pp. 207–16, I try to unravel what is involved in this approach to the use of politics.

What is also remarkable is that there is now available a theory of politics – what I shall call "bourgeois realism" – which forthrightly inverts traditional understandings of abuses of power and redesignates and defends the result as rational, self-interested behavior. In the section "The abuse of power," pp. 216–21, I draw attention to the peculiarities of the self-interest, bourgeois model of politics in contrast to an appreciation of what is at issue in the abuse of power.

Politicians do commit wrongs and lots of them. It is important not to legitimize unethical practices and the final section, "Moral considerations in political practice," pp. 221–8, deals with the question of how we can bring moral considerations to bear on political conduct.

THE PRIVATE AND THE PUBLIC

Both Plato and Aristotle recognized the distinction between a private side to life and a public one. They contrasted life as a householder or a teacher with that of an office-holder or member of the assembly. And while they made much of the distinction they also made much of the relationship between these two modes of experience. For Plato and Aristotle what is good for the good man and what is good for the good state are, if not virtually the same, so closely interwoven that we can say that each is the need of the other; what is conducive to the one is conducive to the other: good men are necessary for a good state, a good state is necessary for the nurturing of good men. One of the major themes of Plato's *The Republic* is that the genuinely good state depends on the moral education of a moral leadership which will "secure the greatest possible happiness for the community as a whole" (1941: 110); and the last chapter of Aristotle's *Nicomachean Ethics* makes it clear that it is only through politics, and especially proper legislation, that a community can see to the moral education which is a condition of the good conduct of its citizens.

According to Plato and Aristotle unethical conduct in public life meant any conscious deviation from the aim of promoting the public interest in order to pursue private, selfish interests. The promotion of such interests, the concern to increase the happiness of some at the expense of others, required intrigue, deception, excess, the distancing of citizens from each other, a breakdown of trust – in short, corruption. Corruption was both cause and consequence of the dissolution of a well-ordered state. It meant or, to be more precise, was most clearly manifested in a derogation of duty by the abuse of public trust: the authority of the state, the advantages of office, were put to private advantage. To be corrupt was to harm the body politic, to treat the public realm as an arena for furthering the privileges of some citizens at the expense of the interests of all. That those with power might rule in their own interest and seek to legitimize such rule by virtue of their power was acknowledged by Plato in his dramatization of Socratic dialogues (especially in debate with Thrasymachus in *The Republic* and with Callicles in *The Gorgias*) but never legitimated. So too, Aristotle shared the conviction that there was a world of difference between political practice and right or legitimate political practice.

Aristotle held that in a lawful system of rule political office is exercised by someone who has no compunction about leaving office because he could assume "that others would take over the duty of considering his benefit, just as he had himself, during his term of office, considered the interest of others." The realities of ruling might sometimes be otherwise: "Today," writes Aristotle in reference to mid-fourth-century BC Athenian politics, "the case is altered. Moved by the profits to be derived from office and the handling of public property, men want to hold office continuously." Now "the conclusion which follows," says Aristotle, "is clear." And it is certainly not that we should alter our notions of what constitutes the proper exercise of office to take account of the "altered case." Rather, it is that, "Those constitutions which consider the common interest are *right* constitutions, judged by the standard of absolute justice. Those constitutions which consider only the personal interest of the rulers are all *wrong* constitutions, or *perversions* of the right forms." Indeed, Aristotle immediately adds that where there is a corrupt form of rule genuinely political relationships, i.e. relationships among citizens who are equals and peers, are excluded and the *raison d'être* of the polis, that it advances the common interest, is undermined. So Aristotle held that a corrupt government is really a despotism resembling a master–slave system of rule "whereas the polis is an association of freemen" (1958: III, 112).

In this light we can appreciate the classical understanding of politics as an ethical science as well as an ethical practice. And we can also see how, for Plato and Aristotle, ethics and politics are inextricably bound.

Now with respect to the tendency of office holders to abuse their positions of trust our day is still very much like Aristotle's. And our own estimation of the illegitimacy of such practices is in many respects not unlike Aristotle's. In most ostensibly constitutional democracies there are laws which are meant to deter bribery, graft and influence peddling. Furthermore, there are widely shared sentiments, often conventions, and now it would seem growing awareness of the need for codes or legislation covering ethical conduct, all of which attest to the view that (a) office-holders should avoid making decisions or exercising influence in situations where their private interests may be involved; and (b) that ethical rules to guide conduct as well as public surveillance to check for abuse are necessary supports for the institutions of government. Inasmuch as Aristotle claimed that the "most important rule of all, in all types of constitution, is that provision should be made – not only by law, but also by the general system of economy – to prevent the magistrates from being able to use their office for their own gain" (1958: V, 228), it would seem that contemporary concern to specify conflict of interest rules is a recollection of the wisdom of ancient political thought.

From Plato to J. S. Mill political philosophy drew attention to the ever present tendencies and dangers of corruption in the body politic. While susceptibility to corruption was readily acknowledged, no major thinker in the tradition, with the possible exceptions of Augustine and Machiavelli, held that by entering public life one is necessarily stepping into an evil domain.

For twentieth-century political realists, however, it is essential to distinguish between a "private" sphere of activity and a "public" one, which, to the extent that the latter is encompassed by politics, "is a second-rate form of human activity ... at once corrupting to the soul and fatiguing to the mind" (Oakeshott 1960: xiv). And it is held that the "sharp distinction" that "must be drawn between the moral and social behaviour of individuals and of social groups... justifies and necessitates political policies which a purely individualistic ethic must always find embarrassing" (Niebuhr 1932: xi). This dogma of separate life worlds holds that politics is an autonomous sphere of study and practice, not only separable from ethics, but from economics, religion, culture;[1] that there is an irresolvable conflict between "private" ethics and politics; that one must, as Hans Morgenthau put it, "know with despair that the political act is inevitably evil" (quoted in Frankel 1978: 72),[2] and still reckon on the place of moral courage and the importance of referring to *some* moral principles.

Now there are a number of items that require unpacking from the realist baggage but several of them can be taken up in the discussion of Weber and the problem of dirty hands since twentieth-century political realism is in major respects an elaboration and restatement of Weber's position.

Here I want to point out first, that the moral perspective and the moral principles which are appealed to by writers like Niebuhr and Morgenthau are derived from a puritanical and fatalistic interpretation of political reality, and second, that such an interpretation expresses a highly individualistic ethic which devalues, if not disavows, the merits of human sociability.

It is literally puritanical because the contrasting notion of private (or individual) morality which is used to illuminate the dark realities of public life is modeled on a divine-like Adam before the fall, before, that is, there were other people and sin. It is fatalistic because corrupt politics is treated on a par with breathing: it is something we must do if we are to do anything; and it is as inescapable as death. "The very act of acting," claims Morgenthau, "destroys our moral integrity" (ibid.). What we are being told is that by definition acting is morally tainted: no matter who is acting and no matter what acts are performed. This of course is not a matter of the difficulties of making difficult moral choices in the context of realities of politics, or any realities; it has nothing to do with what is observable and everything to do with religious metaphysics.

"Men will never be wholly reasonable," says Niebuhr (1932: 34; emphasis added), "and the *proportion of reason to impulse becomes increasingly negative when we proceed from the life of individuals to that of social groups*." The morality of groups is inferior to that of the individual, Niebuhr claims, because there is no way of establishing "a rational social force ... powerful enough" to restrain "natural" social forces; furthermore, the "egoistic impulses of individuals" are aggregated into a "collective egoism" which is "more able to defy any social restraints which might be devised" (Niebuhr 1978: 2–3). Life in society gives rise to an increasing multiplicity of demands which cannot all be satisfied: Morgenthau concludes, "while satisfying one, one must neglect others, and the satisfaction of one may even imply the positive violation of another ... whatever choice we make, we must do evil while we try to do good" (quoted in Frankel 1978: 85). Aside from the obvious problem with assuming that any demand is legitimate and deserves being served and that not doing so implies a positive evil, the thrust of this approach exhibits a bias against collective action as such. The assumption is that as individuals multiply so do competition and conflict, together with an expansion of the realm of the irrational in human affairs. In other words, as social ties widen, as numbers grow, rationality decreases and the propensity for corruption increases. Here is the notion that it is the public in the public realm which cannot be trusted. With respect to the capacity for judgment and moral conduct this is a proposition that there is poverty in numbers. This is proposed as a universal phenomenon, an observable and objective truth of human nature, a political reality.

The trouble here is that this depiction of political reality is highly contentious. And it has been challenged by some acute political observers over time. Aristotle, who as already indicated believed his society was rent by corruption, did not think the proposition about numbers was true. He held rather, that:

> The masses can come to a better decision in many matters, than any one individual ... a numerous body is less likely to be corrupted. A large volume of water is not so liable to contamination as a small; and the people is not so liable to corruption as the few. The judgement of a single man is bound to be corrupted when he is overpowered by anger, or by any other similar emotion, but it is not easy for all to get angry and go wrong simultaneously.
>
> (Aristotle 1958: III, 142)

And to the hypothetical question, if we take a good man and a body of good men, "which will be the more likely to be free from corruption – the one man, or the body of persons?" Aristotle responds rhetorically, "Is not the balance clearly in favour of the latter?" (ibid.).

The observation that collective interaction is likely to sustain ethical conduct rather than undermine it, and that a collective judgment is preferable, on moral grounds, to the judgment of a single individual is not idiosyncratic to Aristotle or Ancient Greece. Rousseau (1972) in the eighteenth century took this sensibility to its participatory democratic conclusion: direct democracy in a small state was preferable to representative democracy because, he thought, a whole citizen body would be impossible to corrupt but representatives easy. And in the nineteenth century John Stuart Mill (who in many respects shared Aristotle's preference for combining features of aristocracy and democracy) maintained that participation in public affairs led to the moral improvement of both those participating and society as a whole.

These references to Aristotle, Rousseau, and Mill are not meant to imply that the question of the relationship between private and public – or any issue for that matter – can be settled by appealing to authorities in the tradition of political thought. Rather, they are meant (a) to provide a reminder that appreciations of the morality of public involvement reflect very differing interpretations of reality which in turn are representative of very differing estimations of the nature of society and the worth of collective action. And (b) they are meant to show that where collective action is highly esteemed we have to take account of the crucial importance of citizenship. And what the notion of citizenship conveys in this respect is participation in collective decision-making. It is through such participation that one exhibits and develops one's sociability while contributing to improving one's society.

Active citizenship, according to Mill, would move individuals away from narrow-minded and self-interested preoccupations of daily life: citizenship would be an educative and socializing process and one that meant *moral* improvement. Indeed, it was the "moral instruction afforded by the participation of the private citizen" that was even "more salutary" than improving people's minds. For the individual as political participant

> is called upon ... to weigh interests not his own; to be guided, in case of conflicting claims, by another rule than his private partialities; to apply, at every turn, principles and maxims which have for their reason of existence the common good: and he usually finds associated with him in the same work minds more familiarized than his own with these ideas and operations, whose study it will be to supply reasons to his understanding, and stimulation to his feeling for the general interest. He is made to feel himself one of the public and whatever is for their benefit to be for his benefit.
>
> (Mill 1910: 217)

I have quoted Mill at some length to point up his enthusiastic convictions about, and the reasons he offers for, the value of public involvement. What needs to be emphasized as well is that Mill believed that public involvement would prevent "every thought or feeling" from being "absorbed in the individual and in the family": where participation was non-existent Mill thought that neighbors would only see one another as rivals: "Thus even private morality suffers, while public is actually extinct" (ibid.). So rather than treat political involvement as some sort of necessary evil which is at odds with the moral integrity of an autonomous, private, individual, Mill sees that public engagement can be a positive good, for the community and the individual. He does so by, on one hand, drawing a connection between the personal and the political – the worth of a state is the worth of the individuals composing it – and on the other by pointing to the distinct character of public activity: there are special obligations to reckon impartially, to recognize canons of fairness, to disseminate information honestly, widely, and efficiently, to subject decision-making to public scrutiny and evaluation.

Mill's estimation of the morally educative role of public involvement was parasitic on an estimation of the dulling, non-participatory mode of existence in the private realm, where there "are narrow circles of personal and family selfishness," and the majority carry out their labors according to the dictates of their employers. In drawing attention to the insularities of everyday routine in a bourgeois world – which he thinks can be compensated by active citizenship – Mill too easily passes over the kinds of intimacies and confidentialities that friends, family, and lovers can share – which he clearly shared with Harriet Taylor – but which are not transferable to public institutions and roles. However, while we may note that it is possible to both over- and underestimate the differences between the public and the private, what we have yet to see is an argument that there is a special ethics which applies to politics, which legitimizes ruthlessness, and which is not subject ultimately to the same moral considerations that inform one's interactions with friends and family.[3] For that we have to turn to deliberations on the problem of dirty hands. In these deliberations, as we shall see, the matter of citizenship matters hardly at all.

DIRTY HANDS

When Plato's Socrates reflected on the difficulties of following a life of philosophy in a corrupt society he confronted the problem of dirty hands. He held that if a lover of truth finds that "there is no soundness in the conduct of public life, nowhere an ally at whose side a champion of justice could hope to escape destruction" he will keep quiet and go his own way, for, "seeing lawlessness spreading on all sides," he should be content "if he can keep his hands clean from iniquity while this life lasts." In the midst of disorder and lawlessness a philosopher is like a fish out of water, or, as Socrates put it, "like a man fallen among wild beasts." Such a man "should refuse to take part in their misdeeds." It is important to note that this is not a recommendation to avoid public life *per se*; it is rather advice to reject corrupt public life, for Socrates quickly adds that, while maintaining one's integrity is no small achievement, if a philosopher could find a society congenial to his nature his accomplishments would be even greater, both for his country and himself (Plato 1941: 204).

This is not a case of contrasting and preferring the sanctity and calm serenity of the private over the inevitably fractious public, or of opting for solitude over social relations. It is rather to emphasize that where good government is lacking neither philosophy nor civil relationships can be properly enjoyed. In this respect it is power-hungry politicians and the struggle for power which are inimical to all three. So while Socrates acknowledged that politics may degenerate into a dirty business he denied such business legitimacy; moreover, he seems to have held that, while one should not participate in ruling where ruling requires dirty hands, ruling does not necessarily require dirty hands, for, when he scornfully sets out his apology to the Athenian Assembly which convicted him he does so clearly as a citizen of Athens who prides himself on having acted ethically and the same in private and public life.

For Machiavelli, however, there are things which must be done to restore, establish, and preserve order and securing these ends overrides commitments to ethical proprieties:

A wise mind will never censure anyone for having employed any extraordinary means for the purpose of establishing a kingdom or constituting a republic. It is well that, when the act accuses him, the result should excuse him. ... For he is to be reprehended who commits violence for the purpose of destroying, and not he who employs it for beneficent purposes.

(Machiavelli 1950: 139)

And for Weber, he who enters politics thereby accepts "power and force as means," effectively sells his soul to the devil, and acknowledges that in politics "it is not true that good can follow only from good and evil only from evil, but that often the opposite is true. Anyone who fails to see this is, indeed, a political infant" (1958: 123).

And Hoederer, the revolutionary hero of Sartre's play, *Dirty Hands*, scolds a young idealist for not understanding that the pursuit of justice requires "using every means at hand to abolish classes," that "all means are good when they're effective," and that one cannot avoid having soiled hands if anything is to be accomplished:

Purity is an idea for a yogi or a monk. You intellectuals and bourgeois anarchists use it as a pretext for doing nothing. ... Well I have dirty hands. Right up to the elbows. I've plunged them in filth and blood. But what do you hope? Do you think you can govern innocently?

(Sartre 1955: 223–4)

And when Michael Walzer attempts to explore "conventional wisdom" and summarizes Machiavelli, Weber, and Sartre, he answers that no one can govern innocently, that "It is easy to get one's hands dirty in politics and it is often right to do so." Walzer notes that what characterizes the dirty hands politician is his experience of "a painful process of having to weigh the wrong he is willing to do in order to do right, and which leaves pain behind, and should do so, even after the decision has been made" (Walzer 1973: 174).

Here we have the main ingredients of the dirty hands theorists' approach to ethics and public action which can be set out as propositions: (1) the crucial reasons for acting are reasons of state; (2) when it comes to considering as well as judging a public act the criterion is the consequence(s); (3) violence and deception, "wicked means," even cruelty can be employed for beneficial as well as destructive ends; (4) when normally reprehensible means are used for "good" purposes their use is morally defensible; (5) public life is carried on in an atmosphere akin to warfare, where social relations are marked by intense rivalry, duplicity and violence; (6) public life requires heroic leadership.

However, not all dirty hands advocates concur on every point. Sartre and Herbert Marcuse reject (1) and Marcuse's agreement with (2) is highly qualified (Marcuse 1966: 133–48). Proposition (1) has long been the lodestar of *realpolitik* and makes sweeping claims about the legitimacy of particular states, the definition of national interest(s), and the identification of statehood in general as the principal factor in politics. Proposition (2) which appears non-controversial (surely, in social relations we should be primarily concerned with the social consequences of our actions), nevertheless is most often a vulgar version of utilitarianism, namely expediency, and carries with it an extreme and therefore dismissive rendering of intentionalist ethics corresponding to the simplistic designation of the "private" we noted on p. 206. It is clear from John Rawls's *A Theory of Justice* (1971) that a modified Kantianism is by no means "non-consequentialist" and can be shown to be directly relevant to morality in public affairs.

Propositions (3) and (5) are meant to be descriptive though both are more questionable as ontological givens than their adherents believe. Despite Weber's injunction that doubting (3) is to render oneself a political infant we might well ask what it means to say that wickedness or deception is beneficial: what is meant here by beneficial? is it the same in every instance? how is it measured or determined? and by whom? and who benefits? – presumably not the people at whom the deception is applied or aimed! If we follow Weber on this point what we find is that what is understood to be beneficial is relative to the capacities of those special people with their hands "on the wheel of history," those select few who have a "calling" for politics, who can discern the "objective interests" of their nation. So part of proposition (3) is contingent on proposition (6), heroic leadership, being practiced.

There is another sense in which (3) could be true but not have the implication that Weber and the ethical realists draw from it, i.e., proposition (4): since the results of political action are often paradoxically at odds with their original intent (good results from evil and vice versa) then one must face up to "these ethical paradoxes" (Weber 1958: 125) and "be willing to pay the price of using morally dubious means or at least dangerous ones ... [with] the possibility or even probability of evil ramifications" (ibid.: 121). But it is surely one thing to note, retrospectively, that a policy or act had unintended consequences quite at variance with expectations, and another to recommend that we can use this kind of experience (which Weber calls the "irrationality of the world") as a principle which will justify morally dubious acts in the present or future. It does not follow that because a good resulted, unintentionally, from evil deeds in the past that we should try to replicate the practice and the consequence, for this would be to intend the unintended.

Proposition (5) provides an ongoing rationale for (4) which constitutes moral advocacy. It is (5) which signifies what Hannah Arendt (1970) has called "a consensus among political theorists from left to right" to the effect that violence is *the* defining characteristic of politics.[4] In this regard twentieth-century political thought has been dominated by a Weberian perspective, for according to Weber, "the decisive means for politics is violence"; and "whosoever contracts with violent means for whatever ends – and every politician does – is exposed to its specific consequences" (Weber 1958: 121, 124). What distinguishes the politician from the thug is that the former uses "legitimate violence." Thus, "He who seeks the salvation of the soul, of his own and of others, should not seek it along the avenue of politics, for the quite different *tasks of politics can only be solved by violence*" (ibid: 126; emphasis added).

This remarkable claim is the view not of a political scientist but of a military commander. Indeed, Weber's understanding of political leadership, even "democratic" political leadership, is that it is a matter of commanding. In Weber's view of democracy, once the people choose their leader, "the chosen leader says, 'Now shut up and obey me'" (ibid.: 42). He has complete discretion and should get complete obedience until the next election. Ergo proposition (6): only great masculine military acumen can keep the many thugs from destroying order (see Elshtain 1985).

This superimposition of a war mentality onto politics is a staple in the realists' and dirty hands theorists' diet. Machiavelli's Prince, it should be remembered, is to have "no other aim or thought, nor take up any other thing for his study, but war and its organization and discipline, for that is the only art that is necessary to one who commands" (1950: 53).

Similarly Hoederer reminds young Hugo that deceiving one's comrades is obviously excusable because "we're at war, and it's not customary to keep each individual soldier posted hour by hour on operations" (Sartre 1955: 222). And while Walzer cautions against overemphasizing the role of violence, two of his three examples of dirty hands are taken from the context of war (firing squad duties and confronting terrorism), and he says: "the men who act for us are often killers, or seem to become killers too quickly and too easily" (1973: 164). It is given this context of widespread violence or "legitimate" violence that the dirty hands proponents make their claim about the legitimacy of employing morally troublesome tactics.

What is sometimes missed in the salience of proposition (4), that good ends justify bad means, is the realists' recommendatory posture, often overlooked because of their penchant for using "is" instead of "ought" while making value judgments (e.g. consider the passage quoted on p. 208, from Machiavelli: "it is well that ... he is to be reprehended who..."). In this regard what is implied in their treatment of public concerns is that there is a difference between recognizing necessities and arguing that some regrettable acts are morally necessary: short-run pain can be justifiably inflicted for long-term gain. Thus, a good leader, says Machiavelli, "must not deviate from what is good, if possible, but be able to do evil if constrained" (1950: 65). This goes beyond a doctrine of inevitability: it is to stress something other than the notion that, to quote Morgenthau again, "whatever choice we make, we must do evil while we try to do good" (quoted in Frankel 1978) for Machiavelli holds that it is "exceedingly rare" to find a good man who is "*willing* to employ wicked means to become prince, even though his final object be good" (1950: 171).

This doctrine of responsibility against a background of

necessity – the perspective here is decidedly misanthropic, the social environment is viewed as constantly precarious, mostly hostile – is a central theme of Sartre's play and is nicely put by Walzer in describing his version of the moral politician:

> It is by his dirty hands that we know [the moral politician]. If he were a moral man and nothing else, his hands would not be dirty; if he were a politician and nothing else, he would pretend that they were clean. ...
> ... politicians necessarily take moral as well as political risks committing crimes that they only think ought to be committed.
>
> (1973: 168, 179)

Weber's heroic politician is really a general with a great capacity for moral expertise and anguish. When such a figure

> is aware of a responsibility for the consequences of his conduct and feels such responsibility with heart and soul ... [then] an ethic of ultimate ends and an ethic of responsibility are not absolute contrasts but rather supplements, which only in unison constitute a genuine man – a man who *can* have the 'calling for politics."
>
> (1958: 127)[5]

There are several problems with the analysis of the problem of dirty hands, particularly insofar as the analysis is a legitimating one. To begin with, the place of violence in politics is terribly distorted, overgeneralized and, in a curious way, reflective of a moral absolutism. The distortion is clear when we stop to think about what is claimed. Why should our attention be directed to the anguish, guilt, or righteousness of the perpetrator(s) of violence, rather than to the suffering of victims? Is violence decisive in politics? Does it make sense to say that only violence solves the tasks of politics?

Given Weber's view of politics as about leadership or the influencing of leadership we can run a short test on his claim that violence is decisive. Let us consider the domestic politics of the world's foremost military empire, a country about which it has been said "violence is as American as apple pie." That country's government experienced two crises of legitimacy in the late 1960s and early 1970s. In 1968 President Lyndon

Johnson refused to run for re-election largely because of his loss of credibility and popularity stemming from his conduct of the war in Vietnam. So the single most important political leader in the country, the commander-in-chief of a nation at war, effectively resigned from political power, and his party also lost the Presidency to the opposition. Of course violence was not absent from American politics in all this, far from it. Furthermore, police forces all across the country were used to beat up war protestors and demonstrators, so clearly Johnson had the decisive element (according to Weber) on his side. Nevertheless, Johnson did not call out the police and the army to keep himself in power; and his opponents, in the streets, in the universities and in the Republican Party, did not call upon them to throw Johnson out. In one of the most divisive times in American history and over the most decisive issue in American politics, leadership of the nation, violence was not decisive.

Example number two: same venue, same position under fire; about six years later: this time Richard Nixon was found to have dirty hands in his 1972 re-election – interestingly enough Walzer provides as one of his justifiable examples of dirty hands the case of an American politician who is willing to rig an election. Again, here was a case of an elected President with all the powers of that office at his command: yet Nixon resigned under pressure of impeachment. It was not violence but the actions of a security guard, investigative journalism, judicial independence, the constitution, and the powers of Congress that were, added up, decisive.

For all of Weber's attention to the analytical and historical differences in legitimations of authority, he failed to comprehend the essence of lawful, constitutional government. And for all his separating of life experiences and activities – into religious ethics, political ethics, green grocers' ethics, marital ethics, among others – Weber for some reason did not see the need to clearly separate the practice of war from the practice of politics, nor could he separate violence and power.

Not everyone experiences the world as a terrain of hot or cold war. It would be difficult for a Canadian, a New Zealander, an Australian, or a Scandinavian to take seriously Walzer's observation that "our leaders are often killers or become killers too easily." Of course if one has in mind

Lebanon or Colombia or sixteenth-century Italy the description takes on meaning: but that is because these are or were societies racked by gang warfare, tribalism, and foreign intervention.

Furthermore, when Weber spoke of violence and power he did so almost in the tones of a born-again evangelist. To employ violence, "legitimate" or not, was to contract with the devil, to give oneself over to "diabolic forces." But here again Weber seems incapable of drawing a distinction between someone beating up someone else while robbing him, and a policeman using physical force to prevent someone from battering a child. He holds – and quite inconsistently, given his views about ethical paradoxes – that all "ideologists," whether "Bolshevik, Spartacist" or whatever must "bring about exactly the same results as any militaristic dictator" because they use the same political means, namely "power, backed up by violence" (Weber 1958: 119). The ideological purchase of this claim should be obvious; Weber is saying that since the consequences of revolutionary methods are the same as the consequences of reactionary militarism then revolutionary socialism has no justification. At the same time he is dismissive of intention and treats politics as an instrumentalist activity.

If the dirty hands position is terribly misleading as description it is also dangerous as prescription and in an important sense is practically incoherent.

Dirty hands defenders arrogate to a heroic leadership the right to exercise a moral autonomy that is denied to the populace at large. The picture painted of such leaders is a composite of wily negotiator, clever manipulator, no-nonsense general and father-knows-best moral actor. Such people will have resolve, a superior strategic sensibility for charting political consequences and, to top it all off, an extraordinary capacity for weighing moral considerations. Only such people have what it takes to face up to the "ethical irrationality" of the world and decide when committing an evil is desirable to bring about some good. Too demanding to be mixed with the *demos*, moral autonomy and commitments to intentionality get checked at the entrance to the public arena. But later these attributes magically reappear as the will and conscience of great leaders.

This is a highly romanticized view of leadership and a dangerous one. It is romanticized because the only place we find such leaders is in hero-producing histories, fiction and Hollywood movies. It is dangerous for precisely those reasons which Acton and Mill appreciated and ethical realists at times so acutely emphasize, but which at other times they conveniently neglect: "power tends to corrupt, absolute power corrupts absolutely."

But dirty hands advocacy can also be instructive, despite itself, when it turns our attention to Presidents, Prime Ministers, Governors, Defense Ministers, and Secretaries of State. For it is hard to take seriously an account of men like Lyndon Johnson, Richard Nixon, Spiro Agnew, Ronald Reagan, Henry Kissinger, or Kurt Waldheim, as moral experts who experience great anguish as they decide "to do what is wrong in order to do what is right." The lesson to be learned is that we should not entrust our political leaders with risking our lives or defer to their great authority. We should institutionalize demands that they provide reasons for their actions, that they provide us with relevant information, that we be consulted and expected to share in extraordinary decisions.

In contrast to this role for citizens, Walzer contends that the only way of dealing with dirty-handed politicians is for citizens to be willing to get their own hands dirty. This is a position which is practically incoherent, and, if not invidious, morally vacuous. Walzer points out that "In most cases of dirty hands moral rules are broken for reasons of state ... moral rules are not usually enforced against [this] sort of actor largely because he acts in an official capacity" (Walzer 1973: 149). But as a defender of dirty hands, Walzer is reduced to emphasizing the need for a political culture which values moral rules highly and takes their violation seriously while acknowledging that it is the remarkable individual who belongs to such a culture who is the quintessential dirty hands politician. This is like recommending a recipe that is bound to be botched before it gets to the table. But why should we assume that so many good people will require special individuals from amongst them to do bad things as a matter of course? Walzer's notion that enforcement of morality against dirty hands involves honoring the man who did bad in order to do good, while at the same time punishing him, is to make double-think into an esteemed principle of political evaluation.

THE ABUSE OF POWER

The highly individualistic, anti-social bias that is found in the realists' rendering of morality in the public realm is paralleled by the account that contemporary bourgeois theorists give of political rationality. In this latter regard it is the calculating, self-interested, behavior of a maximizing consumer or entrepreneur acting essentially in a private capacity which is taken as the model of rationality. From the bourgeois view of *homo economicus*, the self-interested pursuit of infinite appropriation is not only rational, it is also natural and moral. But as soon as an individual moves beyond immediate economic concerns and tries to take account of other concerns or other factors his reasoning abilities become "impaired." On this view, clearly articulated by Joseph Schumpeter some forty years ago, an individual's entry into politics means his mental performance drops "down to a lower level" (1950: 262). In politics, then, a person "argues and analyzes in a way which he would readily recognize as infantile within the sphere of his real interests. He becomes a primitive again. His thinking becomes associative and affective" (ibid.).

These harsh characterizations of the political animal have been up-dated and moderated but the kernel of Schumpeter's idea remains in the work of market-oriented theorists of democratic politics. William Riker and Anthony Downs provide especially instructive examples of this kind of theory.

According to Riker the politically rational man "is the man who would rather win than lose, regardless of the particular stakes." Such a man "will want to make others do things they would not otherwise do, he wants to exploit each situation to his advantage." Such a man, furthermore, always chooses the winning strategy amongst differing alternatives – such a strategy results in a larger payoff "in money or power or success." Riker posits such choice as "definitive" of rational behavior, "while the behaviour of participants who do not so choose will not necessarily be so accepted" (Riker 1962: 22–3).[6]

In his *An Economic Theory of Democracy*, a book that has been widely used in business schools as well as politics departments all over North America, Downs says we must assume that politicians

> act solely in order to attain the income, prestige and power which come from being in office. Thus politicians in our model never seek office as a means of carrying out particular policies, their only goal is to reap the rewards of holding office *per se*. They treat politics purely as a means to the attainment of their private ends, which they can reach only by being elected.
>
> (1957: 28)[7]

And in order to get elected in a democracy they will join with others of their party to promise as much as possible as ambiguously as possible: they will cloud their policies "in a fog of ambiguity." Downs holds that not only do political parties do this but it is rationally compelling that they do so: in other words they systematically must practice skilful deception; but because voters have to expect some degree of predictability and reliability from parties, politicians will avoid blatant lies. There is a public interest assumed: it is a by-product, an unintended consequence, of the competitive struggle for power and office.

Now despite the depiction of ruthlessly obsessive political actors, Downs adds the curious qualifier that his elaboration of the self-interest axiom assumes "at least two limits": his rational politicians will remain within the bounds of legality and they will not try to benefit themselves at the expense of fellow party members. However, Downs readily (and quite consistently) admits that "these limits are unrealistic," but "without them our analysis would have to be extended beyond the purview of this study" (ibid.: 30). In other words, given the "anything goes" nature of this approach to political purpose it is quite realistic to assume that individuals will commit crimes and betray their friends and colleagues so long as they can get away with it – but taking this into account makes a model of rational, economic democracy much less tidy.

In this model everyone treats everyone else as an object of manipulation. Each is a means to another's ends. There is no need for "a perception of good and evil, of the just and the unjust" – attributes that, Aristotle (1958: 6) held, when shared

217

with others, are constitutive of families and a polis. Nothing stands in the way of a single-minded pursuit of selfish interests. Indeed the singleness of purpose is so marked that a rational actor – in this model, to be sure – will not be deterred by considerations which may be crucial to his psychic well-being or relations with intimates: primary social and psychological needs are treated as subordinate factors.

Furthermore, it is assumed that major decision-making will be carried out by and in the interests of people with the highest stake in expanding and perpetuating their power. In short, unequal influence over decision-making, inequalities in social and economic life and political inequality generally – with the exception of an equal franchise – are all reconciled as conforming to the requirements of this "rational" model. Indeed, inequality is treated as a functional norm of this kind of authority structure: it is anticipated that relatively few will actually engage in the decision-making process after election day because it is taken for granted that only a small minority will have the wherewithal to play what is treated as an expensive game, wherein, it is further assumed, there is increasing cost to increasing public participation.

So it is rational for "those who have what it takes" to get highly involved (since the benefits/utilities are considerable), and it is also rational for the vast majority to refrain from costly participation once they have cast their ballots. The result is a conception of citizenship which is remarkably truncated: it means a right to vote, little else; for the average citizen is likened to a consumer with little influence over what he is being sold and no reason to want anything different; "in general, it is irrational to be politically well-informed because the low returns from data simply do not justify their cost in time and other scarce resources" (Downs 1957: 259). And, in contrast to the relative impotence of ordinary citizens, government is described as "that specialized agency in the division of labour which is able to enforce its decisions" (ibid.: 34) upon all others. Thus there are active, well-off, powerful decision-makers who command at one end of the hierarchy, and passively obedient, less fortunate, manipulated citizens at the other.

Where politics is understood as continuing conflict among congeries of interests – parties and interest groups – competing to maximize their members' self-interests, the practice of buying and selling influence, exchanging favors, jobbing, patronage in general – which Walter Lippman once described superbly as the "traffic in privileges" (1970: 294) – are treated as normal, expected, legitimate aspects of political activities.

Christian Bay's designation of such activities as *pseudopolitics* serves as the clearest articulation of an ethical response to the positivist pretensions of the *homo economicus* model and the social pathology of the practices described by it. Bay uses the term *pseudopolitics* to refer to

> activity that resembles political activity but is exclusively concerned with either the alleviation of personal neurosis or with promoting private or private interest group advantage, deterred by no articulate or disinterested conception of what would be just or fair to other groups.

> (Bay 1967: 15)

And when he turns to the proper meaning of politics Bay reformulates some of the key considerations we have seen in the reflections of Aristotle, Rousseau, and Mill. Politics, Bay states, is "all activity which is aimed at improving or protecting conditions for the satisfaction of human needs and demands in a given society or community according to some universalistic scheme of priorities, implicit or explicit" (ibid.).

The bourgeois theorist's response to Bay is either to decry the loading of value into a "value-free" account of power struggles, or to maintain that ethical theories can only be tested using a value-free model. But here the problem is that, protestations notwithstanding – Downs (1957: 31) says his study "contains no ethical postulates" – certain values get submerged, either in definitions of rational conduct, or in "enlightened" commitment to the ongoing system. In bourgeois theory when somebody prefers more material utilities to fewer and is concerned to bargain for them such behavior is treated as "a matter of scientific report," but "whenever any other goal is mentioned, its 'ethical a-scientific' status is heavily emphasized" (Stretton 1969: 348–9).[8]

Nevertheless, there is a sense in which it is correct to acknowledge the amoral and anti-social character of quintessentially selfish behavior. Where such behavior is the norm moral considerations have to be brought in from outside the context and standards of the conduct itself. An appreciation of corruption or abuse of office is simply not possible from within a context which deems such behavior normal and rational.

Inasmuch as this kind of theory treats public life as hazardous (people could become "primitive"), and the enterprise of politics as too demanding for many, there are similarities with ethical realism and the dirty hands advocates. But the differences are marked. Thinkers like Machiavelli, Weber, Sartre, Marcuse, Morgenthau, and Walzer address moral problems which surface because people are motivated to use power for state, revolutionary, public, or common ends. For bourgeois theorists such motivations are extraordinary and generally signs of irrational conduct. And the problem of dirty hands disappears since morally dubious politics is not a dirty business; it is just business. What this also means is that the capitalist virtues of calculating, possessive, and competitive behavior are indices of rational behavior in politics. Bourgeois theory holds that the private–public divide can be crossed most expeditiously if one applies the mentality and talent honed in the former to decision-making in the latter. Through the promulgation of a particular notion of rational conduct the classical concept of corruption is negated and the scope of what is acceptable and desirable is radically transformed.

What is lacking in the bourgeois account of public practice is any sense that something other than an egoist's consequentialism is required. There is no place here for

> a positively sympathetic disposition toward others, a
> preparedness to be genuinely concerned with "their"
> interests *per se*, as well as [one's] own, a preparedness to be
> "objective" not in a merely logical, but also in a distinctively
> moral sense.

> (Sibley 1953: 557)

This is a disposition that W. M. Sibley refers to as the disposition to be reasonable. This disposition – in contrast to the disposition to pursue one's own interests in a prudent, calculating way – is crucially linked to the disposition to act morally and it is fundamental to what John Rawls (1980: 528–32) has called the sense of justice.

What the pseudopolitics of private advantage conveys is something completely different. Rather than commitment to fairness, to keeping one's word, capitalist politics has to be grounded on lying. This is no extremist charge from the perspective of moral absolutism in an ivory tower. If a capitalist politician were honest he would have to preface and end every appeal to voters roughly as follows: "Remember, no matter what I say about this or that policy, you should vote for me because I'm going to make my interests, and not yours, my first priority." The fact that politicians do not appeal to voters in this way is one reason that the *homo economicus* model cannot be grafted onto, or made to fit, democracy. Unless one assumes considerable ignorance and gullibility on the part of the electorate and a pivotal role of the disposition to lie on the part of politicians, the relationship of democracy and pseudopolitics is theoretically and practically incoherent.

MORAL CONSIDERATIONS IN POLITICAL PRACTICE

Dirty hands and *homo economicus* are obstacles to the reconciliation of ethics and power. They both represent distortions of politics and the proper use of power. They both address in different ways the corruption of politics.

Both, as practices, presuppose an environment marked by hostility and considerable socio-economic and political inequalities. It would be well in this regard to heed Aristotle's advice that we need to bring about changes not only in law but in the general system of economy. Both, as practices, require political actors to flout basic principles of justice such as treating others fairly, and respecting persons as moral agents.

This is not to make a case for moral absolutism against the consequentialists; it is, rather, to contend that consequentialism must not be divorced from non-consequentialist considerations. Moral expertise entails taking both kinds of ethical consideration into account without in principle subordinating the one to the other. This is to say, that, contra Weber, the consequences of integrating consequentialist reasoning with commitments to integrity and veracity, and acceptance of the rights of active citizenship, will generally prove more beneficial (i.e. rewarding) to politicians and publics than realists imagine. Put another way, if a party, government, or decision-maker factored in – rather than excluded – a reputation for trustworthiness along with discernible contributions to a general interest as an essential ingredient of what constitutes any consequence, then we would be linking an ethics of ultimate ends with an ethics of responsibility.

Furthermore, when order has broken down, or when oppression becomes intolerable, and a case for the employment of violence seems unavoidable, there are still moral considerations that limit what is permissible. Here it is well to remember that a just war or revolution does not legitimize unjust practices in war. Against Hoederer's claim that "all means are good when they're effective" (Sartre 1955: 223) Marcuse states that "there are forms of violence and suppression which no revolutionary situation can justify because they negate the very end for which the revolution is a means. Such are arbitrary violence, cruelty, and indiscriminate terror" (Marcuse 1966: 140–1).

Despite overgeneralizations in the two approaches examined there are some truths contained therein. There are leaders who act as though they are engaged in warfare. There are officials whose actions are designed to fill their pockets and stroke their egos. And there are those who combine both propensities.[9] It is important to try to restrict the scope and discretion of such figures. The machinations of the powerful and power-hungry need to be closely scrutinized and checked.

Although numbers of people may habitually act in these ways, that ought not to prevent us from identifying such acts as bad habits, injurious to the health of a body politic. Bad habits, like smoking cigarettes, drinking to excess, drug addiction, and family battering, are hard to break, but that should not prevent us from trying to break them. Likewise, we need to confront corruption. In one respect that means taking a leaf out of the pages of the dirty hands advocates; power is required to check the abuse of power.

What is required is the protection and establishment of agencies and institutional mechanisms whose independence and impartiality should be modeled on the judiciary and whose *raison d'être* should be the surveillance of ethical conduct by public officials. An example here is the role of the Auditor

General in Canada's Parliamentary system. The Auditor General is a non-elected officer of Parliament, rather than a member of government, and his task is to scrutinize and annually produce a public report on the accounting and spending practices of government. In principle this officer has access to all public spending and he can only be fired if there is a joint address by the two chambers of Parliament. Expanded roles for bi-partisan public accounts committees would also be useful. In addition there is need for a non-governmental, but public, commission responsible for administering the provisions of a code of ethical conduct. Codes should be enacted: since moral suasion is futile in deterring abuses by those who are moved by selfishness, there is a case for legislating morality and stipulating penalties for abuse; in-house, Prime Ministerial or Presidential guidelines are inappropriate since chief executive officers have more incentive to cover up than disclose abuses.

Legislation is also important for another reason: a large number of public officials are lawyers and many lawyers appear to act on the principle that "if it's not illegal it's not forbidden." What should be required of every elected office-holder and a great many appointed officials is accountability and full disclosure of material holdings, including (to recognize the arm's-length principle of material interest) the holdings of spouses and immediate family members. Holdings must be placed in trusts which are administered at arm's length by a professional agency with whom the official would be expected to have no future public concern. This could result in wealthy businessmen and aspiring entrepreneurs deciding to forgo political careers. It is sometimes editorialized that this would be a great loss to the political process. On my reading, it would be a substantial gain. The aim should be to have the interest of an office-holder coincide with the duties of his office, not with his investment opportunities.

In this respect as well, patronage appointments have to be understood as making party and personal interests coincide. These become the interests of an office-holder rather than duty to office. Patronage is a system of rewards and inducements through job provision which makes access to power a matter of who you are, who you know and what party you have supported. Because patronage presupposes both favoritism and unaccountability in the appointing process it is a practice which flouts the principles of impartiality, independence and equality – principles which are integral to constitutionalism (Green 1988).[10] It is of course unrealistic not to expect that there will be highly partisan, personal consultants and assistants to politicians. But the numbers of such appointments should be strictly limited and their salaries and functions kept distinct from those of public servants.

And, in order to reduce the opportunities of exchanging privileges and buying and selling influence, all government contracts should be advertised and tendered. Whenever the lowest bidder is passed over the reasons for doing so would have to be set out publicly for the benefit of legislators and citizens and tabled before an appropriate watch-dog committee. Consistent with such proposals would be a requirement that contact with lobby groups be subject to full disclosure (with the onus on both parties to report the contact, its nature and purpose) – and this assumes that such groups as well as individual lobbyists are required to register their activity and those whom they represent.

Indeed, the principle of publicity, implying full disclosure and accountability, is so important that there is a need for laws which stipulate conditions under which people who learn about particular abuses must report them and are legally protected from reprisals when they do so (Bok 1982: 227–8). As Sissela Bok has noted, such laws have to be "limited to clear-cut improprieties; and the lines must be firmly drawn against requiring reporting on political dissent or on purely personal matters" (ibid.: 228).

There are two main objections that can be raised to the thrust of the recommendations I have been making. The first is that an expanded array of legislative and administrative checks and balances will increase the amount of red tape that already hampers government, that it will diminish the discretionary authority of dynamic individuals who are innovative and productive. This objection conjures up the specter of big brother and everyone looking over everyone else's shoulder and is usually accompanied by the sentiment that a "little larceny" is acceptable if it accompanies efficiency. From this perspective it is suggested that "in spite of the evil involved political corruption nevertheless has certain resultants which are advantageous, not simply to those who profit directly by crooked devices, but to society in general" (Brooks 1970: 501).[11]

This of course is the dirty hands rationale – in this case used to defend venality! It is, to emphasize the point once more, the perspective of a commander – here the general and the chief executive officer are interchangeable – who has little use for collective decision-making. So this objection assumes the decision-making superiority of a combination of possessive individualism and authoritarianism in contrast to democratic practices and procedures. On this level the argument has little to do with either the peculiar nature of ethical considerations in politics or the matter of efficiency (which appears descriptive and calculable but is value-loaded); it rather turns, as we saw earlier, on estimations of the citizenry, of the public in the public realm.

The second objection was clearly put by J. S. Mill in his reflections on representative government: all the institutional checks in the world will be of little avail,

> If the checking functionaries are as corrupt or as negligent as those whom they ought to check, and if the public, the mainspring of the whole checking machinery, are too ignorant, too passive, or too careless and inattentive, to do their part.
>
> (Mill 1910: 194)

Mill offered a rejoinder and it is still relevant. His rejoinder I shall reconstruct as having two claims. First, with respect to the potential weakness of any check, he said "a good apparatus is always preferable to a bad," and he immediately turned to a very strange example to make his point: "Publicity, for instance, is no impediment to evil nor stimulus to good if the public will not look at what is done; but without publicity, how could they either check or encourage what they were not permitted to see" (ibid.). What Mill says about the importance of publicity can hardly be overemphasized, but it is a principle of representative democracy, not an administrative apparatus or institutional mechanism. Neither in Mill's day nor our own have we managed to convert this principle into an administrative practice. Rather, what is normal is to have a wide range of government activity covered by national security, official secrets, rules of public service confidentiality, executive privilege, and cabinet secrecy. So this part of Mill's rejoinder should remind us of how much needs to be done and undone in order to check power. There have been some useful moves in this direction through freedom of information regulations and laws, along with the establishment of agencies and commissions to provide for dissemination of and access to information. But this is only a beginning.

The second part of Mill's rejoinder should be understood as what he takes to be "the first element of good government: the virtue and intelligence" of those composing the community. The argument is that in order for the checking apparatuses to work, the citizenry need to understand how to use power and how to guard against its misuse. And in this respect, as pointed out on pp. 205–6, Mill emphasized the importance of political education, which for him, as for Plato, Aristotle, and Rousseau, meant moral education, which in turn was something learned in participating, collectively, with others in public life.

In this connection something has to be added to the account of moral education. For this account corresponds to what H. L. A. Hart (1966: 20) has referred to as "positive morality" – "the morality actually accepted and shared by a given social group." Hart draws attention to the importance of "critical morality." A critical morality raises questions about the morality of prevailing institutions and practices; it inquires into the morality of positive morality. And it raises the question of justification, as in when or why might such and such a use of legal coercion be justified? When or why not?

The development of a critical morality, a critical ethical consciousness, is a crucial ingredient in the restraint of power and in checking its abuses, given the duplicitous language and practices of pseudopoliticians. Educating and sharing moral expertise involves teaching the values of critical analysis, impartiality, independence, objectivity and the duty to blow the whistle on corruption. These are the special responsibilities of educators. Unfortunately, the responsible teaching of ethical issues and problems may be put in jeopardy by growing concentrations of economic power and the increasing presence of the corporate world in the daily lives of everyone. I am especially troubled about the consequences for journalism and the professoriate, two professions traditionally concerned with applying a critical dimension to political affairs.

It has taken universities hundreds of years to develop a small space somewhat apart from the orthodoxies of Church and State. Universities now appear to be enveloped by and may soon be integrated in the marketplace of power and money. Instead of rational criticism, academics may become adept at the soft sell, the hard sell and the middle sell. Instead of having an incentive to review and publicize abuses of power, those whose livelihood is the university may feel obliged to discover beneficial public consequences wherever, whenever, dirty hands and "rational" self-interest have had their way. There are reasons, certainly, to be pessimistic. But that is no reason to drown in pessimism.

It is not of course always clear what the "right" thing to do is, whether in or out of politics. In many practical issues there may not be an ethical resolution which is simple and straightforward. How to tell what's best for oneself, for one's family and friends, and for others, and how to resolve what to do in cases of conflict make for ethical problems. This is as true in the private realm as it is in the public. If all one considers is oneself or if one treats all others' interests as functions of oneself there are no ethical problems or dilemmas. If one doesn't see any difficulty, any conflict between others' interests and one's own, and no conflict between or among others, again, there will be no dilemma: like nihilism, narcissism and absolute altruism take one beyond good and evil. What has to be confronted is the always incomplete task of working through to a tentative, "time and circumstance-bound" solution. To claim that politics and ethics are complementary, that they "need" one another, that they go together in a symbiotic relationship, is not to imply that a concern for political right ensures political right. Applying moral expertise to politics should make us more aware that being committed to doing right, believing that one is doing right, and actually doing right are not, unfortunately, the same things.

Being ethical doesn't mean being right; it means that our actions and judgments concerning others are informed by dispositions of reasonableness and sociability, of respect for individuals as moral beings, and of integrity, and this in the context of an appreciation of the difference between the ways things are in contrast to the way they ought to be and the way they might be, always remembering that they might be better and they might be worse. Such dispositions as these can be felt, learned, experienced, and practiced by everyone; so there is no need to privilege a particular group or class of moral experts. When such an appreciation is extended throughout the populace moral expertise is democratized. If this were to take place alongside a diffusion of power and growing participation in community decision-making we would expect that politics and ethics would be more fully integrated and that a rational exercise of power would be founded on moral considerations.[12]

NOTES

1. A rather different view was assumed by Jean-Jacques Rousseau who held (in *Emile*) that, "One must study society through men and men through society: those who would treat politics and ethics separately will never understand either" (trans. Barbara Foxley, London: Dent, 1974).
2. Frankel's article is an excellent introduction to and critique of realism as it has been applied to international politics.
3. Thomas Nagel argues that "sometimes ... ruthlessness is acceptable in public life," because there are some significant differences in the nature of obligations which pertain to the two spheres of conduct. He nevertheless holds that, while the morality of one may not be derivable from the other, the morality of public action is justified "by ultimate considerations that underlie individual morality as well." Nagel attributes "added weight" to consequentialism, as opposed to a morality of actions, in the public sector. But this is to neglect the terrible significance in our century of those public officials who did their duty and followed orders, rather than concern themselves with the "moral outcomes" or "consequences" of their actions. Steadfastness to duty, or a concentration on immediacy, may be taken as licenses of ruthlessness no more and no less than can a commitment to outcomes. The grounds for issuing such licenses are always morally dubious.
4. See especially pp. 35–56.
5. Leo Strauss's thoughtful and often incisive critique of Weber is unfortunately misleading when it maintains that, for Weber, "the conflict between ethics and politics is insoluble" (Leo Strauss (1965) *Natural Right and History*, Chicago: University of Chicago

Press, p. 64). Weber's contention is that there is a *particular* ethic that is appropriate to politics just as there is a shopkeeper ethic, a religious ethic, a marital ethic, a competition ethic, etc. On this, see Weber (1958: 118–19).

6. It is clear that most people will not and cannot be rational, according to Riker's definition.

7. See the excellent article and critique of Downs by Joel L. Fleishman, "Self-Interest and Political Integrity," in Joel Fleishman, Lance Liebman and Mark H. Moore (eds) (1981) *Public Duties: the Moral Obligations of Government Officials*, Cambridge: Harvard University Press.

8. Downs's "value-freedom" is nicely evinced in his summary of the political importance of information: "Political information is *valuable* because it helps citizens make the *best* possible decisions" (Downs 1957: 258; emphasis added).

9. In late 1987 and early 1988 two former top officials in President Reagan's White House were convicted of various crimes having to do with their activities as lobbyists in contravention of the US 1978 Ethics in Government Act. The two were Lyn Nofziger, Reagan's political director in 1981–2, and Michael Deaver, Mr Reagan's former deputy Chief of Staff. More than one hundred US Administration personnel have been linked to scandal in Reagan's seven years in office. At time of writing, six had been convicted on numerous criminal charges. In addition a former national security adviser, Robert McFarlane, pleaded guilty early in March 1988 to withholding information from Congress about secret US operations to support the Nicaraguan Contras. His assistant, Lt Col Oliver North, had earlier testified before a Congressional investigating committee that he had lied to Congress about his involvement in the matter. Since several millions of dollars have been unaccounted for in this secret government operation involving arms sales to Iran and money transfers to the Contras it appears that several of the people who "dirtied their hands for their country" also made substantial profits.

10. In addition to an excellent summary of constitutional principles and their relation to conflict of interest issues, Green has compiled from media reports a list of thirty-five prominent cases of alleged conflict of interest involving Canadian federal or provincial cabinet ministers or their aides which became public in the period January 1986 to February 1988.

11. Brooks is in fact a critic not an advocate of the quoted lines. Brooks's criticisms were set out in 1910. They did not persuade more recent apologists of corruption like James C. Scott, who writes that "other things being equal, corruption which secures greater freedom of operation for the private sector will generally promote economic growth" (cited in Heidenheimer 1970: 481).

12. In addition to the references cited, I have borrowed from chs VI and VII of my *Rationality in Contemporary Political Thought* (Ph.D.

dissertation, University of Toronto, 1976). And I have benefited more than I have been able to indicate from the considerations advanced by Sissela Bok (1978) *Lying: Moral Choice in Public and Private Life*, New York: Pantheon Books; Virginia Held (1975) "Justification: Legal and Political," *Ethics* 86 (1): 1–16; and William J. Meyer (1975) "Political Ethics and Political Authority," *Ethics* 86 (1). J. Patrick Dobel (1978) has provided a very insightful summary of corruption as seen by five major theorists in the history of political thought: see his "The Corruption of a State," *American Political Science Review* 72 (3): 958–73.

Noam Chomsky is the unrivalled chronicler of the abuses of power in contemporary politics though his focus is on the American empire. See Chomsky (1973) *For Reasons of State*, New York: Vintage Books; Noam Chomsky and Edward S. Herman (1979) *The Washington Connection and Third World Fascism*, vol. 1 of *The Political Economy of Human Rights*, Montreal: Black Rose Books.

It should be clear that I share C. D. MacNiven's perspective that moral reasoning is integral to personal and social development. I share as well and have benefited from his holistic approach to the relationship among the three branches of ethical inquiry. See MacNiven's article in this volume.

REFERENCES

Arendt, Hannah (1970) *On Violence*, New York: Harcourt, Brace & World.

Aristotle (1958) *The Politics of Aristotle*, ed. E. Barker, London: Oxford University Press.

—— (1962) *Nicomachean Ethics*, trans. M. Ostwald, New York: Bobbs-Merrill.

Bay, Christian (1967) "Politics and Pseudopolitics: A Critical Evaluation of Some Behavioural Literature," in Charles A. McCoy and John Playford (eds) *Apolitical Politics: a Critique of Behaviouralism*, New York: Thomas Crowell.

Bok, Sissela (1982) *Secrets*, New York: Pantheon.

Brooks, Robert C. (1970) "Apologies for Political Corruption," in Arnold J. Heidenheimer (ed.) *Political Corruption: Readings in Comparative Analysis*, New York: Holt, Rinehart & Winston.

Downs, Anthony (1957) *An Economic Theory of Democracy*, New York: Harper & Row.

Elshtain, Jean Bethke (1985) "Reflections on War and Political Discourse: Realism, Just War, and Feminism in a Nuclear Age," *Political Theory* 13(1).

Frankel, Charles (1978) "Morality and U.S. Foreign Policy," in Donald G. Jones (ed.) *Private and Public Ethics: Tensions Between Conscience and Institutional Responsibility*, New York: E. Mellen Press.

Green, Ian (1988) "Conflict of Interest and the Constitution: An Analysis of Conflict of Interest Rules for Canadian Cabinet Ministers" (mimeo).

Hart, H. L. A. (1966) *Law, Liberty, and Morality*, New York: Vintage Books.
Lippman, Walter (1970) "A Theory about Corruption," in Arnold J. Heidenheimer (ed.) *Political Corruption: Readings in Comparative Analysis*, New York: Holt, Rinehart & Winston.
Machiavelli, N. (1950) *The Prince and the Discourses*, New York: Modern Library.
Marcuse, Herbert (1966) "Ethics and Revolution," in Richard T. De George (ed.) *Ethics and Society: Original Essays on Contemporary Moral Problems*, New York: Anchor Books.
Mill, John Stuart (1910) *Utilitarianism, Liberty, Representative Government*, London: J. M. Dent & Sons.
Nagel, Thomas (1978) "Ruthlessness in Public Life," in Stuart Hampshire (ed.) *Public and Private Morality*, Cambridge: Cambridge University Press.
Niebuhr, Reinhold (1932) *Moral Man and Immoral Society*, New York: Charles Scribner's Sons.
—— (1978) "Ethics and Power Politics," in Donald G. Jones (ed.) *Private and Public Ethics: Tensions Between Conscience and Institutional Responsibility*, New York: E. Mellen Press.
Oakeshott, Michael (1960) Introduction to *Leviathan* by Thomas Hobbes, Oxford: Blackwell.
Plato (1941) *The Republic*, ed. F. C. Cornford, London: Oxford University Press.
—— (1952) *The Gorgias*, trans. W. C. Hembold, New York: Bobbs-Merrill.
—— *Apology*, in *Great Dialogues of Plato*, trans. W. H. D. Rouse, New York: Mentor Books.
Rawls, John (1971) *A Theory of Justice*, Cambridge, Mass.: Harvard University Press.
—— (1980) "Kantian Constructivisim in Moral Theory," *Journal of Philosophy* 77: 528–32.
Riker, William H. (1962) *The Theory of Political Coalitions*, New Haven: Yale University Press.
Rousseau, Jean-Jacques (1972) *The Government of Poland*, trans. Willmoore Kendall, New York: Bobbs-Merril.
Sartre, Jean-Paul (1955) *Dirty Hands*, in *No Exit and Three Other Plays*, trans. Lionel Abel, New York: Vintage Books.
Schumpeter, Joseph (1950) *Capitalism, Socialism and Democracy*, New York: Harper & Row.
Sibley, W. M. (1953) "The Rational versus the Reasonable," *Philosophical Review* 62.
Stretton, Hugh (1969) *The Political Sciences*, London: Routledge & Kegan Paul.
Walzer, Michael (1973) "Political Action: The Problem of Dirty Hands," *Philosophy and Public Affairs* 2.
Weber, Max (1958) "Politics as a Vocation," in H. H. Gerth and C. Wright Mills (eds) *From Max Weber: Essays in Sociology*, New York: Oxford University Press.